D0339230

Also by Herbert Gold

Bohemia

DIGGING THE ROOTS OF COOL

Herbert Gold

A TOUCHSTONE BOOK
Published by Simon & Schuster
New York   London   Toronto
Sydney   Tokyo   Singapore

TOUCHSTONE
Rockefeller Center
1230 Avenue of the Americas
New York, New York 10020

Copyright © 1993 by Herbert Gold

First Touchstone Edition 1994
TOUCHSTONE and colophon are registered trademarks
of Simon & Schuster Inc.

Designed by Irving Perkins Associates
Manufactured in the United States of America

1   2   3   4   5   6   7   8   9   10

Library of Congress Cataloging-in-Publication Data
Gold, Herbert, date.
Bohemia: digging the roots of cool / Herbert Gold,
p. cm
1. Gold, Herbert, date.—Biography. 2. Authors, American—20th
century—Biography. 3. Bohemianism. I. Title.
PS3557.034Z464 1993
813'.54—dc20
92-30521
CIP

ISBN   0-671-76781-X
ISBN   0-671-88608-8(PBK)

For Melissa.
In Memory.

Contents

1

Protocols of the Elders of Bohemia

San Francisco.

I live on Russian Hill, which seeps downward into Chinatown, the Barbary Coast, the International Settlement, and the traditional Italian-fisherman settlement of North Beach. Vines cling to the wall opposite my house, there's a fig tree bearing inedible, fog-stunted figs, but the dappled sun and green make it resemble a wall and fig trees I remember in Fiesole. Sometimes the street outside smells like the harbor of Port-au-Prince—the drains have been clogged during my thirty-two years here—but most often the sweet sea fog and currents of wind keep the air crisply laundered.

A few days after I arrived to settle forever, at least temporarily, taking my dinner one night at the "lonely table" of the New Pisa Restaurant—seven courses plus wine, $1.75—I was startled at the end of my meal, apple with a slice of Monterey jack, coffee poured into the wineglass, when an entire Japanese opera troupe arose to do honor to the cook. In 1960 we still imported courtesy, not Hondas, from Japan. They sang, in Japanese, every verse of "Oh! Susanna."

I realized I had fumbled my way into a very important corner of the universe.

Later that evening I met a young woman in the basement of City Lights Bookstore. She was reading the *Hudson Review*, and she had been the drum-majorette champion of the state of California, and she had a jeweled baton given her at the Orange Bowl by the very hands of Debbie Reynolds.

I realized this important corner of the universe was a congenial place for me.

Michael McClure offered to read his beast poems aloud, in the beast language, sonnets composed by lions, tigers, and bears through the medium of Michael's tongue and palate, in the privacy of my monkish flat. To an audience of the drum-majorette champion and me.

I realized I would find friends in this corner of the universe. Michael told me that silly putty had been invented here. Someone dug a hole in his backyard, and by morning it was filled with silly putty. I realized that irony and fun would not be omitted, even in the place of beast poetry.

Home at last!

I know third-generation beatniks now. At the farewell party of an actor friend who periodically moves to Los Angeles, I met teenagers whose grandparents smoked grass. I keep up with a whole emergent phalanx of Bohemians through the welcome-home and farewell parties of Garry Goodrow, who constantly heads down the highway to Hollywood or Manhattan but somehow manages never to leave San Francisco. A few weeks after his most recent good-bye party, a young rock bureaucrat calls to say, "Garry's back! From one o'clock Saturday afternoon till, oh, maybe Sunday morning. Bring bottle, chemical, or fruit salad."

For all these years I've occupied the same temporary pad on Russian Hill, but my roots in Bohemia go back even further, to college and graduate school and the lines of force that spread from Greenwich Village to Chelsea, from Rush Street to the Sunset Strip, from the Blue Bird Café in Moscow to the Bodeghita del Media in Havana, from Saint-Germain-des-Prés and Montparnasse through time to Montmartre and Soho and across time to all the previously named depots, from the Haight-Ashbury and Telegraph Avenue to the coffeehouses at a host of colleges and universities across America. The international brotherhood of Bohemia even has outposts in my native town of Cleveland, Ohio—a few health-food stores, espresso machines, and bookshops at Euclid Heights Boulevard and Coventry. Where the time-unstrung gather—in Lahaina or Maui and in Provincetown and Key West and both Venices; in the real estate promotional "Old Towns" and in shopping malls; in all the interstices of a society that still requires art, imagination, laziness, adventure, and possibility unwilled by family and employment—the Bohemian unpacks his tender roots.

Naturally, if this is a mass movement, as indeed it is, it runs the danger of becoming a herd of independent minds taking on a national costume and official smoking habits. Well, too bad. Conformity is inevitable when folks huddle together in rebellion. Seekers grasping in deep need of genius or nonsense, whatever works for them, are not necessarily rigorous thinkers and profound sensibilities. The mechanical repetition of a style achieves unintentional comedy; few are called, but many are funny.

The arriviste imitates the manners of the class above him; the Bohemian takes his stand imitating the manners of the class *below* him—grandly. There is a relationship in yearning and need. Both arriviste and Bohemian choose new roles for themselves, hoping to become authentic.

The frazzled beatnik, pretending he's a French-Canadian country-western Zen Buddhist mafioso, is a groupie to be found any evening at City Lights, Vesuvio's, or the No Name Bar. Tirelessly he digs the scene, still rebelling from his parents all these years as his prostate gives out. During college vacations and at graduation or dropout time, fresh blood flows onto the Beach. "Hey, you mean you really knew Kerouac?" "Jack, Allen, Gregory, they all knew me."

Fellow travelers in the life of art provide the support system, the social context, the economic basis of the bookshops and coffeehouses, maybe even a few audiences for the other-language and revival movies, street fairs, and performances that the religion of Bohemia requires. Dietary laws are loose. In recent times health food has replaced junk food, which replaced spaghetti. Permissiveness is an ironclad rule. If someone wants to walk around with an ancient paperback of *Under Milk Wood* or *Gravity's Rainbow* in his jeans pocket, and spend a life seducing men or women, why, let him do so. It means the streets are populated. For many years I used to see such a man, always with his volume of Dylan Thomas, and when it frayed and wore out, he managed to pick up another at Discovery Bookshop on Columbus, down the street from City Lights, where he used to shoplift in the evenings. Oddly enough, I saw the same man—or at least the same book-stuffed back pocket—in Harvard Square one summer.

In Paris I found a book called *Le flâneur des deux rives,* and a new word came down the mountain of Parnassus like an eleventh commandment. *Flâneur.* It means wanderer, ambler, stroller; it means a nosy, curious, and receptive harvesting of the pleasures of street life. "Se promener sans but" is the way one dictionary defines the verb *flâner;* "perdre son temps en bagatelles." To stroll with no defined goal. To spend time in playfulness. *The Stroller of the Left and the Right Banks* doesn't adequately interpret the smoky poetry of that title, stained by red wine and *caca de chien.*

The street idler, the person who browses and wanders, who seeks the comfort of crowds, the spectacle and entertainment of loveliness or folly is a close cousin to the Bohemian. He is nourished by the fashions in clothes or ideology which he finds during his irresolute routines. He treats the city and all of civilization as a commodity for entertainment. William S. Burroughs, sitting near his hot plate in a hotel on the rue Gît-le-Coeur in Paris, explained why he had been a heroin addict so long: "It's something to do." It occupied the hours, but when he discovered writing and found success at that enterprise, he was able to give up the heroin remedy for boredom.

I believe I asked if his choice of the rue Gît-le-Coeur—Here-Lies-the-Heart—was made because of the name. In typical layabout Bohemian fashion, I don't remember his answer.

Bohemia is not a secret society limited to actual practicing artists, innovators, and revolutionaries, although of course some are required to justify all this turmoil. Consumers, life-stylers, and hopefuls, those who survive best in a tentative and prospective atmosphere, form the Bohemian masses. One of the variant terms in fashion during the sixties was "the underground." The *Evergreen Review* and Grove Press had a brief success with the slogan "Join the Underground!" which they advertised like a brand of jeans. In the days of prosperous revolutionaries—here comes some nostalgia for the Aquarian dawn and instant sunset—contributors to the *Evergreen Review* were invited to receptions at the Kennedy White House. File this history under the heading "Co-optation." Through all this funning and styling, the taste-making and joy-making aboveground of the underground, a Bohemian style succeeded in disseminating its firm rootlessness throughout the world, even unto the suburban tracts. The black light shading an important part of our inner and outer lives is not emitted by the Communists, the Jews, the Church, the Masons, the Trilateral Commission, or Mobil Oil. What came blowing in the wind is still eddying about us. America may not have been greened, but it was boheemed.

What needs to be called Bohemia—although the word has purplish, archaic edges—has provided a lingua franca to generations and nations. You can start a sentence in North Beach in San Francisco, continue it in Greenwich Village, finish it in Chelsea, Saint-Germain-des Prés, or at the Blue Bird Café, and be speaking a common language although the cities surrounding these enclaves are strange to each other. The artists and their satellites—coffee drinkers, trendsetters, talkers, and strollers—form a permanent brotherhood which recognizes itself at a glance in Copenhagen, Havana, Port-au-Prince, or Lawrence, Kansas.

"Where are we meeting now?" I asked a group of students in Lawrence, and there was a bar which was the answer to my question.

In San Antonio, Memphis, Atlanta, and Charleston, in most ripened cities of the American South, the classic nonuniversity style of Bohemia is practiced—drinking, loafing, idling, and freaky. In Cleveland there used to be Bellflower Road, the Monkey House, Adele's Bar in a fertile enclave between a ghetto, a university, and an art school, a faded settlement of Rockefeller money. In Detroit there were small assemblage and collage workshops on Woodward and Cass. In a hot-dog-and-sauerkraut joint called Hot Dogs! Sauerkraut! an industrial junk happening welder explained how eleven years of Freudian therapy enabled him to go out into the world to eat hot dogs dripping with sauerkraut in public without embarrassment.

Now Cleveland's Bohemia is displaced to the Flats and to Coventry and Euclid Heights Boulevard, Detroit's is shot all over town by redevelopment, but wherever Bohemia used to be, it also still is. Those who hung out at Adele's in Cleveland now keep the faith at the several Arabica's on Shaker Square or at Euclid Heights Boulevard and Coventry. Like ailanthus, the tree of heaven, Bohemia grows in any alley where there's a bit of fertile dirt and noninterference. Born-again existentialism and folk-song revival never die; they return between the seasons, like Indian summer, the swallows of spring, improvisational theater. Soho seems to pass the torch to Chelsea and then perhaps to Knightsbridge, Montmartre to Montparnasse to Saint-Germain-des-Prés to the Marais, Greenwich Village to the Upper West Side to Soho to the East Village, North Beach to the Haight to the Mission— the spoor of Bohemia blows in the wind and leaves its traces everywhere.

Sometimes, of course, the genetic mutation of Bohemian is hard to separate in the Caffe Trieste, drinking his cappuccino, from purest eccentric, flake, or turkey. This confusion forms part of the hospitality of Bohemian nationality. Once a turkey claims citizenship, he enjoys all the rights thereunto allowed, including the invention of new art forms, the sampling of banned pharmaceuticals, the choice of parasitism or creativity, and the privilege of attending the coffeehouse of his choice. If he's a scientific flake, he can organize seminars on perpetual motion, chickenshit-powered automobiles, or the energy to be drawn from right-thinking. The Bohemian physicist, psychodynamist, or channeling chiropractor contributes a balanced scientific nonestablishment for this expanding society. I don't mean to disparage the work, either. It turns out that wind, sun, and chickenshit really can run machines, the mind has its powers, and among all the blatherers there sometimes appears a breakthrough thinker. Originality has always required a fertile expanse of fumble and mistake. That's the beauty of the option. Your wastrel life might turn out to be just what's required to save the planet.

Plato's allegory of the cave was a metaphor to describe how we see reality, dimly flickering and distorted through the fire between our dark presence and the universe out there. We don't—we can't see reality. All we know, or think we know, is shadow play on the walls of the cave. Plato's cave evokes our human need to huddle, our will to heat our bodies and light our souls in company and shelter, our smallness within the immense mystery of the universe.

Sarfatti's Cave is the name I'll give the Caffe Trieste in San Francisco, where Jack Sarfatti, Ph.D. in physics, writes his poetry, evokes his mystical, miracle-working ancestors, and has conducted a several-decade-long seminar on the nature of reality and his own love life to a rapt succession of espresso scholars. He sings Gilbert and Sullivan songs. He suffers tragic reverses among women. He issues ultimatums to the CIA, the FBI, Werner Erhard, the navy, the KGB, and the Esalen Institute. With ample charm and boyish smiles he issues nonnegotiable demands. He has access to a photocopying machine. It's Jack Sarfatti against the world, and he is indomitable.

One of his soaring theories is that things which have not happened yet can cause events in the present; in other words, time is shaped like a wounded corkscrew. Obviously this has consequences for prediction, the nature of causality, our conceptions of logic. Although few in the outside world, other than the elect at his front table who listen to his smiling and eloquent rapping, are willing to follow him, occasionally he finds support from one of the moneyed seekers passing bemusedly through the Trieste, which is now the oldest living coffeehouse in North Beach. With just a little more, one more grant, one venturesome patron, one young woman with a trust fund, he can build the machine to prove his theories. Already in his possession are the theorems, formula, algebra, and poetry for it. He covers sheets of paper. He can prove everything—here's a sheet of paper with guaranteed algebra, physics, and citations from *Faust*.

The money runs out before his work is completed and he has to take a job, working in a bookshop, lecturing on a navy battleship, teaching at various private schools, giving an acclaimed series of speeches in San Jose at the Rosicrucian University, the

University of the Rosy Cross. He has published papers in respectable physics journals. His poetry is widely photocopied. His correspondence with the great in several fields is voluminous, recorded on computer disks. Cornell University B.A., University of California Ph.D., his credentials are impeccable.

Following is a quotation from a lecture given to a San Francisco State University physics seminar on 30 April 1991:

CAUSALITY VIOLATING QUANTUM ACTION AT A DISTANCE?
by Dr. Jack Sarfatti

. . . the universe is created by intelligent design but the Designer lives in our far future and has evolved *from* us . . .

Perhaps, all of the works of cultural genius, from the music of Mozart to the physics of Einstein, have their real origin in the future. The genius may be a *real* psychic channeler whose mind is open to telepathic messages from the future. The genius must be well trained in his or her craft and intellectually disciplined with the integrity of the warrior in order to properly decode the quantum signals from the future. The *purpose* of our existence would then be to ensure, not only the creation of life on earth, but the creation of the big bang itself! We obviously cannot fail since the universe cannot have come into existence without us in this extreme example of Borgesian quantum solipsism. Existentialism is wrong because it is an incorrect extrapolation of the old physics. Breton's surrealism, with its Jungian idea of meaningful coincidence, is closer to the truth. This would then be the final secret of the Illuminati—that charismatic chain of adepts in quixotic quest of their "Impossible Dream" of the Grail. Enough of my subjective vision. Now on to the objective physics.

In Plato's story, prisoners in the cave see only the shadows cast by the fire on the back wall. Then they may turn around to see the fire itself and the objects casting the shadow. Later perhaps they escape the cave to stand amazed before the world in the light of the sun, and then perhaps they gaze upon the sun, the Form, the Good, God, the Source.

In Sarfatti's version, it seems possible to shortcut all these difficult stages by listening to Jack himself. The Bohemian is fortunate to find comfortable shortcuts in his quest for the Grail of Reality. In this case, by following the wisdom of a maestro, guru, and genius, they also leave time for fun and parties when the Trieste closes for the night.

The story of Bohemia is not a sex, dope, jazz, or rock story, or a romance of radical politics, or a chronicle of mad scientists, or even a case study of outpatients, although it includes all these elements. In the Modern English Language Deceased Literary Division, Bohemia is also the distinguished international community to which e. e. cummings, James Joyce, Gertrude Stein, Sherwood Anderson, Brendan Behan, Jack Kerouac, Anaïs Nin, and Henry Miller belonged. It thrives today, expanded by recent beat and hip recruits. The great contemporaries need not be named because, as Nabokov said, anonymous praise hurts nobody. Bohemia has climbed toward power, making art into a career and setting styles in clothes, journalism, advertising, recreation. As the context grows familiar and unnoticed, it is even more important.

At Bohemia's best (let's name one figure: Allen Ginsberg), the virtues of sacrifice, social intimacy, idealism, availability to experience, acceptance of both pleasure and suffering, and talent come together. It brings the news of the world to the world without transistors or word-processing equipment. Within the universe of mass culture, it smuggles a ripe whiff of village life, of an extended family, with all the turmoil of quarrels and the coziness of mutual need. Absent a leader, a pope, or an Oral Roberts, a president of Bohemia, anyone can appoint himself Minister of Propaganda and Secretary of Organic Gardening. Margo St. James went from hooking to organizing a hooker's union to becoming a scholar of hookpersonship on campus, talk-show, and international podiums. Lacking a defined dogma, although "life-style" sometimes trespasses close to dogma, any laggard great mind can set itself up in the prophecy trade. On Russian Hill I find more world-historical manifestos under my windshield wiper than invitations to the sales at K-Mart. Punk theater and scratches on 8-millimeter film may yet save us from Armageddon, or bring us Armageddon, or make use of Armageddon (pick one of the above). There's a poet in North Beach who saves the world by wearing, speaking, reciting, and singing blue; she calls herself Blue, so it's not difficult to fix her idea in the mind. She smiles a lot. It's always a pleasure to catch her blue self pursuing blue destiny.

When Jack Kerouac's daughter, a lovely young writer, appeared at one of her father's posthumous birthday celebrations at the Old Spaghetti Factory, I told her I had met him twice, and she said, "Me too, but I also talked to him on the phone once," so she was ahead of me there.

The person coming toward me as I walk in North Beach in the forever springtime of San Francisco might be a panhandler or he might be a part of history and he often is both, like Lawrence the Young Poet, who says he's "six-seven years old, because that's younger than sixty-seven." We were all younger once, and older than that now.

My whitewashed monk's roost has gradually become stuffed with the debris of life. Books, music, paintings, prints, files, clothes I didn't wear yesterday or even the day before that; carbon copies, notebooks, the poetry I won't publish, journals, and income-tax records. Yet when I arrived in San Francisco, I came stripped to the bone—two barracks bags and the intention to live on pure spirit. (I may have meant nerve.) What stuck in my mind about *Walden,* which I had read like the Torah, was Thoreau spying a hobo crossing a field with all his possessions in two sacks. And Thoreau was filled with pity, because the hobo *still had to carry those two sacks.*

It's easy to cry "Simplify! simplify!" Complication is inexorable, inexorable. My formerly monkish roost now has children's drawings on the walls. I bought silly putty for the kids. I couldn't escape the common destiny, thank God.

Nevertheless, Thoreau's impulse toward purity, spirit, and lonely nerve provides an enduring subtext to American ambition. It's one of the most moving nostalgias we keep amid all the noise and hustle.

A whole dissertation could be written about nostalgia as the dominating climate of Bohemia, a longing for we-know-not-what

—oh, love, kindness, ease—some Arcadia where the Grail is filled with Integrity and Inspiration. This will not be that dissertation. But it turns out that we know what the longing is for. (*Oh, love,* etcetera.) Memory and childhood nourish both art and neurosis, and perhaps it's only stubborn persistence that makes the difference. Nostalgia, hope, and desire, the fuels of art, turn to grief unless they are transformed and re-created by imagination. Ambition needs persistence and energy. Discipline doesn't need to be visible, but it needs to be present.

In North Beach we pay homage to the jolly old Bohemian survivors. We also remember those who don't make it, and go down with their bottles, with methamphetamine, with automobiles on Route 1, or simply dwindle into crotchet and vanquished hope. A novelist tells me he has learned to live on air and brandy—he's a breatharian—and the impurity of my character indicates that I have not learned this. A painter comes screaming to gallery openings, wants to invent painting defacement as his art form. Various babas and swamis dressed in orange, wiping their noses with orange washcloths, reap good harvest among those tired of dignified loneliness over Jack-in-the-Box turkey nuggets on national holidays. Needless to report, there are borrowers of money who hate those who lend. There are outpatients. There are the disappeared.

As I take my nightly walk in North Beach, down to City Lights, over to the Trieste or the Puccini, I am testing myself against history. Mostly I enjoy the smells and sounds, and the sense of being in a place I've known for a generation now, a happy, unhappy, and familiar place, complicated as the places are that one comes to know. I also want to make sure I'm still a survivor.

I've written several stories about the drum-majorette champion in which I switched her around, like silly putty, into several different people. In real life she made me happy and she made me unhappy. In the stories she did the same. And now, in real life, many years later, we are still friends and this handsome middle-aged businesswoman is still my nineteen-year-old drum-majorette champion who never missed an issue of the *Hudson Review*.

. . .

The sons and daughters of Bohemia can be seen as the modern gypsies, traveling widely, telling ill-founded fortunes, with semisecret communication and ticklish devices and the proud mission to fulfill their destinies. They are chosen; they have chosen themselves. There may be some vanity here, even some solipsism and paranoia. I also know third-generation printmakers, but the world of art intersects the world of Bohemia as those who drink beer in stadiums intersect the world of athletics. They need each other. One pays admission and offers applause; the other sweats. Those who hang out are those who *live like* artists. Sometimes, of course, there is a crossover. e.e. cummings said the poet is a poet only during a few blessed moments of his lifetime; the rest of the time he is a would-be poet.

The buzz of the would-bees provides the consoling street sounds of Bohemia. For a hundred years or so, Bohemia was a way of life to which travelers might voyage and not bother to return; or if they did, they "settled down" and it was a forgotten episode. Things have changed now. Peccadillo has become a capital city. Dropping no bombs, exploiting no races, owning no air force, the legions of Bohemia occupy unresisting towns with guerrilla peacefare. It's still not too late to surrender.

If a culture finds relative peace and prosperity, the persistence of Bohemia provides an outpost of loose-limbed style in a standard-brand world. In the shifting hunt for meaning, a blending of individualism and community becomes increasingly popular. In fact, the herd of independent minds has multiplied since World War II, when Bohemianism meant going to Paris and buying a beret and an Olympia Press edition of *Tropic of Cancer*. The gallery-and-coffeehouse block can be found on Main Street. Henry Miller, barely a hundred years old, is an Honored Ancestor. Long banned, his books are now found in Chico, California, and Grass Lake, Michigan, along with New Wave record shops and local productions of Genet's *The Maids*.

In this world of impermanence, a sustaining force comes from the hope of joining a community with linkage through times, cultures, languages, sexes. The history of Bohemia brings everything back home through the tide of connection. A hundred and forty years ago, when Henri Murger in *La vie de bohème* wrote about *déménagement par la cheminée*—the process of moving by burning your furniture for heat—he was not too far from the concept of Goodwill and Salvation Army outfitters. The dispersed race of Bohemia retains its careless, troubled traditions, seeking to make love and art, seeking to defeat grief and death, and winks at the rest of the world, "winks most when widows wince."

I remembered that phrase from a poem by Wallace Stevens in l'Escale, a waterfront bar on the island of Saint Pierre, where a Quebec broadcaster and a French rag salesman questioned me about whether "Allen-Geensbairg" still lives in San Francisco, whether the proper translation of *désinvolte* is still "coule," and if "notre Kerouac" remains the idol of the young. The shirt-peddling person from the seventeenth arrondissement of Paris explained that through the Beatles and "les Stones" he found black rock 'n' roll, and through rock 'n' roll he found jazz, and through jazz he found poetry, hashish, and the meaning of life. The broadcaster from Québec makes sound collages on tape, inspired by the talk in the Co-Existence Bagel Shop and the Coffee Gallery; the one long gone, alas, the other still dealing in interracial chess matches, with an occasional festival of heavy metal or saxophone revival.

"Where are we meeting now?" asked the Québecois, and the answer might be: *Anywhere.* Even at l'Escale, a café on a foggy rock of France lost in the Labrador current fifteen miles from Newfoundland.

When I found San Francisco, I found my home. I found Left Bank Paris and Greenwich Village in a permanent laboratory condition, wrapped in a convoluted time warp of past and future within the instant present tense of California. Oddly enough for a committed wanderer in this land of loose nuts, I have dwelled in the same flat on Russian Hill for over thirty years now. The more things change, the more they become different. But this is *com-*

munitas. This is, despite everything, a variety of stability. These sticky things are roots.

The Bohemian culture of North Beach has elaborated an urgent hundred-year-long operetta for the entertainment of San Francisco and the world. While this corner of America seemed at first to have the same connection with real life that *The Mikado* has with Japan, I gradually came to realize that "North Beach," "Bohemian," "beatnik," "hippie," "New Wave," are not substitutes for real life but metaphors of reality. North Beach is not *really* an operetta: three of my children were conceived here; there are schools, strikes, and churches; people get rich and go bankrupt; my beard turns gray and the wrinkles of my face grow more wrinkly. I see a neighbor who used to ride a bicycle now hobbling with an aluminum walker. The crowded hills and flatlands are not inhabited by stand-ins and chorus; those are genuine Italians, Chinese, Australians, castaways, alcoholics and nonalcoholics (some of the latter, like me, the worst kind), dropouts from the Midwest, remittance persons from Texas and New York and Boston, Californicaters—all the men and women in funny clothes who give flesh to the metaphor—plus a genuine residential neighborhood, shops and houses and flats, filled with people who pass the time by working and looking out for themselves as sensibly as possible.

The world is not always sweet and hospitable to strangers. In moments of optimism and euphoria on Russian Hill, which is sweet and hospitable, I feel like a part of some marvelous ongoing enterprise, and that I am not alone, not part of a gang or secret society; my family is growing. Bohemian American is Middle American turned peculiar. But here in North Beach, even the Middle Americans seem to have curlicues at their edges. I said I know third-generation marijuana smokers. I also know third-generation *square* marijuana smokers.

A beautiful coffee-colored girl, driving a red MG with the top open, noticed me watching her swing the car gracefully, with one neat parabola, into a parking space on Upper Grant. She looked familiar; even if she didn't, she needed to look familiar. I asked, "Vous êtes haïtienne, mademoiselle?"

"You bet," she said. "How 'bout you?"

We headed for coffee while I hastened to explain that the streets of North Beach, Port-au-Prince, and Paris are my favorite theaters.

"Personally I like a good dinner show at the Fairmont," she said.

But the thing about it is: I didn't surprise her. She knows what North Beach is for.

Thanks to the audience climbing onto the scenery, thanks to the players climbing back into the audience, North Beach remains a stage for ongoing rehearsal of that urgent Bohemian operetta. We are not just singing our arias, opening our mouths like the birds and letting it peep out; we are doing the work of the world.

Thank you, Henri Murger.

Thank you, creators of sourdough bread, Monterey jack cheese, red wine, and getting there on foot.

Thank you, whichever unknown geniuses deep in human history invented the soulful metaphor and goofing around. Wouldn't it be marvelous if it could have been the same person? But even if it wasn't, Bohemia demonstrates that the creators must have been related.

2

When North Beach Made an Offer, Old Bohemia Couldn't Refuse

Thank the gods that protect writers from the obligation to write: the phone just rang. It's an old acquaintance from North Beach days whom I haven't seen since breakfast at the Trieste Caffe this morning. We Bohemians in our red-lined satin capes and berets believe in mystic synchronicities.

Ffrank Ffollet (don't forget the extra f's, to differentiate him from the bogged-down Irish one-f Francises) is writing his own version of *Roots*—in this case, the roots of a Welshman, since Dylan Thomas just didn't have enough genius to do the job right. You need *spark*. You need *fire*. You need *Ffrank Ffollett*.

But now my friend's wife has been laid off from her job as a teacher's aide, and the IRS says he owes $623 in taxes from four years ago when he briefly sold out to the military-industrial-bucketshop complex and took a job selling circus tickets by phone for the Firemen's Alzheimer's Benefit. Those bastards were supposed to forget to report his earnings, but you can't count on the boojwah to do it right by not doing it, despite the promise that their brains have turned to tofu.

Since Ffrank owes such a small amount, the whole force of the government was coming down on him in a strike force of attack helicopters filled with auditors from the Federal Building. It makes him nervous. Even after three double espressos, his stomach is still jumpy. How can a person sing the truth of the Welsh race, their sagas, their kings in fur hats, under such pressure? As a member of an ethnic group myself, can I dig what he's saying, brother?

That's his story. And since I bought a pair of circus tickets from him, I'm partly to blame.

"Okay," I said, "I'll lend you a hundred. Come and pick up the check."

"Jeez," he said, "couldn't you meet me at the Puccini? I'm pretty busy right now, got to make a couple more calls, but I could take a break in an hour. Can I lay a cappuccino on you, pal?"

Ffrank qualified. The Christmas Alzheimer's circus ticket salesman and Welsh epic poet knows I won't change my mind. He's got other trapezes to fly. And I'm a sucker for a free cappuccino.

Among my early memories of San Francisco's Old Bohemia, then bivouacked in a North Beach concentration so dense that one strategic bomb could have wiped out most of the nation's resources of unrhymed verse, are the even older Bohemians of the late fifties and early sixties, complaining, "I remember the *real* Bohemia of the thirties . . . Wobblies, anarchists, jug wine toters, poets, and you could get a big dollar dinner for seventy-nine cents. There were giants in those days, young feller."

Well, when I roamed North Beach with Allen Ginsberg in 1957—hadn't yet come to live in San Francisco, but was scouting the terrain—the prix fixe dinners at the Hôtel du Midi (upstairs Basque), Ripley's (sort of French), the Pisa (definitely Italian), and a half dozen other all-you-can resorts cost in the neighborhood of a buck seventy-five, red wine a quarter extra. Allen preferred the New Cup Café (Chinese) because it was less expensive. But we are all artists here, our heads in the clouds; let's not emphasize vulgar inflation. The young whippersnapper eventually becomes an old whippersnapper.

Surely the Bohemians of the twenties and thirties ran into garrulous veterans at the Black Cat or in their studios in the Monkey Block, now buried under the TransAmerica Building, who remembered the carefree, romantic, and sexy pre-earth-quake San Francisco Bohemia described by Frank Norris in his novel *Blix*. This picture of lazy young would-bees buzzing over the seven, count 'em, well maybe nine hills of the Bay was published in 1899, the same year as his better-known *McTeague,* a gritty story of Zolaesque misfortune on Polk Street. One of the miracles of my early discovery of San Francisco was to find that Polk Street, adapted into Eric von Stroheim's great and doomed film *Greed,* was psychically intact—still very much as Norris described it, even with the hint of homosexuality discreetly foreshadowed nearly a hundred years ago.

When *Greed* was shot, von Stroheim used a corner apartment on Columbus in North Beach to represent the Polk Street dentist's office. When I used to visit, it was the house and studio of a cigarette-addicted abstract-expressionist painter who moved out from New York after one of his lungs was removed. "If I'm gonna die," he said, "might as well have some fun before I go."

It was a time of great fun in North Beach. We watched Officer Bigaroni enter the life of poetry by rousting poets guilty of interracial marijuana smoking. (A bar on Upper Grant had a swinging outdoor sign which announced: HEADQUARTERS FOR ETHNICS.) The black Jewish abominist poet Bob Kauffman wrote his "Notes Found at the Tomb of the Unknown Draft Dodger." We broke sourdough together at the old Pisa (it was called the New Pisa) and melted with feeling as that Japanese opera troupe arose after the family-style dinner to sing "Oh! Susanna" in Japanese. We should have suspected, when they took over Stephen Foster, they would move next into the automobile industry.

The San Francisco Renaissance, nationally celebrated and therefore validated by Grove Press in a special issue of the *Evergreen Review,* laid waste the terrain, reciting to jazz and pillaging, shooting paint onto canvas, smoking, and attacking New York while Kenneth Rexroth beamed and Zen pioneers learned how to pronounce Om. Heroes arrived from Manhattan by thumb, by driveaway car, and by prop plane, as brave in their hearts as Cortez, Richard Henry Dana, Robert Louis Stevenson, and Fatty Arbuckle, who made the trip to San Francisco a little earlier by . . . was it covered wagons?

Allen Ginsberg recited "Howl," with its famous results in destroying the very fabric of western civilization.

The Circle Gallery dropped the scales from our eyes.

Michael McClure snarled, growled, snuffled, and purred his beast poems in front of my fireplace, scaring my young woman friend, who spoke only English and French, not Beast.

Ron Boise's *Kama Sutra* instruction sculptures were arrested, jailed by the police, and ultimately acquitted. I have a mug shot of a cast-iron couple caught in flagrante and tagged: BOOKED. S.F.P.D. One gaunt erotic enigma stood for years on the roof of the Anchor Steam Beer factory, where it was visible from the freeway, improving the sex life of commuters, until Fritz Maytag took over the native brew.

Katharine Ross, later to star in *The Graduate* and *Butch Cassidy and the Sundance Kid*, was a lovely young understudy in Actor's Workshop productions. She lived upstairs of a grocery on Stockton near Filbert; she stood nude on stage in a daring version of Jean Genet's *The Balcony*. When I lent her my prewar Citroën gangster getaway car—it had running boards—she wisely used convenient parking in front of her building. When I returned from a trip to Saint-Germain-des-Prés, the North Beach of Paris, I found that she had collected one fire hydrant parking ticket for each day I had been obliviously dreaming at the Flore, the Deux Magots, and the Bonaparte.

She had the bedrock solidity of a true North Beach believer. Everything was for the best in the best of all possible worlds if you remember to tuck the tickets neatly into the glove compartment . . . especially if you look like Katharine Ross. The first time I was ever comp'd for a meal was at Cho-Cho, the Japanese restaurant near City Lights Bookstore, when Jimmy, the proprietor, said: "You come in with a person who looks like her, you don't ever have to pay."

I'll tell you how long ago that was: sushi hadn't yet made it past Hawaii, crossing the Pacific. California cuisine meant Hangtown fry. Natural foods were Bird's-eye frozen instead of Libby's canned peas.

My excuse for moving to San Francisco—the excuse that paid my child support—was a grant to do a play at the Actor's Workshop. If I took kindly, sweet-tempered, high-cheekboned Katharine Ross to dinner, you see—the logic should be clear to any other pure soul—it was only because we needed to exchange hints on success in show business. In the great tradition of noncommercial theater, my play was not performed here because I wouldn't consent to the director's wish to cast his wife in a role for which she was of the wrong generation. The play was later given an undeserved run in Los Angeles.

Katharine was itching to get away from Vesuvio's. When she returned to Adler Alley, now called Jack Kerouac Street, it was with makeup personnel, trailer, canvas chair with her name stenciled on it, and a full crew. The ghost of Kathie Past haunted this set. I watched in the crowd of gawkers, along with Jimmy from Cho-Cho, who said, "Just as pretty. Just as pretty."

Across from City Lights and Vesuvio's ("We Are Itching to Get Away from Portland, Oregon") there used to be the Bodega, flamenco dancing, cans of tomato sauce over rice at night, guitar lessons during the day. A psychiatrist's ex-wife told me that her guitar would never betray her as her husband did. (He lied to her, like a banjo.) Where there is now an "adult" screening room–bookshop there was then an art cinema and a restaurateur who liked to relax by wearing spike heels during his at-home hours. Kenneth Anger, film collagist of *Scorpio Rising*, lived upstairs with his fan magazines and his leather collection. At Vesuvio's, another psychiatrist's ex-wife, author of *I'm Sorry, Darling*, the story of premature ejaculation, sat patiently for two years, analyzing her divorce. She said everything many times, like a balalaika. The Discovery Bookshop, a treasure trove presided over by Frederick Roscoe, rhymemaster, world champion in the Indoor Olympic Doggerel Competition, gave employment to such clerks as David Meltzer, who now teaches poetry at New College in the Mission, and Peter Edler, a German beatnik known as "the Hip Hun" because he had been expelled from the Hitler Youth for talking in class. He later married a Swedish woman, ran a child-care service in Marin, and moved to Stockholm when she came into her inheritance.

Prominent vegetarians and the founder of Breatharianism,

which taught people how to nourish themselves without eating, a recipe using the native chlorophyll in their skins plus a dash of the sunlight over the miracle church of Peter & Paul, hung out in the Bermuda triangle of Grant, Broadway, Union, and Columbus. The geometry might suggest a rectangle to some, but at least it's not square. The prophet of Breatharianism sat at the bar of the Washington Square Bar & Grill, tossing popcorn and pretzels into his mouth while he promised to reveal the secrets of foodless feeding to anyone who bought him a brandy. "That cognac is pure sunlight, it's a known fact," he explained. A friend remembers Joan Baez crooning softly on a bench in front of the church while an admirer brushed her long, dark, glossy hair. It was a scene of peace and love until Joan said to her fan, "Get your sticky fingers the fuck away from my guitar." Peace, Sister.

The spike-heeled restaurant owner on Columbus near the Hungry i entertained his patrons by singing and dancing "Tiptoe through the Tulips." His ambition was to grow up to be Tiny Tim, but twinkletoes was stilled, due to murder by his late-night busboy. An occasional crime of passion is part of the Bohemian tradition called Going Too Far. Later there was another musical tragedy, the case of the killer piano which crushed a bouncer who happened to be embracing a lady after hours at the Condor. It crushed him against the *ceiling*. Some prankster pressed the button that raised this traditional platform on which Paderewski and Carol Doda cavorted, and in his ardor the lover failed to notice that the earth was moving toward heaven. The couple lay pinned together until cleaning folks arrived in the morning. The woman survived but, wishing to change her karma, departed North Beach for North Dakota.

Did the Vesuvio's psychiatrist's wife, author of *I'm Sorry, Darling*, preoccupied with sexual persistence, lean on the button? History cannot tell us everything; that's why we need rhetorical questions.

Mort Sahl used to get his exercise sprinting to the bank when it opened to cash his paychecks from Enrico Banducci's Hungry i. Other employees were often ahead of him in line, rubbing the sleep from their eyes and praying. Enrico was an entrepreneur with ample soul but loosely wrapped accounting skills. The one-legged hooker at his bar entertained seekers of oddness, including Alvah Bessie, the Hollywood Ten blacklisted writer who came to work the nightclub's light and sound system after he was released from prison. I walked out on Barbra Streisand because she sang too loud; I blushed for Woody Allen, who panicked on stage and forgot his lines. The next day we drove to Berkeley because he said he needed to get over his trauma by viewing "girls with major hair."

When Lenny Bruce thought he was a bird and flew out a window of the Swiss-American Hotel on Broadway, near Enrico's Coffee House, which provided an outdoor office for entertainers, mobsters, financial-district employees, and sixties grokkers and groovers—also Vietnam service people on R&R—Ralph Gleason, jazz and rock critic, stood by taking notes. The medical emergency crew that came to carry Lenny to the hospital taped his mouth shut because the disappointed bird was using language not in the vocabulary of your average fallen eagle. "Is there anything I can do?" I asked Gleason.

"There's nothing anyone can do now," intoned the philosopher.

The Hip Hun strolled past in his medal-bedecked caftan, which looked like a ball gown. The wife of a stage manager at The Committee offered me a fuzzy capsule from her private stash. What's this? I asked her. "A dream of truth," she said. "Try it."

The ambulance went sirening off, carrying a bird with his wing broken and his mouth taped.

Old cities are better than rapidly evolving new communities at offering enclaves and backwashes in which Bohemians can set down their lightly packaged roots. In the late nineteenth and early twentieth centuries, Montparnasse and Montmartre in Paris, Soho in London, Greenwich Village in New York—and the ancient inner cities of Rome, Athens, even such buttoned-up places as Geneva, Switzerland, and less buttoned-up Stockholm, Copenhagen, Buenos Aires—discovered that gypsylike strangeness could sprout in alleyways like the ailanthus tree in my native Cleveland.

Sometimes a college neighborhood helped to provide the necessary cheap eats, lodging, and companionship. San Francisco's street ambling, its site as a hilly port, as destination for Latin folks, its speculative fervor, its early prosperity, its newness and oldness, gave it unique advantages. This city has studied hard how to entertain itself and others. Mark Twain came for the gold rush; Ambrose Bierce, Joaquin Miller, Bret Harte, Isadora Duncan, and the Emperor Norton were famous beatniks and hippies before the words. The Emperor Norton wore flowers, dressed like a burning bush, printed his own currency; now street poets hawk their wares in North Beach and at the Café Picaro in the Mission—still living off the yearning for distraction a Mediterranean, forever-springtime climate helps to nurture.

Even businesses with a sordid criminal aroma elsewhere assume a genuinely playful form where the yerba buena grows. The Mitchell brothers, Artie and Jim, hippie filmmakers out of San Francisco State University, were official pornographers-in-chief, avuncular sex-show operators. They followed their bliss. The outdoor mural at their erotic world headquarters in the Tenderloin propagandizes for the rain forest; the one it replaced dealt in nymphs and myths. Unfortunately the brothers, intimate friends and fishing companions, raising a flock of children together, seem to have had a falling out and Jim shot Artie to death. Naughtiness crossed the edge to violence in the real world of money, power, and fraternal rivalries.

Pure naughtiness has always had a central position in San Francisco Bohemia, in keeping with the city's tradition of taking its frivolity seriously. The Barbary Coast and the International Settlement, archaeological remnants of which can still be found in the bidets and outdoor erotic murals not yet extirpated on the Jackson Square area, specialized in drink, sex, and the genial spending of money. This was a port, after all. The Sexual Freedom League, sponsored by the Reverend Jefferson Fuck Poland in the sixties and early seventies, hasn't been heard from lately. The Kerista Commune, a group marriage, men and women who share everything, including children, used to provide me with house-cleaning service, arriving in a group marriage of three, one sanitary expert carrying a snakelike vacuum cleaner draped like a Jungian symbol about his upper body. In response to my application to visit their commune as research for this report, they said they would take a vote. They discussed; they voted. "We've consensussed," one of them responded by telephone, and the answer came to my request: they noed.

Margo St. James started the first hooker's union, Call Off Your Old Tired Ethics (COYOTE), in North Beach. "Since I didn't find a nice old man, preferably an invalid, to support me, I went into business," she explained. "I like giving shampoos."

Another enterprising young woman, a nurse from Boston, started the Golden Gate Foundation to guide libidinous men back toward karmic tranquility. She thrived for a few years. A receptionist used to say to the waiting clients, "The therapist will see you now, big boy."

I was invited to the Christmas party given at a popular North Beach restaurant by a woman I might call Ilse von Braunschlofer (not her real name, if you plan to look her up in the S&M yellow pages), whose business was the constant care of men devoted to leather and severe discipline. Like hay fever, this seems to require regular visits for skin tests and prickly inoculation. Aside from me, the other male guests were clients. The disciplinarians were schoolteachers, parole officers, motorcycle-repair ladies, except for one who told me she was a nuclear physicist. "Aw," I said, "you look more like a molecular biologist."

"Caught again," she exclaimed, snapping her fingers. "Hey, promise you won't tell my mother?"

What in other climates might be called prostitution came to be a slightly eccentric work-study program in San Francisco. A young woman who took showers with visitors at the Mitchell brothers' emporium ("Take a Shower with a Feminist") was a graduate student in clinical psychology. "We're pioneering in the safe-sex field," she said. Another groundbreaker was my friend Judy Roe, author of *The Same Old Grind*, writer, stripteaser, set designer, costume maker, now retired to full-time authorship and the occasional painting of "Nymphs from Hell" backdrops for an erotic live show. When I asked why she corresponded with me before we met, she said, "Because you're the only stranger I know."

My sons keep asking me, "Dad, were you alive before there was AIDS and herpes?"

There were giants in those days, my boys.

Besides the ever-popular sex adventurers, chafing at the limits, there are San Francisco's Bohemian stockbrokers, lawyers, physicians (Dr. Flash Gordon, the motorcycle specialist, for example), even real estate speculators. A Zen Center musician from Green Gulch Farm leaned on my shoulder, crossing Upper Grant, muttering, "The punk monk is drunk." Part-time, many try for Bohemianism, and the nice thing is, all can succeed. Why not? The rules are generous in San Francisco, unlike the rules for major-league basketball, where you have to be tall.

One of the less benign elements of the sixties flower epoch was the discovery of drugs as a shortcut to satori, nirvana, dream therapy, relief from parental nagging, esthetic fulfillment, preparing for final exams, and foreplay. Bad drugs came into the mainstream. Thank you, Dr. Leary, Dr. Alpert, and the other Dr. Feelgoods. A poet-filmmaker-cabdriver-stand-up comedian named Chris preached his new discovery, chanting: "If coffee, tea, or Ovaltine don't do it, try Meth." He had a way of injecting friends so that he would be murmuring, "Now don't you feel . . ." and just as the speed hit their bloodstreams, he would utter the lyrical word *"bettah?"*

It was magic. He had a gig as a stand-up comic at the Hungry i, he charmed everyone, he made a prizewinning film, and within a couple of years he gave himself a Methedrine lobotomy. His IQ went from something near genius to moron and below. He became nearly blind. He wandered North Beach and panhandled and pretended he still knew me. "Chris, remember we first met at the Crystal Palace in St. Louis? Remember Gaslight Square?"

"Yeah man. Yeah man."

Bohemia promises eventual performance; not everyone fakes it very well (Ffrank Ffollet and his telephone solicitation for the charities of his choice). Another poet saw me with Allen Ginsberg on Grant a few years ago, and said, "Hey, how's it feel to be the eastern establishment?"

Allen looked quizzical, he looked bemused. He was worried about a friend's upset stomach and was heading for a store to buy a roll of Tums.

"Back east," muttered the young middle-aged poet of the Golden West, "they just don't understand the post-Ginsbergian revolution."

"Pardon?"

"They're Eurocentric. Gender chauvinists. Deconstruction is a hegemony racket, man."

The 12 Adler Place poet gave me high fives and slapped my palm. Power to the post-Ginsbergians! Down with the *Paris Review*!

A hyphen and overlap between my old Bohemia and the even older Bohemia of a previous generation is exemplified by William Saroyan, whom I met by accident as he was boisterously touring the San Francisco Museum of Modern Art, explaining matters to his son and daughter. He came to visit my flat on Russian Hill above North Beach—Charles Reich, author of *The Greening of America,* and also the sculptor who did the fakes for William Randolph Hearst's San Simeon have been my neighbors. Saroyan, a lover of Strange, adored the fresh plaster smells when newly minted Renaissance masterpieces were moved onto the sidewalk out of the defunct artist's studio after the sculptor's untimely death. When I introduced Saroyan to Reich, the two gentlemen stared at each other and said, like gentlemen: "Good day."

In the early sixties, since I was five or ten years younger than I am now, I had the right to a young woman friend (called "girlfriend" in those dear dead days beyond recall). She had a roommate who admired William Saroyan. We decided to . . . please recall this quaint Mickey Rooney language . . . "double-date." The two young women arrived at my apartment and I lit a fire. Saroyan arrived and a burning crate leapt out of the fireplace, due to the draft of his entrance. "That's the tiger in the fireplace," he explained, as we ran about, stifling the conflagration.

The evening had begun nicely: warm hearts and singed rug.

But Saroyan decided, to her great disappointment, that his date was too young for more than avuncular attention. He gave us a tour of his—an earlier—North Beach Bohemia, Barbary Coast, International Settlement. We had dinner at the Brighton Express. He asked the cook if she would like to be God in his new play. She giggled prettily, wiped her hands on her apron, and said she might consider the job if it didn't conflict with her schedule for making mud pies, the ice cream dessert she had invented.

The question of the existence of God resolved, Saroyan took us to Earthquake McGoon's to hear Turk Murphy, the great Dixieland horn player, another old San Francisco Bohemian from that border where North Beach fades into the waterfront, the longshoreman's union of Harry Bridges, and the spiritual link of two raffish ports, San Francisco and New Orleans.

Late that night, we said our prayers with an Irish-coffee ritual on the terrace at Enrico's, where a famous pair of call girls used to cruise in their jointly owned Thunderbird. They parked in the no-parking zone reserved for taxis, callperson Thunderbirds, Zen real estate showoffs, and close personal friends of Enrico Banducci, and then strolled over for an exchange of sociability in the 2:00 A.M. damp. The outdoor heaters sizzled. Saroyan peered with his ardent dark eyes into their faces and began to discuss their ethnic heritages "because such things are *very interesting.*" And when they left, he reminisced about the call girls of yore, who didn't drive Thunderbirds.

Our young women were charmed by this contact with the literature of the thirties. And then, ever courtly, Saroyan doffed his fedora to his date, the deep Saroyan scholar, said goodnight (her eyes were gleaming with pride and frustration), and began to trudge across town to his sister's house. The scholar was thankful for a glimpse of "The Daring Young Man on the Flying Trapeze," that great early story about a starving writer in San Francisco. She remembered that his Pulitzer Prize play, *The Time of Your Life,* was inspired by Izzy Gomez's saloon nearby on Pacific. "That's cool, Herb, I can make do with insight," she said, "even if he's gotten kind of lazy."

When I see my friend of thirty years ago, she still sometimes recalls that evening and says, "Poor Debbie. She thought Saroyan would be more . . . Bohemian. But she said the same thing about a wing of the Jefferson Airplane and a vice president of Merrill Lynch."

North Beach was still a place for seekers who came seeking. The working artists couldn't stay up all night, liked to tuck themselves in at closing time.

Bohemians are not what weekend visitors, bridge and tunnel folks, think they are. Bohemians may look like outcasts and scapegoats, cultivators of private gardens, but in fact, they want to run things, define the taste, preach the theories, support the arts, make the music, write the literature, and drink the coffee and wine that keeps society jumping, vigorous, and fun. Even Bohemian dead-beats and panhandlers help give body to the soup.

A CBS producer and I strolled around North Beach, he carrying a tape recorder while I chatted with the turbulent Bohemian masses, which include few actual artists, of course, but many profound lumpens living off the land. I interviewed Lawrence the Young Poet, who hoped people would confuse him with Lawrence Ferlinghetti.

At City Lights, Mad Alex, a handsome, tall, black street rapper, said to us by way of introduction: "I got the bucket if you got the water."

What could be a better, more mysterious, yet strangely coherent description of the marginalized performers who enact our street theater?

America needs to match up the buckets and the waters. I'll drink to that.

Hube the Cube, retired dope dealer to the beat generation— "Hey, man, *Jack Kerouac* bought from him!"—later peddled the early streets edition of the San Francisco *Chronicle* to the folks on the terrace of Enrico's, audience and actors in the hundred-and-fifty-year-long operetta. In 1957, when Allen Ginsberg introduced me to Mad Alex at the Co-Existence Bagel Shop on Upper Grant, he acknowledged my presence with bucket and water riddles. Alex returned from some kind of forced vacation to stand in front of City Lights, haggard, gaunt, white haired, but still reciting his paradoxes. Bob Kauffman, our Rimbaud, our champion of doom, took a vow of silence except for harrowing croaking demands for rent or food money. A toothless novelist and poet whose exercise consisted of hiking to City Lights to pick up his mail, whom I used to invite to Enrico's for hot chocolate—all he could chew—met a schoolteacher from Sacramento, married her, and grew teeth. Henri Lenoir, ballet dancer, proprietor of Vesuvio's, patron of the beat painters, permanent honorary mayor of North Beach, came in his retirement to the meals offered him by Enrico Banducci. Occasionally he raised cash by selling off part of his art collection. At the Hôtel du Midi, a prix fixe Basque restaurant, I met temporary true love in the early sixties. Richard Brautigan, suddenly the rage in his Confederate general disguise, handed out free poetry:

I give her an A+ for long blond hair . . .

and curtseyed winsomely when college women asked for his autograph. Later he shot himself.

The hum and whir of the late fifties, early sixties mimeograph machines, churning out beat poetry, deafening me as I walked down North Beach alleys, grew still. The preeminence of rock 'n' roll slowed poetry production to a torrent. The Reverend Pierre de Lattre, the Congregational minister who founded the Bread & Wine Mission to the beats, hoping to convert them to Christianity, was instead converted himself and now lives and writes in New Mexico.

The Black Cat, a link with ancient North Beach Bohemia, became a gay bar and then closed. There was another dark side here, too. Bunny Simon, the stately New Orleans Creole gentleman who owned The Anxious Asp, moved his bar to Haight Street. "Some folks in North Beach didn't want a man of color doing business," he told me. Officer Bigaroni, who harassed the beats, flailing with his club, ran into his own troubles with fraud charges during his retirement. As Bohemia made North Beach chic, rents became confiscatory, driving out theaters, cheap restaurants, artists, and the old radicals. Greenwich Village and Saint-Germain-des-Prés followed the same pattern, the iron grip of real estate speculation closing upon the graceful swan necks.

Irascible Fred Roscoe, rhymemaster with his Santa Claus beard and pinkness, closed Discovery Bookshop and moved to San Anselmo. Enrico Banducci lives with his son back east in Virginia. A few grizzled veterans still hang out at Gino & Carlo's, remembering grand old poets, grand old pool-cue fights. A few stubborn radicals like Jack Hirschman still sell their verse and their manifestos at 12 Adler Place. The countercultural physicist Jack Sarfatti, Ph.D., preaches the corkscrew shape of time to his permanent seminar at the Trieste. "Things that haven't happened yet can cause events in the past."

I know, I know, Jack.

Occasionally, I still see Lawrence the Young Poet on the bus. He's retired from seeking patronage up and down Columbus, Broadway, and Grant. A young poet who was once five-seven years old, then six-seven, eventually gets to be eight-zero.

A few cafés, bars, restaurants, bookshops still keep the faith. Beautiful Clara Bellino, actress, poet, and founder of the rock group The Flying Monkeys, stands at the microphone with her delicate pale face and leather miniskirt, singing her tender lyric to some lucky lover:

> *You're lying on a cloud*
> *My lipstick on your ass . . .*

An occasional brave entrepreneur prevents North Beach from becoming a Bohemia theme park, a kind of Beatnikworld. Recently Rumors, on the corner across the street from boarded-up Enrico's, has been trying to put together the right ingredients— cheap food, warm hearts, a hospitable eccentric proprietor in the form of James Swim, a Chinese-speaking former U.S. Army intelligence expert. There were blabbermouth nights, occasional fits of reggae, waitresses with metal decor pinned through haphazard parts of their lovely countenances, whispered conferences among pursuers of beauty and truth, an easy layabout atmosphere, and most basic of all . . . *Cheap Pasta.* In North Beach today, this miracle makes a person weep with gratitude and nostalgia. The sourdough bread was baked on the premises. It's not gourmet dining; this was comfortable, adequate feeding in a world of congenial loafing. Eureka, we can go home again. I met Ffrank Ffollet there in the company of a daughter by a marriage he had forgotten. They explained that they had just happened to notice each other, found something familiar in their faces, and realized . . .

"Hey, Dad? Is that you?"

"Fflorence?"

The miracle of a third-generation Bohemian meeting a second-generation beatnik.

I blessed them and found my own table under a light in the corner. A tall fellow, the ghost of Mad Alex, pale, with a fragile beard, introduced himself. "My name is Wo," he said.

"That's funny, you don't look Chinese. How'd you get that name?"

"Because Wo is me," he said. "Now will you buy one of my poems?"

3

Coffee, Sex, Art, Terror, Money, and Other Rituals—France, Boheem Mamas, and the Pursuit of Pleasure in the Bohemian Religion—Some Necessary Histories

An Arab legend credits Solomon, king of the Jews, with the first use of coffee, at the command of the angel Gabriel, in order to cure some unspecified disease (anomie?). Then it's fast forward to Yemen and Ethiopia, the fifteenth century, and the Sufis, who used the roasted bean to drive away fatigue and lethargy, bringing to the body "a certain sprightliness and vigor." The recipe for Sufi ecstasies and dancing doesn't call for decaf. Sufi practice did not "take" coffee as American morning commuters on the run might do; they *drank* it in a ceremony of sociability and appreciation. They noticed that wine reduced the need to eat, but coffee chased the need to sleep.

One Arab scholar said coffee made his brain "nimble."

The Sufis stayed awake, sang, danced, and nimbly conversed with spirits.

Inevitably the rumor of coffee's power traveled, traveled well, and soon reached Cairo. Along the way, some of the mysticism fell off. Places to drink coffee—coffeehouses—grew up in the vicinity of mosques and markets. They provided alternative occasions for meeting. God and commerce could be reconciled, pleasures proposed. In the normal course, prohibition of something so delightful had to be the next step. The first incident of prohibition took place in Mecca, where a holy man noticed men having fun, chatting, laughing, drinking *qahwa*. Must stop this, mustn't we? Jurists, priests, physicians, promptly joined the thought police with legal, religious, and medical reasons for banning the African brew. God, the State, and vital humors were all opposed. The drinking of coffee was forbidden in 1511.

This edict worked as well as prohibition usually does.

In Cairo, bands of righteous thugs destroyed coffeehouses and attacked coffee drinkers. Resistants received seventeen lashes for persisting in their evil ways. The number 17 was specified for reasons beyond my knowledge.

The punishment worked as well as it usually does.

Nocturnal meetings for fun and talk continued to alarm both religous and civil authorities. Coffee among the Arabs, as later in Europe, encouraged staying up after dark and cultivating adventurous thoughts. Sixteenth-century Turkish engravings depict crowded coffeehouses with the typical activities proper to such a place: the brewing of beverage, reading and discussion, playing backgammon and other games, flirting, singing, smoking, plucking stringed instruments. One can imagine hubbub. Morris Lapp, an artist in San Francisco, has been engaged for years in a project to paint all the coffeehouses of this metropolitan village in their variety mostly south of pious but north of bawdy. The ritual is consistent from medieval Istanbul to contemporary California.

Angelic distinctions needed to be developed in order to separate the idea of coffee from the idea of wine. Was "intoxication" the word for coffee-induced nimbleness? Generations of Arab savants debated this issue. Some compared coffee with hashish, which was generally forbidden. A defender of coffee summed up his apology:

> One drinks coffee with the name of the Lord on his lips, and stays awake. The person who seeks wanton delights in intoxicants disregards the Lord, and gets drunk.

This sprightliness of affect tended to win the day against rigid piety. If coffee modifies the spirit, as it does, and therefore should be banned, what to do about garlic, onions, cloves, spices? What about steam baths, where people also gathered to make secular communion and sometimes tickle each other? There seemed to be no way to remove pleasure from life; people wouldn't consent to it.

The early Middle Eastern medical scholars of coffee, who were echoed later by Europeans, believed that coffee cured and caused melancholia, depending on temperament. It excited and disturbed the mind. It calmed the spirit. It reduced sexual desire. It stimulated sexual desire. It prevented the bubbling of blood, but since blood doesn't bubble much, this virtue tended to be forgotten. It also cured smallpox, especially in those who had not been exposed to the disease.

One quality which seemed to check out over the hectic centuries was that coffee enabled people to stay awake at night. For the pious, it meant that they could perform additional devotions. Through that option it stimulated religion, unlike excess use of wine, which might make a person forget his vows.

The brew changed social life. Places to drink coffee, coffeehouses, joined restaurants and taverns to different purposes. Generally, if prohibition was attempted, the doctors were called in to discuss the health menace of coffee *after* the decision to prohibit. By the sixteenth century coffeehouses had spread throughout the Middle East. Men left their dwellings in order to share the ritual. There were storytellers, gossipers, gamblers and gamers, sometimes things to read, sometimes male or female prostitutes. There were puppet shows and shadow plays, drummers and fiddlers. If coffee led to melancholia, coffeehouses also provided remedies: symposia, dancing and singing girls, beautiful boys, relaxed and public scheming. . . . Sometimes even hashish or opium found its way here.

The coffeehouse changed social life, anticipating the revolution created by Lloyd's of London, the coffee resort which developed the practice of insuring ship travel and trade and thus made the industrial revolution possible. This is the sort of change that can occur if you don't go to bed at nightfall, instead remaining alert and full of ambition in the tavern-without-wine. People wanted to get out, and having gotten out without getting drunk, they wanted to do things. They did things, shared risks, participated in profits, and sipped a beverage made in gleaming and treasured machines, like temple objects.

The coffeehouse corrupted strictness about social standing and unnecessary speech. Even the passing of the cup or the pot was a leveling gesture. Drinking coffee together leads to eating together, talking together, perhaps bathing together and wickedness. And all this sometimes led to working together. In Cairo, Istanbul, London, and Paris, both noisy contemplation and silent euphoria encouraged the development of new social and business arrangements in the temples of coffee.

The wakeful enthusiasm of the café breathes a different atmosphere from the ebullience, ecstasy, and despair of the tavern. People don't generally leave off an excess of alcohol to rush with renewed energy toward their labors. The savor and energy of coffee, and the atmosphere of the places where it is shared, became linked with the effort at tribal cohesion which Bohemians longed for.

At a café in Manhattan's East Village, which for a time was called The Sixties, the afternoon table talk was about being dangerous. The artist is a terrorist; the heavy-metal musician forces us to live in an amplified world, giving us the moral bends along with hearing loss. The poet snaps our morality between his pens, puts everything we think we hold dear on a soft disk and then wipes it out. The philosopher is a computer virus, spreading silently, a thief in the night.

I wondered if the abovementioned poet with a pen in each hand was using them like drumsticks. Two-handed poets were new to me.

During extended visits to New York in the late eighties, I sat among these revolutionaries of cruel vision every afternoon, often eating fruit and yogurt. Greenwich Village has split like an amoeba into its Soho, Tribeca, Noho, Upper West Side, Brooklyn Heights, and East Village overflows. The East Village was the place of strictest theory; this café was a refuge for floating certainties. On nearby streets, others were defending Tompkins Square as a people's park for the homeless, or driving the crack dealers from entrenched positions, or demonstrating against absentee landlords, gentrification, or New York University while their video cameras and tape machines recorded it for the future. At The Sixties the light was good, the yogurt organic, the fruit fresh, the waitpersons agreeable, the prices right. When the weather was warm, there were tables outside and you chained your bicycle to a fence and watched it like a hawk, despite prudent kryptonite locks almost as heavy as the bikes.

Down the block a bit there was a good selection of East Indian restaurants, some featuring live sitar music in the evenings.

I made friends among the café revolutionaries. Their ecology required an audience and I qualified. They were somewhat chagrined by the attention paid their startling integrity, which they tried modestly to conceal in cafés, bars, and occasional public proclamations. It was none of their concern if people tended to spy and eavesdrop while, in righteous indignation, they raised their voices in protest at the corruption all around us. It was lonely out there in the world of unique virtue. They were surrounded by the envious and the indifferent—two faces of the same monster, which failed to see them correctly and agree with what they said.

No matter. They would go their solitary way. The cult of personality was one solution to the problem, but it depended on the selection of the personality. Theirs, for example, would be a daring choice.

The Bohemians at this East Village extremity of ambition and need often attach themselves to causes and gurus because it's hard to survive as a solo practitioner in the Truth trade. Mysticisms, cults, fanatical politics, books of miracles and miracle-declaring leaders find fertile ground among those who have cut themselves away from the other conformities. It's always a strain to practice originality and art, especially if one is neither original nor an artist—and even the real artists gather their strength only while they are working. At the other lonely times, they are as susceptible as any mortal, and vulnerable to doubts and the night terrors.

Lean, long, lanky Ichabod (not his real name) has a talented body, dramatic cheekbones, a loft full of state-of-the-art workout equipment. By profession he is a terrorist mime; he's definitely not one of your whiteface jokesters with a franchise on a street corner frequented by tourists (had graduated from that school). He is a theatrical performer with exceptional gifts—also problems about working with others. When he played a rooster in a stage version of an old Chinese story, he asked the director, "What's my relationship with the landlords?"

"Just flap your arms like a chicken," said the director. "We're trying to open a play here."

"If I'm not helping to bring revolution to this village, I'm part of the problem."

"Your problem, Ich, is that this is fourteenth-century China. You should have thought about your political role six hundred years ago. When you flap, point your elbows out."

"I can't do it if you're just horsing around."

"Ich, look at it this way. You're the conscience of the community. You arouse the other chickens. Flap and go in French: Ko-ko-ri-ko! Okay? Can you learn the line? Put all your resources of alienation into it, Pops."

In this and other cafés on the St. Mark's Place axis, some of the revolutionaries are doing sexual politics. A would-be necrophiliac argued against "vivationist chauvinism"—the prejudice people express for living, breathing sexual partners. The anticircumcision forces gathered to protest mutilation and demand job preference quotas for the foreskin-deprived, prepuce-handicapped. "I'm differently abled," I argued, defending my people against the idea of disability. "I'm a Person Living with Circumcision."

My woman companion silently mouthed the acronym, PLWC, and later told me it wasn't catchy enough. She suggested: Person Really into Circumcision Knowledge.

When I asked the anticircumcision activist, who earlier had been noted for campaigning against the closure of group-sex bathhouses, whether there could be a double-blind experiment to treat levels of impotence caused by traditional mutilation, he said, "You're rationalizing."

"Irrationally speaking, then, how can we know how much we have lost?"

"You fight the battle first. Then you tote up the cost. That's real life, asshole."

At the next table, someone else hip to real life was saying that Samuel Beckett, "his oov-ver," comes closest to a bomb on an aircraft killing 272 men, women, and innocent children—"not that the *adults* are all that guilty."

"Terrorism as existentialist theater. I get the picture," said his companion, a person in an Esprit tee shirt probably intended for a woman.

"We've all got the picture," mournfully intoned the coffeehouse terrorist. "That's why we don't write plays anymore."

"Did you ever?" asked the Esprit tee-shirt person.

Rudeness hung in the air like the steam from the espresso machine. Some of those children on the imagined airplane explosion might, in fact, not be innocent. A certain percentage would surely have grown up to be suit-wearing white males.

In California, one of my favorite terrorist Bohemians is a lovely Finnish artist whose painting specialty is portraits of Middle Eastern families now residing in the suburbs of San Francisco, San Jose, and Los Angeles. They are families temporarily installed with swimming pools and electric gates while lawyers help them expedite fund transfers from their native lands. They are patriotic and nostalgic for home. My friend—call her Inga—knows how to help them express their emotions. Fifteen-year-old Kuwaiti sons are posed in front of Matisse-y rolling hills with AKA assault rifles crossing their chests, a furriest suggestion of the beginning mustache on their upper lips. Or dad appears with his sailboat in a Dufy-like scene of naval grandeur at the St. Francis Yacht Club. Mom? Nestled at the fireplace among her heirs, holding the youngest in her lap. Inga feels bad about asking so much money for her work, but otherwise they wouldn't hire her. And she has her own children to support ("their father, that bastard, he is no good").

Art provides a vision of the superior reality. The Kuwaiti dad might well be inspired to take a frogman course in response to Inga's maritime vision. The fifteen-year-old son must be thinking of his oppressed brethren throughout the Gulf; that's the import of the shadow across his eyes.

"I do what I can," says Inga. "Someday I'll be free, I'll paint what people really look like inside. Someday."

When I returned to the East Village, the café called The Sixties—on a corner of East Sixth Street—was called something else. Retro Aquarian hadn't worked out, but there were echoes of the Summer of Love. At the tables on the street bicyclists still paused for fruit and yogurt, and when I met the lovely waitress from Lanciani's on West Fourth Street, she confessed that she was into health more than revolution, theory less than love.

With a California-like "have a nice day," she resumed gazing into the eyes of her companion.

Money is a dirty secret in the archipelago of Bohemia. A fair sampling of the Maoist and Weather Underground revolutionaries I've encountered operate with the help of tidy little annuities. They might have preferred us to think their funds come from bank robberies, but the shadow of remittance falls over their lives. Anarchism thrives on tamper-free fiscal provision. An actor who practiced spitting on stage and calls for strict destruction of the bourgeoisie has a strictly managed trust fund. He rode calmly over my accusations of drug use, corruption of minors, betrayal of friends, and lazy exercise of the mime he studied with Marcel Marceau in Paris. But when, in rude temper, I accused him of money from his dad, he didn't speak to me for years.

The program of the enraged is to be poor and revolutionary.

The program of the charmed, the Upper Bohemians, is to be patrons, organizers, enlightened consumers.

Sometimes there are crossover folks, patrons of revolution, drawn by nostalgia for a struggle and a poverty they had never been lucky enough to earn in their very own lives. Grandaddy was rich; *darn*. As the poet Theodore Roethke wrote,

Money money money
Water water water.

The chic of Madison Avenue Second Time Around shops helps to make some feel in touch with the culture. A used-clothing culture has emerged, Boheem chic, in which even Goodwill opens top-tier stores for the well-to-do in yuppie neighborhoods. In some cities you have to get down to the Purple Heart store on the other side of town to find traditional prices and shabbiness, or look to the sidewalks of St. Mark's Place.

Many of the remittance Bohemians inherited hard for their money. It's not as if they don't deserve it. They worked long minutes in lawyers' offices listening to the reading of the will. They had to write down the family lawyer's hot line phone numbers in case of emergency while seeking their misfortunes under foreign skies. If they never feel pinched by the two-drink minimum, that's fate smiling upon them. They are people of dependent means.

My friends in Paris, Lawrence Vail and his son, Sindbad— Lawrence once married to Peggy Guggenheim; Sindbad sometimes the son of Peggy Guggenheim—were fighting and throwing tables at each other at the Old Navy on the boulevard Saint-Germain. It was a voluptuously operatic public quarrel, scraping the inside of the Oedipus complex with an extravagance befitting their expatriated money and self-indulgence, Americans in Paris enjoying café life while trying to beat the shit out of each other. Not quite traditional father-son stuff.

The whistle, club, and cape-bearing police hate to arrest Americans but needed to interrupt the fight because it was disturbing the flow of Paris lovemaking and political discussion. A couple of *flics* engaged the battlers in conversation. When they asked the Vails what was their occupation, the words "tourist," "painter," "writer," or "editor"—all somewhat applicable—would have appeased them.

Lawrence, who exhibited his old wine bottles with tasteful wax drippings in a Left Bank Gallery, drew himself up with cool dignity and said: "Rentier."

Man who lives by his income. Remittance individual. Dependently wealthy.

The cop arrested them both.

Sindbad published a literary magazine, *Points,* in both French and English. He played cricket and married less frequently than his father and mother. As a third-generation American in Paris, he spoke with an odd Azorean accent, a mixture of American, English, and French. He was generous with his mother's dole, generous within his means, and printed the early writing of Brendan Behan, fresh out of jail, James Baldwin, and young Americans in postwar Europe.

He could have said he worked, but chose not to. It was none of the cop's business—this was principle.

The battling father and son act was carried off to a few hours of jail and then something to talk about during the weekend in the country. Upper Bohemians tend to be subsidized folks with soul and a need beyond what they have been given. They want to have more on their minds than miracle hair-care products. They take to collecting art and artists, or hanging out with art and artists, because life is too short and this seems to be a way of making it seem longer. Immortality is an option some seek through children or good works; Upper Bohemians believe money gives them further options. Occasionally even an artist, a very successful painter, writer, or filmmaker can join their ranks. "How can we die," the symbolist painter and poet Mina Loy asked, "when we haven't finished talking yet?"

During the glory days of abstract expressionism in New York— the fifties, early sixties—painters and sculptors pioneered in hiring rock bands to accompany their opening nights. Alfred Leslie, painter, kept black chalk in the pocket of his raincoat in case his fingers ever happened, by some unfortunate accident, to get clean. "My patrons expect it of me," he explained. "Who wants to shake hands with a pinkish artist?"

In the Hamptons there were softball games with Marilyn Monroe and Willem de Kooning on the team. (Maybe it was Shelley Winters and Mike Goldberg—these are mere details.) Someone painted a grapefruit to look like a ball and the first successful batter splattered grapefruit juice and seeds over the happy crowd in Westhampton (or was it Central Park?). Picasso and his friends at the Bâteau Lavoir in Paris did well by peddling their legend along with their work; so did the high-living artists of postwar New York. At the Cedar Tavern, and the Eighth Street Artists Club (which met on Fourteenth Street when I attended), reputations were promoted before Andy Warhol had bought his first wig.

Larry Rivers, visiting San Francisco, described being taken prisoner by revolutionaries in Africa. It really happened; he said so. The painter, making a film for television, found himself in the middle of a war. His captors planned to stand him up before a firing squad; they marched him to the wall; but the leader of the executioners wanted to learn French. Larry offered to teach. He gave him French lessons, making up a language he called "French" until arrangements could be made for his rescue.

The northern California poet George Sterling, whose most quoted line describes San Francisco as "the cool gray city of love," drank and spent himself in a series of love scandals in order to occupy the cool gray hours of San Francisco and Carmel. "There are two elements, at least," he said, "that are essential to Bohemianism. The first is devotion to one or more of the seven arts; the other is poverty.

Sterling was an early member of the Bohemian Club, now an enclave and resort for the rich and powerful who like to engage in high jinks. In 1926, Sterling bit down on the cyanide capsule he always carried for emergency suicide use.

As Bohemianism becomes a mass movement, a few Bohemians seize the opportunity to become the businessfolks, entrepreneurs, and service-industry moguls of herbal tea, music promotion, boutique costuming, book, poster, or health-food shops, not to speak of the less legal occupations, dealers of dope and chemists of psychedelia. A few communes have become thriving farms and light-industry sanctuaries. Some gurus have made fortunes. A dropout English professor from San Francisco State University, who used to run Aquarian seminars for flower children at Ocean Beach in San Francisco, now runs a small conglomerate of country communards doing his bidding in Tennessee.

A resident of his commune, traveling on business, a drummer for New Age books produced by the guru, visited San Francisco to push the product. I met him at a shop that sold a mix of word-processing equipment, crystals, incense, candles, CDs, and books. (For herbal remedies, you have to go elsewhere.) I invited him for an overflowing sandwich, sprouts and avocado, at All You Knead on Haight Street. They serve meat and dairy products, but he didn't fear contagion.

"I don't fear animals," he said. "I fear men. So why should I eat animals? I should be eating—"

BOHEEM MAMAS

Certain Bohemian patterns recur everywhere; they recur but differ. For example, the ample, laughing, hospitable keeper of a stage for eating, performing, and being seen is exemplified by New York's Elaine of Elaine's, the East Side Manhattan restaurant which serves Upper Bohemia—George Plimpton, Woody Allen, Bruce J. Friedman—the artists, theater, and film celebrities whom she places at tables in harmony with their ranking. Perhaps one might say snobbery is in action here (one does say it), and perhaps Henry Kissinger needs to come in with Jules Feiffer to get a good table. I got a *fair* table because I had known Elaine when she was a young hostess at the Limelight in Greenwich Village, or it could be because I arrived with a moderately well known actor. Perhaps otherwise I would only have been assigned another table. But I did proudly receive a strong, focused, lubricated, sincere hello, kiss-kiss, kiss-kiss, just as if Elaine in all her regal vastness remembered me from her well-spent Greenwich Village youth. Noblesse obliges generic total recall.

Nothing incomprehensible about this variety of insulating her Upper Bohemian celebrities from the rest of the world. I don't live in Manhattan; I'm not a regular; coming in from the cold world out there, Elaine's people like the comfort of her embrace and protection. It's part of the nourishment; the food matters less. To the extent that others don't feel like members, just to that degree the Chosen feel like part of a warm and welcoming family. "Nothing human is alien to me," Goethe said, so perhaps in another life, if being a literary genius didn't work out, he could have managed the door of an exclusive Manhattan club.

Tosca, a bar in San Francisco's North Beach, enjoys the Boheem Mama radiance generated by its proprietor, Jeannette Ethridge, and her mother, Armin Bali. They have made it a club for ballet dancers and film celebrities, Francis Coppola and Baryshnikov when he's in town, with a pool table in a back room for the elect. They transmit the gossip; they provide a cozy resort on chilly evenings; people meet in an atmosphere of family, carrying on their feuds and love affairs under the caring eyes of watchful but nonjudging women. Actually, they continually judge, but they instantly forgive.

Hunter Thompson danced off a table here and broke his ankle. Marriages also have been broken, and recombinant DNA has found ways to recombinate among the smells of chocolate cappuccino, leather banquettes, and the sounds of a jukebox traditionally filled with old opera recordings.

City Lights Bookstore stands nearby, and so do Vesuvio's and 12 Adler Place, drinking resorts and mail drops for several generations of our kind. Their alleys have now been officially renamed for William Saroyan and Jack Kerouac. Theme-park fixative can't hold a neighborhood together; North Beach is also becoming a Chinese shopping bazaar, no longer officially groovy, but Jeannette and Armin at Tosca, Lawrence Ferlinghetti at City Lights, open late into the night, do their best to keep the spark glowing. The Upper Bohemians who come to inhale the steam off chocolate cappuccinos, and even to drink them if their stomachs, livers, and teeth can bear the strain, like to see themselves in a historical continuum. As long as there are Boheem Mamas to nourish the terrain, the stoves remain warm. A Chinese poet lives in the Sam Wong Hotel, which used to be the Colombo Hotel, a residence for lonely old Italian men, including a lonely old Italian poet.

Like a forest leveled by the lava flow off a volcanic irruption, the ecology of North Beach seems to regenerate after periods of fallowness. The Mamas never quite leave.

A more louche (translation: "funky") eating and drinking asylum for Bohemians of less exalted station was Juanita's Galley on the Sausalito waterfront. Hell's Angels, artists, ceramacists, insomniacs, dope dealers, members of the Sausalito bargeoisie, speedfreaks and freaks with no particular adjective in front of the word, showed up at Juanita's all-night, all-day public kitchen on the mud-sunk decaying ferryboat *Charles Van Damme.* It was open continuously unless it happened to be closed; if so, tough titty, try again. Juanita Musson, several hundred wild pounds of her, more vast than Elaine, West Coast majestic, uniquely saturated, carried her hospitality to a generation's eating and drinking. When her Galley on the *Van Damme* died, she took it to the Valley of the Moon, where Jack London used to live, and then to Port Costa, all places within striking or biking or hitchhiking distance from San Francisco. Sometimes stretch limousines would bring postopera social-register folks, afflicted with *nostalgie de la boue,* the yearning for mud, to her swinging door and raucous or surly welcome. The mix helped to form the Boheem stew of Northern California.

Meals at Juanita's Galley were great, in the sense of size, but breakfast was *great,* in the sense of cholesterol. Sometimes a pet deer, turkey, ducks, or chickens followed Mama Juanita around as she delivered coffee, off-menu insults, random kindness. Once she gave a visiting Japanese tourist an "ear job," enveloping his head between and under her breasts. He had not heard about this quaint American custom; he asked her to repeat it while his friends photographed the event. Then each member of the group asked for the same perfumed smothering and slathering. Sometimes Juanita didn't oblige visitors; this time, for the sake of international friendship and misunderstanding, she complied. Ear jobs were not on the regular menu.

During the glory days of Juanita's Galley in Sausalito, the bargeoisie and anchor-outs were fighting the city, the state, pollution laws, and each other. They were an ardent motley of seaborne Bohemians. Some had to row out to their floating wrecks; blessed by the vibes of fate, few fell into the briny bay and drowned. It was an amphibian tribe. Shel Silverstein owned a houseboat nearby, magazines were published from houseboats, marriages began in this romantic tidal slum and didn't end any worse than landlocked marriages. For a time it seemed that the main occupation, even ahead of illegal pharmaceuticals, was the making of documentary films about their own lives. In a burst of enthusiasm one Saturday afternoon I bought shares in a film company floating on a barge. Later, when I asked for the stock I had purchased, the movie magnate, call him Steve, informed me he had used it to satisfy a court order for child-support-payment arrearage. "Goddamn ex-wife of mine got no concept of responsibility," he raged. "And now you'll think I let you down, too, won't you?"

Juanita let him run up a tab with the promise that she would play the romantic lead in a story of overweight love. When he was served with a subpoena on behalf of his irate ex-wife and hungry children at his table at the Galley, he explained that this was a sort of contemporary art form, the running of court orders, like the Christo Running Fence. Everything that happened to him in Marin County was grist and gruel for Steve's mill. Sometimes fervently hot tempered, Juanita doted on this nonfilmmaking filmmaker, bringing him free french fries without being asked, filling his thermos with liquids for the lonely creative hours aboard his houseboat.

The Boheem Mamas show the human economy working to balance things out in patterns of need. Gay men often enjoy companionable women; many companionable women relish the charm of gay men without the risks of sexual obligation. It works for the men; it works for the women; it works. Bohemian communities encourage such arrangements, although the sexual details may differ. A woman can be married to the mob, and not in the way of the available music groupie. Beauty is not a requirement, although style and individuality are requested. When Bohemians tear up their old roots, it doesn't mean they don't want new ones, mentor fathers and mentor mothers, a reconstituted extended family.

No wonder the chief expatriate café in Palma, near the Plaza Gomila, was called Mom's Place until the Franco authorities demanded an authentic Spanish name and it became Chez Jose (FORMERLY MOM'S PLACE).

In Rome, the Illustrissima ma Principessa Marguerite Caetani di Bassiano—originally named something like Margie and from Missouri—supported the trilingual book-size magazine *Botteghe Oscure,* named after the via Botteghe Oscure, where her husband's ancestral house stood. The check for my contribution to *Botteghe Oscure* was delivered to the room where I was staying by a uniformed servant, the envelope on a silver tray, along with an invitation to meet the princess. I traveled to her city estate on the back of a Lambretta with my friend Ben Johnson, led through the mansion by a series of door-opening servants. Momentarily blocked by a thick white rug like a snowdrift, we paused to take thought. Ben leapt over the whiteness; I waded through it. Finally arriving at our destination, the princess in her study, we found her wearing American sneakers and eager to reminisce about growing up with T. S. Eliot in St. Louis. Her magazine published early work by Dylan Thomas, Brendan Behan, Truman Capote, English, French, and Italian postwar writers, and a small group of expatriate Americans.

Tea was served. Port. Cookies. Crumbs dropped from my lips; the resinous wine curdled my shyness into garrulity.

Conversing with Illustrissima ma Principessa, I described my revelation as a student in existentialist Paris that Nietzsche was right. I hoped I was bringing her good tidings. What he said about poets applies to all artists and also to Bohemians: "sensual, absurd, fivefold, irresponsible, and sudden in mistrust and trust . . . idealists from the vicinity of swamps." What he (probably) meant by swamps are the greedy needs of dreaming children. They lived vexed by the dreams they can never, talented or not, decipher into the final decisive clarity. As for everyone else, artists or not, Bohemian or not, the mysteries of love, yearning, loss, and death can only be celebrated. They can never become nonmysteries.

I was exalted by food, drink, and the conviction that publication in *Botteghe Oscure* would reveal my genius to the world, thereby persuading my mother and father to stop asking me to move back to Cleveland and be sensible. I overestimated the circulation of *Botteghe Oscure* in Cleveland.

As I explained about Nietzsche and me to Marguerite Caetani di etc. etc. etc., I ate her cookies, she poured the tea, I drank her port, and perhaps I astonished her with my depth. More likely I burbled an arrogant and timid twenty-four-year-old's gratitude for her perception of genius in sending me a check and printing my story in her magazine. I too was defying the mysteries, wading bootless in the swamps, greedily dreaming.

In Europe, France particularly, the tradition of the salon hostess—often with a dimly smiling, agreeable, or absent husband—continues. She feeds the artists and seeks to absorb their secrets, a task which can never be completed. When I lived in postwar Paris among the returning colony of sentimental Francophiles, late forties, early fifties, several American women carried on the tradition. The dollar was strong; it didn't cost them too much to entertain Saul Bellow, James Baldwin, Jean-Paul Sartre—that group—and some who are less well known. There was a predatory motherliness about the attention. One, more frankly American about it, used to say to my then wife and me: "We're having some people to dinner Saturday night. Why don't you come for coffee and a drink afterward?"

I was twenty-two, unknown, unresentful, and eager to meet the great artists of the two banks of the Seine. When the lady invited us for coffee after dinner, I was grateful.

Years later when I met her again, her salon now transferred to the East Side of Manhattan, she said, "Hey, if we'd known you were going to be important, we'd have had you for *dinner.*"

I felt a surprising surge of lack of gratitude. And here I thought I had always been unresentful.

"You want to?" she went on. "Sunday afternoon, brunch, I've got this terrific gay activist from Atlanta, and Lenny Bernstein, and some people I'm sure you must know . . ."

I was lonely and free on Sunday afternoon. I went. A boy's got to eat, doesn't he? Otherwise I'd just have been having dinner alone.

BOHEMIA AND FRANCE

The troubadors and the goliards of medieval times wandered about with their baggage of songs and stories, enjoying the unpolluted air of freedom and poverty, sometimes precariously adopted by the aristocracy, sometimes begging like gypsies, or stealing, or gleaning, hoping to be tossed coins as reward for their songs, stories, and craft. The word *bohemian* may have derived from a name given the gypsies, who, when they were not considered to be from Egypt, were thought to be from an alternative vague middle-European distance called Bohemia. Geography was not the strong suit here.

Like the gypsies, Bohemians sang and made music, worked at odd jobs or no jobs, stole a little or at least didn't feel responsible for paying their debts, and probably had a special dispensation from God. A gypsy legend, which I heard as a teenage runaway among carnival people, explains to interested parties that Jesus spied the gypsy in the crowd along the Via Dolorosa who had forged the nails for his cross and pronounced upon him an ambiguous blurse, a combination blessing and curse:

> Because you made the nails with which I am crucified, you must wander the earth until my return. But because you skillfully made the nails sharp, so that they would hurt less, you may steal and beg and. . . .

What else? Wear funny clothes?

It may be that, unlike gypsies, who roam in their gypsy raiments because of convenience, a love of color, and ancient tradition, the Bohemian wanders and dresses peculiar in order to shock the bourgeoisie (read: his/her parents). Enveloped in a particular history and support system, the gypsy finds it difficult to become a non-gypsy. The Bohemian can drop back into the bourgeois world by changing his wardrobe, switching his style to a new channel. Bohemianism is a *role* even if it acts like a race, class, or ethnic affiliation. The element of play makes it unusual among allegiances. Voluntary poverty is not the same as poverty. And the Bohemian, however poor, considers himself among the elect, chosen to an elite of abstention from workaday society. The fortune he tells is mainly his own.

This kindly or extravagant hedonism sometimes gives way to monkish abstention from the joys of the world. I knew a painter in Mendocino, California, who wore a tee shirt inscribed INTERNATIONALLY UNKNOWN ARTIST. Tee shirt irony: By announcing the fact he contradicted it, at least in Mendocino. He deconstructed, he ironized, he reasserted—all on one Fruit of the Loom all-natural fiber artistic medium.

Extravagant haberdashery life-stylers, bangles and spangles and soul-testing music, Bohemian swank, coexist alongside the strict mystics or modest artists in their garrets, basements, or country cottages. The decision to belong is what defines the Bohemian; he can come from anywhere to declare himself a member of the band. Conversion may mean only that he knows where to hang out. He may be eccentric, or may just need a rest from his past. He can be James Joyce or Charles Manson. She can be Djuna Barnes, defiantly a novelist, lesbian, and recluse amid the turbulence of Greenwich Village, choosing to drop out of Bohemia while remaining at its center. Traditional Bohemia reflected traditional sex roles; women were asked to feel free to serve men. Gradually militant women have taken to Bohemian life as women, undefined by their men or their menlessness, leading the way for women in the larger society. Upper Bohemians like Virginia Woolf, George Sand, and Isadora Duncan pioneered as artist-Bohemians, escaping the roles of model, muse, and nurse. The anarchist-Bohemian Emma Goldman led men as well as women, accepting male followers as her due.

Although Bohemia took its modern name and form about a hundred and fifty years ago in Paris, when *la vie de bohème* was immortalized by Henri Murger, then put into pretty song by Puccini, the practice of breaking class restraints in something like the Bohemian manner runs as a continuous thread in history. The Diggers of medieval England, the troubadors of medieval France, the goliards of Germany, England, and France—twelfth- and thirteenth-century wandering scholar-bards who performed bawdy verses in Latin—carry the message of defying convention, living for free spiritedness, making do with what comes along, forming allegiances with a class of artists and rebels separated from the rigidity of feudal status. They didn't have garage sales and rent parties, but then they didn't have garages or proper landlords, either.

An imagery of Bohemia—an Eden without guilt or pain, in which folks laugh and gambol free—seems to have provided a consistent release from the irksomeness of society. Carnivals and circuses go back to Roman times and probably have links with ecstatic mystery cults, worships, and orgies venturing beyond the limits and rules. Brueghel's painting *The Land of Cockaigne* portrays a pagan extravagance of pleasure—wine, pigs, drunks, smiles, dancing, pleasure. It still looks good. Hormones of adolescence and the hope of freedom are celebrated, even as they were celebrated in the Summer of Love in San Francisco. The *fêtes foraines* I used to visit on the boulevard Richard-Lenoir, near the Bastille in Paris, had the wild gurdy music, performing monkeys, fire-eaters, and even some of the smells of American midwestern and southern carnivals. They were mystery rites, plus fortune-telling and kootchy dancing. There is still an underground "Gathering of the Tribes" every year in some woodsy place which gets mysteriously to be known worldwide, hippies materializing out of the mists and fens as they do for Grateful Dead concerts, heedless, miraculous, wearing funny clothes. When life is a festival, a group can make Halloween when it chooses, inviting all the devils back.

Shakespeare's seacoast of Bohemia, "a desert country near the sea," is a movable feast whose unique geography requires only people, not property. This real estate is not really real; its inhabitants define it. Paris provides the most enduring place image for the Bohemian tradition—wine, song, compliant lovers, berets, vagabonds and apache dancers, pleasure-seekers and pleasure-givers, cafés haunted by art, fun, and the triste whine of musettes, that accordion with soul. Some of the details shift; the beret now tends to be associated with the fake-folk yearnings of both Pétainists and Communists.

The dream of *la vie de bohème* endures despite the remark of a sour theorist that France was so beautiful that God decided to offer proper balance by creating French people. At least He also provided enough constriction for French Bohemians to have something rigid to rebel against. In different generations, different sections of Paris housed the Bohemians of the time—Montmartre, Montparnasse, the Latin Quarter, Saint-Germain-des-Prés, the Marais, all still floating atop this city of light and surly shopkeepers which we persistently view through the kaleidoscope of myth. The feast could indeed be moved. It is a feast still needed by bohemians from Oak Park, Dakar, and Tokyo.

A few years ago my friend Claude Roy, poet, journalist, existentialist, rebel, and heavy smoker, strolled with me down the rue de Seine and suddenly stopped, grimacing, gasping for breath: "Alas, the peasant of Paris can no longer breathe the air of Paris."

The myth endures; the need is great. The constraints of French society and history—it is a Catholic nation, and one which has angrily suffered many defeats in modern times—seem to compress out successive generations of rebels, artists, and dreamers who head for Paris just as did Balzac and Diderot, Rastignac and Rameau's nephew. The philosopher Denis Diderot's ironic chronicle *Rameau's Nephew*, about a Paris wastrel who lived mostly off the story that he was related to the composer Rameau, can be called the first novel about a Bohemian. I went to Paris first as a student, with a fellowship to write a dissertation in philosophy, tracing the links between Diderot and Bergson. Instead, reading Diderot and riding my bike, I decided to be a wastrel like the nephew of Rameau. I wondered, in those damp, shabby, gloriously happy postwar years, if I might learn to shamble into the gardens of the Palais Royale every afternoon. This task turned out not to be too difficult; the project was within my means.

A fellow Fulbright scholar, studying in Belgium, happened to arrive for his first visit to Paris on July 14, Bastille Day, when the entire city was strung with colored lights. Bands played on every corner, or at least flutes and musettes; people were dancing, singing, embracing, inviting us and anyone else nearby to join them for their wine and food. It recalled the *soupers fraternels* of revolutionary times, when the people of Paris set their tables outside, lay extra places for hungry or convivial passersby who wished to share bread, wine, and cheese. This Bastille Day mood, after war and Nazi occupation, was one of spiritual orgy, a festival nourished by deep griefs. My friend saw only the gaiety. He looked about at the hubbub, sighed, and said, "I always knew Paris would be like this."

Paris, of course, is not really like this. But we know it must be, therefore it is; the Paris of our dreams is a required course.

"Youth is a disease which time cures"—Goethe. "Ugliness is superior to beauty because it lasts longer"—Serge Gainsbourg.

The French *chanteur* Serge Gainsbourg died the "slow-motion suicide" he predicted for himself in his celebration of cigarettes, alcohol, and the lust for teenie-tinies. He even wrote a song in praise of incest, sung as a duet with his daughter. When folks wondered why his baggy eyes, poisonous breath, and shaggy unkemptness attracted a succession of fresh young beauties, he modestly quoted himself, cited above, to explain the matter. A person can count on ugliness, but beauty passes. A Harley-Davidson lasts, or you can buy another. Depression is a welcome friend at times; *le cafard* belongs in the Paris of Juliette Gréco, Mouloudji, and the green-skinned beauties huddled outdoors on the terraces during the autumn rains. It's lovely to be young and melancholy.

Serge Gainsbourg dramatized the Left Bank in a time of rapid erosion of the Bohemian ideal, Paris threatening to become Alphaville. For the artist, truth is in the details, even if the details seem to be more nostalgia than contemporary reality. Perhaps this successfully scandalous song writer and café performer was more Bohemian than artist; he made festival of a personal style and became, even into his sixties, an icon. They still love their games and image in the Île de France, best formal garden of the world.

When I revisited Paris during the fall of 1991, I found a mysterious epidemic of men carrying poodles or terriers, live fur hugged in their arms as they strolled out to dinner. I tried to deconstruct its meaning. I consulted Foucault, Lacan, Derrida. I tried semiotics. I went all the way back to Lévi-Strauss, Robbe-Grillet, and

Nathalie Sarraute, honored ancestors of another decade. I tried every goddamn French theory which had recently floated through the crowded and polluted air.

Then I saw a photograph in *Paris-Match* of Jean-Paul Belmondo, movie star and man about town, carrying his dog under his arm. Mais oui! These independent minds on the boulevard Saint-Germain were imitating Belmondo the way, a few years ago, rebellious teenagers wore one glove like Michael Jackson or leather drag and a crucifix to do their Madonna act. That's what they were saying: *I'm hip.* Plus, of course, that they love their pooches and can afford to feed the perky things off their plates at the Brasserie Lipp.

By the time I go to Paris next, there will be another star setting another fashion for the same revolutionary accessory wearers.

One of the first stories I published was inspired by contemplation of Rodin's statue of Balzac in the green triangle at the intersection of the rue Vavin and the boulevard Montparnasse. This masterpiece, leaning ferociously, balancing the belly under a regal or priestly cloak, seemed to express both the struggle of artists to become artists and the tragic triumph of the author of *The Human Comedy*. Rodin cast many versions of the work, struggling to get it right. Some of them were censored by the burghers of Paris because of the flagrant, pupick-bearing nakedness of Balzac's belly. Genitalia didn't help, either.

In the version approved for public use, the novelist wears a cloak over his body. But both Rodin and Balzac managed to express their will anyway—the hard bulge of excess suggested by stance under the cloak was more convincing than mere nudity. The statue communicated the power of both writer and sculptor, and that it stood at an intersection beloved of artists, café sitters, and strollers made a declaration about Paris, too.

Recently I revisited the statue at Vavin-Montparnasse. Think of it as pilgrimage; think of it as a believer going back to the shrine of revelation and epiphany. But now the sharpness of Balzac's features, the commanding frown, the protruding belly have been softened by corrosion and stain. At first I thought my vision had degenerated with time. The image I had carried so long seemed to be clearer than the reality. As I stood there amid the surrounding whoosh of traffic, I remembered pedaling my eight-dollar bicycle to these corners, studying the lessons of Balzac and Rodin, two rebels who dominated and worked their will. I used to fall into a state which some might call worship or meditation, and then I headed with my velo and my notebook to the Dôme or the Select to bite my pencil and make tracks on the pages bought or shoplifted from Gilbert Jeune. I too would invent and enforce my world.

Why was Rodin's Balzac no longer the slab of triumphantly articulated power which had so inspired an American would-be? It was time and the acid air of Paris which changed this presence, aged it in this way. And I was forced to reckon with the fact that I have known Rodin's Balzac for more than forty years now— more than half of its life. It begins to seem that even immortality doesn't last forever.

Kenneth Rexroth described a snob as a person who imitates the manners of the class above him, probably inaccurately. Rexroth himself, a poet, critic, translator, professor, revolutionary, father to the beatniks and then would-be executioner, inventor and reinventor of his own life—a hardworking loafer who never rested—led the traditional Bohemian chieftain's life in Chicago, New York, and San Francisco. World-famous but unappreciated, overflowing with Zen peace and mad at everybody, he kept his books in crates, scavenged money from rich men and indulgent women, served spaghetti and wine on red-checked tablecloths (stained ones) to an artistic circle (hub: Kenneth Rexroth). He attacked Henry James for his aristocratic pretensions. With nice symmetry, Rexroth had proletarian pretensions. His Bohemianism imitated the manners of the class below him.

Sometimes I stood with him in his kitchen while he decanted California beach-party jug wine into French bottles, all the while lecturing about the need to be authentic. For a time we didn't speak because he thought I had written an essay criticizing him under the name Noel Clad. He discovered there was another Noel Clad, I was not the offender, and he forgave me my sin of deluding him into thinking I was Noel Clad. (My denials had convinced him I was lying.)

Rexroth lived in a neighborhood which was then part of the black ghetto; he liked to shock visitors by referring to "niggers." "They know I love them," he declared. As admiral of the arts in San Francisco, he enlisted a group of local folks to meet a distinguished visiting French critic, introducing each of them as they sat in a circle: "This is the best harpsichordist . . . the best poet . . . the novelist . . . the greatest painter." And then he introduced a high school senior with a Beatles haircut as "the American Rimbaud." The French critic was stimulated out of his jet-lag daze by this Francophile reference. He asked the American Rimbaud what it was like to be a seventeen-year-old genius poet in San Francisco.

"They won't let me graduate from high school," said the American Rimbaud, bitterly shaking his Beatle shag. "They say I have to take required courses. I gave them poems, but they say I have to take geography and history. They don't appreciate poetry in my high school. This country is fucked."

As I drove the critic back to his hotel, stopping carefully at all Stop signs, both of us filled with spaghetti and red wine, he kept repeating an astonished chant, like one of those toys where the sound comes when you pull a cord: "C'est lui le Rimbaud américain? C'est lui le Rimbaud américain?"

That's the American Rimbaud? That's the American Rimbaud?

Most years I try to attend the Gay Freedom, Gay Pride parade in San Francisco—hundreds of massed motorcycles, protests, demonstrations both touching and comic, floats and trucks and specialty causes on foot, vehicle, or animal; leather, S&M, a series of Black & White Together delegations carrying their banners from such varied locales as Frankfurt, Germany, Atlanta, Georgia, and even a brave couple of couples from my hometown, Cleveland, Ohio. There were bands, floats, costumes, chorales, dancers, singers, male nuns, female paratroopers. There were Differently Abled S&M Lesbians—a woman in a wheelchair chained to a woman with a whip who spurred her to roll the wheelchair faster, faster. There was the Boy Lovers Association, which elicits controversy because of its insistence that sexual free choice should begin in infancy. There were the Radical Faeries and, of course, the many passionate AIDS support, advocacy, and protest groups. The Chicano Queens for Christ in shades of pink and lavender, dancing and squealing. Samoans, Nigerians, Finns, all uncloseted together and free at last. Ethnic diversity.

Following the ominous but cheerful phalanx of motorcycle lesbians, gunning their Harleys, came a bicycle built for two, furiously pedaling. The spokes flashed in the sunlight with tampon streamers. The riders hoisted a banner: THE MENSTRUAL CYCLE. The crowd burst into applause. I saw a child on the shoulders of his dad put his fingers to his mouth and give out a perfect adult shrill whistle. This is a trick not many four-year-olds can master.

There was food and drink, there were smiling cops, there were engrossed tourists and sightseers and journalists from the world over. It was reported that a quarter of a million people came out to watch the parade and join the festival. They had always known San Francisco would be like this.

After the 1990 event, a group of Young Turks in the San Francisco gay community sued to overthrow the established gay leaders who had organized the day with the help of city funds. The charge? "The parade wasn't fabulous enough."

Insufficient fabulosity is a complaint that rebel Bohemians of all sexual varieties bear against life as it is lived in the workaday world. Even within groups like the gay community, which some would consider Bohemian by definition—separated, establishing its own standards and styles—each generation wants to be Bohemianer than its forerunners.

"Of all the manifestations of power," Thucydides said, "restraint impresses men most." This Greek notion has been slightly modified. Now yelling, screaming, crying, complaining, and the spilling of guts impress the folks. We live in less aristocratic times.

4

Search for a Star, Finding a Bliss, Demanding Correct Pronunciation

A fertile crescent of islands scattered in the ocean of ordinary life, the Bohemian archipelago stretches through time and across space with a population that keeps the ambiguous faith: to be bemused and filled with remorse; to be amused and filled with reasonless hope. This is far from that Bohemia in the neighborhood of Prague, once a province of the Austro-Hungarian Empire ruled by Franz Joseph with his solemn, impeccably bearded slow stare. Those who preside over the islands of Bohemia have darting glances, sometimes ragged beards and scruffy robes. Stodge is not their art form. They are not yet sure what they really rule; maybe only the earth and the sky for an hour or two, the stars, and especially the moon.

Despite indecision about powers given, the empire of Bohemia has been expanding since it first found its name and definition out of a population of gypsies, layabouts, lazy students, would-bees buzzing, folks wandering lost in the cities of Europe. Now the archipelago includes urban places, college towns, encampments everywhere, in the new world and the old, in Africa, the Caribbean, Indian Ocean, the South Pacific and South America, wherever the enterprising can make a nest without too much work or get others to make the nest for them. In Ubud, in Bali, an action theater commune gathered, and I met a middle-aged matron who had left her husband and children in Scarsdale while she spent "a year on Me." She was taping herself doing Balinese dances while a gamelan orchestra played (her husband paid).

In a village on Galapagos I found a young man taking notes on the poems dictated by the fearless birds that sat on his finger. Walt Whitman posed with a bird on his finger, said the poet, but it was a paper bird. "This is a *bird* bird."

The Rainbow Family, a floating group of sixties seekers, meets every summer for the Fourth of July weekend in a different national forest. Some of them come out of the disguise of normal life—engineers, professional people, blue-collar workers—into their real life as Bohemians. They were touched by a vision and they take on their magic clothes once a year, bringing their children, performing their ceremonies, occasionally giving birth to their babies in the forest, often conceiving them there.

In cafés in far corners of the world, in Boulder (Colorado) or Athens (Greece), I sometimes read the notice asking RAINBOW FAMILY! WHERE ARE WE MEETING? and the answer, telling which forest and what date. Once I came upon the news on the cork board of a laundromat near a boat basin in Pointe du Bout, Martinique, and knew I could find hippie seekers in this Caribbean French department, perhaps working on a yacht or folding yachting whites in the wash-and-fold section of the laundromat.

It's not a tiny group. From ten to twenty thousand hippie Aquarian survivalists gathered in the Green Mountain National Forest in Vermont for the 1991 conclave. Some drove their Volvos to the party, swanked up in NORML tee shirts, or tie-dye yellow at the edges, and exchanged memories of The Band's *Big Pink* album heard on a sweltering late-spring evening in Chapel Hill when the conversation seems to have been about paper furniture and underwear you'd never have to wash because it was disposable, biodegradable, before that was an everyday word. When they parked near the forest, marching into the shade with the other druids, they tried not to worry about damage, theft, or pine resin droppings on their Volvos. The Goddess worshippers,

Gaia-greedy, kept a little distance from the plain old pantheists, nudists, deadheads. Those who had given up psychedelics in their other lives took the sacrament again as part of the Family's ritual. A baby called Forest Moon was born to a mother called Sunshine amid the rapture of nudists and Buddhists, gays and straights, tepee builders and drum beaters, wild men from the bog, hairy, frantic, with graduate degrees in the helping professions; all bringers of peace and good vibes to themselves and the planet.

Some remembered the Harmonic Convergence and crystals.

Some remembered all the way back to mandalas and the Free Store.

Some couldn't remember very much because they believed in living for the Now. It was a matter of principle.

Many of the Rainbow Family had gathered for the Harmonic Convergence a few years ago in Hawaii, ushering in the New Age, communicating and channeling with each other, their ancestors, and Shirley MacLaine. A Vietnam veteran named Wobbling Jim (probably not his real name) was asked what qualifications a person needed to join the group. He pulled up his shirt, showed his navel, and asked, "Do you have one of these? Used to be we all had blue VWs. Now all we all got is belly buttons."

The rule is that nothing ever dies. The Rainbow Family represents the immortality of the sixties flower child, taking acid and chanting Om. And in an act of forest Zen, they clean up afterward.

Their Aquarian peace was modified for me by the visit of a German member of the Family, Gottfried X, fresh from his week in the forest. We were driving through Golden Gate Park to see the buffalo. He believed that American bison could understand German when it was spoken with sincerity and he wanted to try out his theory. Waving his arms as he explained Rainbow matters, he grieved about acid rain in the Black Forest of the Jungian gods, blocked my view, and I drove into a highway stanchion, blowing out a tire. "Vunderbahr! Vunderbahr!" he cried. It was another American adventure. "Vait, I do it!"

He changed my tire in five speedy minutes, sharing all the while.

But it seemed that we arrived at the buffalo pasture late. By the time we got there the bison had forgotten their German, muttered only in Buffalo. As we turned to go, one answered the visitor's saddened "auf Wiedersehen" by dropping a noisy and soggy buffalo turd, ponderously putting distance between human discourse and the green fields which are real life. He lumbered away.

My friend Gottfried wistfully described the departing buffalo in a way probably learned at language class deep in the Vermont forest primeval: "Great ass, man."

Parents are in the business of wondering if someday the dropouts, layabouts, beatniks, hippies will settle down to a decent normal life. It's the job of parents. Bohemians have their reasons for thinking they have already found their decent normal life. It's an act of continuous becoming which is profoundly human. Animals grow up without much time spent in contemplation and the exploration of appetite.

This empire, this archipelago, this milky way of flickering outposts in capitals, ports, college towns, and the Green Mountain Forest, this purgatory garden where boys and girls in the bodies of men and women sit staring at the meaning of life as hidden and revealed in wine, coffee, and dreams, this Bohemia has no clear geographical frontiers. It is girt by seas of aspiration and fantasy, melancholy and elation, the resort of folks proud not to be outpatients because they are artists, or know an artist, or believe they think for themselves and therefore must stand apart. Or at least have picked a good thinker to do the thinking for them and help them stand out of the crowd in a privately illuminated gang. "Had some terrific thinks today," said the young actor in Collegetown, adjacent to the Cornell campus. He tapped his notebook as proof. "Wrote them down right here."

Bohemians freely offer patriotic allegiance to their nation, the republican empire, the dictatorship of the illuminati. Sometimes revelation seems dim and flickering, and the expression of the think stutters, but it's hope that counts. They have ample supplies. They intend to have a good time and ingest favorable substances,

or at least find lots of free time and acceptable substances. The
actor at Cornell told me he was writing a play with a terrific part
for himself and he was going to call it *Under Milk Wood.*

I told him that the title sounded familiar. He stared me down.
I was a graybeard from earlier times, hung up on originality.

I wished I could tell him I understood the problem—could
deconstruct it. So much has already been written; why write
something new? When asked what was his favorite wine, even
Diogenes answered: "Other people's."

The citizen of Bohemia seems to have tentacles rather than
roots. He can hardly cross a frontier, because when he gets to the
new place, he finds his kind again, in the districts of Copenhagen,
Nice, Chicago, or Dakar where the art fanciers and dropouts
gather. And yet he can hardly stay in one place, because when he
leaves the Bohemian enclave in his hometown, or adopted hometown, he crosses into that Other life abruptly at a boulevard, a set
of tracks, some unmarked frontier. In Greenwich Village and the
East Village, it's Fourteenth Street, though of course the border
leaks, just as the borders of the United States leak in Texas where
Mexico begins. In San Francisco, I climb out of North Beach onto
proper Russian Hill, or trudge across Market at Valencia, and
now I am among the Others. There is the Adobe Bookshop on
Sixteenth Street, run by the Columbia Mafia, a crew of recent
Columbia College graduates with the beatnik dream of Frisco still
alive in their hearts. Or I can cross the Golden Gate Bridge to the
Book Depot in Mill Valley, which offers cadenced words, healthy
food, and spiritual community in a village center like the market-
place in front of a cathedral (no soaring Gothic towers, but lots of
tall caffe lattes).

The Bohemian traveler easily finds both foreign and familiar in
his hometown and abroad. It's not simply a matter of keeping his
eyes open and his nostrils sniffing. It's how he—as Vladimir Nabokov said of himself—travels through life in a space helmet. That
space out there is crowded with more and more satellites, adding
their allotment of soul to the universe.

They are subject to gravity or degeneration into junk in their
own ways. Just as the hack writer is still a writer, even if a bad one

("after weeks of painstaking research, I finally finished this useless book"), so the hack Bohemian is still a Bohemian. Painstakingly, without fear or favor or relief to his liver and arteries, he drinks his beverage, sniffs or injects or inhales his drug of choice. A cheating politician is still a politician—he runs something—even if all he wants is his perks and power. Fake love still involves (insincere) contact of intimate parts. There's a dreamy-eyed child in everyone's past.

In a pensione in Florence I met Alfred Idwal, an expatriate wanderer, who claimed he had quit the U.S. because he couldn't stand American abuse of the mighty English language which Alfred Idwal shared with William Shakespeare. In Italy he could hear the beautiful language of Dante, which he didn't speak very well, since he did most of his talking with tourists and expatriates. He was writing "denunciations," he said, "like Mencken."

"Are you being a little, uh, judgmental?"

"They been telling me that all my life, only now they say elitist. It's the same old same old, man. They said the same thing to Mencken in that bookstore in Baltimore. The Peabody Bookshop. They had a back room where people ate honest pumpernickel, decent Lebensraum cheese, they drank beer like gentlemen and protected the language. Mencken was in charge, man, he didn't let them fuck up. . . . So just if they'll pronounce the English-American language right I'd be quiet. Like the song says, I'll be a satisfied man. I don't need great sex anymore—okay sex is good enough. H. L. Mencken's on my side if he were alive."

He drank beer, ate cheese, and looked for pumpernickel bread in Italy. He drew the line at living in Baltimore; wasn't a fanatic.

The voyager into Bohemia feels like a tourist sliding on banana skins, except that his fall doesn't hurt—he laughs, they laugh, a pretty young woman turns back to her lover, and then the traveler can go home. If he has a deeper agenda—love, allegiance, escape from a reality which no longer fits—he can find possibilities in this elsewhere which floats unmoored to the quotidian. It's been a long time since children stayed where they were born. Risky voyages of discovery are part of our routines.

As a young writer in Haiti, I passed some years among a circle of Haitian poets and philosophers, dressed in skin which marked me off, a *blanc,* speaking their French with the sense that I was a stranger, taking affection greedily but knowing I would eventually go home to my own language and nation. For me, it was the most blessed of Bohemias, that golden age of the arts in Port-au-Prince of the fifties. It was based on illusion? Of course. Was it therefore meaningless? It was the tragedy all Haitians danced to and which the poets and artists celebrated. I partook of Strange for a while, until it became my familiar companion and the Haitian reality of my poet and artist friends became a part of my ecology. I could never go back to Lakewood, Ohio—had taken out citizenship in the smoke, laughter, and disaster of Port-au-Prince.

In the dream nation of Bohemia, the archaeology is of nostalgia and the new construction is of illusion. Armies fight wars for the right to mope. Grief and dismay are major transactions; slyness and mad hope rule the sidelong glances in the cafés. Today is quickly turned into yesterday, then treasured; tomorrow is welcomed but the dawn of the new day never comes.

Bohemian nostalgia, customarily for a better place in the past, directs itself into the future for the political Bohemian. The revolutionary sits in his commune, his rural hideaway with his old Fillmore posters, or his urban safehouse, and remembers the lilacs which bloomed in some not yet doorway. Bob Dylan sang,

> *There was music in the cafés at night,*
> *And revolution in the air*

and for the folk-rock Weatherperson, the revolution seems to be an afterthought, following the music. When I hear café talk of fire in the streets, I look for the guitars rather than hoses. The scowling warrior armed with guitar and stool, cigarette tastefully dangling from his lip, his tip jar inviting, evokes anarchy and the apocalypse and beckons to the freshest young thing he sees.

There is a weight of absence in the Bohemian life which drives the ambitious into a mixture of energetic sociability and lonely isolation. James Joyce's silence, exile, and cunning—minus the silence—were answers not only to the need for freedom but also to his disappointment in Ireland, in home. To build his work Joyce dwelled elsewhere, in Trieste, Paris, and the various non-homes to which he wandered, alone among the sociable cele-brants of his own lost kind.

"I'm like a dog looking for the meaning of life," Alfred Idwal said.

"What'll you do when you find it?"

"Hey, when a dog chases a car, what does it do if it catches it? Hell if I know."

"What are you chasing?"

He gave me a lopsided, language-defending grin. "A star, man."

5

Colonial Outposts/World Headquarters/Downtown Bohemia

PALMA, BAJA, VENICE, MAURITIUS, BUDAPEST
ONCE UPON A TIME, TONOPAH, CHARLESTON,
OTHER PLACES, AND...*YUBA CITY*.

Americans are Johnny Appleseeds of Bohemia, fertilizing everywhere, depending on preference for dope (Nepal, Goa), wine (southern Europe), women (Scandinavian countries, Italy, and everywhere), boys or men (Haiti, West Africa, Venice). These distinctions are also multiple-purposed and nonpurposed except to be Elsewhere.

Some Bohemians are revelers, like the black American poet Ted Joans, who lives much of his time in Africa, bringing his internal sunshine to the continent of his ancestors. In Dakar and St. Louis, Senegal, I met French Marxist Bohemians, deconstructed anthropologists, and the filmmaker and novelist Ousmane Sembene, who had a black American wife from Chicago. He was testy with me in French and English, but grew more cordial (only a little) when I spoke Russian with him. Some Bohemians are begrudgers, like the angry poet Jack Hirschman in

San Francisco's North Beach, who defended Soviet communism when he was almost the last to do so; said everyone knew who paid writers to attack the proletariat. Others wander such lost places as Belfast with "a dirty dog and fiery gin" to keep them company in the troubles of continuing civil wars.

A Big Sur tree-dwelling convert to saving an endangered resource—the foreskin—proposed a new National Priorities Czar to launch a lightning campaign to reverse circumcision, save the ozone layer, and decipher the zip code. "Only prompt action can bring America to its knees," she proclaimed. She was deconstructing the idea of fanatic causeism.

The tradition of surrealist and dadaist café parodies of public life became popular in Switzerland, Germany, and France, where authority traditionally chafed against the forces of anarchism. Rhinocerus parties and pataphysicians, followers of the prankster playwright Alfred Jarry, author of *King Ubu,* enlisted tiny legions of supporters. The yippie nomination of a pig for president, and the run for office in Mayor Daley's Chicago, carried on the tradition in the U.S. In San Francisco, traditionally hospitable both to rebellion and its parodies, the Saint Stupid's Day parade has become a tradition during the past decade or so—a ragtag band of out-of-key musicians in out-of-sense costumes to celebrate the Dumbing of America. Just as for any other carnival event, creative energy is spent devising new masques and songs in honor of Saint Stupid, patron saint of those who just don't get the picture.

One of the reasons for the Attack of the Bohemian Hordes is that many of the young and not-so-young were raised in suburban places where, as someone said, "suicide would be redundant." They seek alternate allegiances, a freer choice of families, an escape from history into a tradition they turn even more congenial by making it up as they go along. In North Beach and Greenwich Village, there are third-generation Bohemians, although another frequent scenario among the children of sixties communards is a rebellion against rebellion. A responsible young mother seeking to buy a house in suburbia was raised in Project Artaud, a group artists' commune where parenthood was shared and a group family was the ideal. Now she seeks monogamy, although her father lives in a van someplace in the desert, occasionally harangu-ing her by letter or, if short of ideas, by postcard.

PALMA, SPAIN

Contemporary generations of writer-groupie dropout Bohemians can be partly charted by their subject matter. There is an age which studies Jack Kerouac, there was an age which studied Ernest Hemingway. In Palma, Mallorca, I met the man who dined out (drank out) on his thirty-year literary project. Call him Crandall. "I'm writing the only definitive biography of Brendan Behan—not many people can say that."

"I thought it was Dylan Thomas, last time I saw you."

"Yup, him too—next," he said crisply. As a young graduate student he had worked on Hemingway.

I thought of the wild, wasted, fructifying lives of Behan and Thomas, how they spent their strength and lost their teeth, refus-ing to go gentle into that good night. "You took on a real job with those two English stars."

"Irish." Crandall corrected me disdainfully. "Welshish. And 'stars'? Meteors is more like it."

I agreed that an astronomer charting the passage of meteors, assessing their history and destruction, might need eons before he could offer the world full understanding of Brendan Behan and Dylan Thomas. It's easy to predict the future; the past is more complicated. Crandall might need to brood forever at his regular café on the Plaza Gomila.

Suffering from imperfect Spanish, I had taken to calling the Plaza Gomila the Plaza Gonorrhea. The foreign artists, men and women, and artists' molls, both men and women, found living here no worse than a bad cold. They beamed into the sun when a new Swede or German found his or her way during the months that, rumor had it, were elsewhere inclement. Neither the weather nor painful urination interrupted my pal Crandall in his relentless pursuit of the means to climb over his writer's block.

"Quoting is the sincerest form of plagiarism," he said. "If I could just quote from the works of Brendan or Dylan, I could get home free with a masterpiece like *that.*" (Expertly snapped his fingers.) "But people want you to do more."

"How about quoting half from Thomas and half from Behan?"

He blew smoke, he blew cognac fumes, he exhaled. He was considering a joint biography of the two poets who should have met. They had so much in common—women troubles, alcohol troubles, Celtic troubles, genius. Welsh/Celtic isn't quite the same as Irish Celtic, but that's a pedantic detail. The broad lines were clear. If a person quoted from several different poets, then it was more like research than what those fuckers back in London and New York call plagiarism. "I'm taking my time because that's what it needs and that's what I've got." He scanned the Plaza Gomila, pinched the bridge of his nose, squinted at the years stretching ahead. Mom's Place became Casa Jose and might become Mom's Place again in the new Common Market Europe. He would roll the rock up the hill as long as there was strength in his arms and a check from home. Brandy, chemistry, and an occasional temporary muse among the winter visitors would not let him down. The world waited for Crandall. Crandall waited for inspiration.

The Wandering Bohemian is limited only by his ability to live off the land. The Remittance Bohemian can work his whole life at his novel or, like Crandall, at his café in the Plaza Gomila in Palma on the lovely, tourist-infested Spanish island of Mallorca, on his definitive biography of some poet or other. Dylan Thomas was a creating and writing Bohemian; those who suck the milk of his legend are the ones who keep the cafés and taverns in business. Although his reminiscences of Dylan Thomas and Brendan Behan were shifty and misty, Crandall was a fount of specific information about the Bohemian enclave in which we sat, drinking old but not expensive brandy. This was something he knew from real experience, sincere study.

Crandall's companion that winter was a once beautiful English woman who owed her cachet to having been, in the distant past, the alleged lover of Henry Miller, a reputed visitor to him in California, a perhaps rival to the eleven or twelve important women in his later career. I chose to believe it; why not? I could see the ruins of good looks. She would have been a stately older lady except for the missing front teeth and a certain distractedness in her gaze. Her once long fair hair was now long and white. As she drank her brandy, she shivered and I wondered why. "Brandy always does that to me," she explained, and I started to ask What? And then I noticed what. She was sitting on her chair in the puddle she had made.

"Doesn't make any difference," she explained, "cheap or good, even the best. It's in the nature of brandy."

In the jungles of Elsewhere, the Bohemian finds a roost, not a nest; and then later, if things grow too crowded, another. If companions become judgmental because of difficulties in bladder control, one can move along to other companions. Crandall shrugged off the stately Englishwoman's problems. After all, Dylan Thomas suffered from sudden relaxations, and nevertheless wrote, "Do not go gentle into that good night."

The world is full of sorrows. But the wise Bohemian—like an advisor to rulers—sleeps a little better, knowing that he or she is there. Available to complain, suffer, enjoy the sun, and wait. Looking forward to tonight's fun, tomorrow's masterpiece.

LA PAZ, BAJA CALIFORNIA, MEXICO

Baja, sparsely populated, desert and cactus, with a highway to the southernmost resort of Cabo San Lucas, looked like an afterthought hanging from the continent below the U.S. and alongside traditional Mexico. The main industry of the village of Cabo was honeymooning, whale watching, tourism. La Paz, a port partway down the peninsula, was something like a real Mexican town. The beer was Mexican and good—this is a redundant statement. The tourists mostly passed overhead on their Mexicana Airline flights, leaving all the beer for the thirsty local population and a select group of North American dropouts. Glamorous traditions of artists, patrons, galleries, magazines were not the history here. La Paz was a place of waiting for something to happen, siestas, visitors lulled to sleep by the sounds of pores opening in the afternoon heat.

In La Paz I precariously floated—combed the beaches—lodging near a curve of sea where the chief esthetic yearning of the expatriate community seemed to be to capture the perfect sunset. They watched, they predicted, they intuited, they angled . . . it's coming . . . they raised a glass to welcome inspiration. . . . THERE IT IS! . . . at a bar promontory on the bay. The winner in La Paz was not, in those go-go eighties, the one who collected the most goodies. It was the one who meditated over the deepest world-historical vision from the stained white tablecloths on a shaded terrace stretching out toward sky, sun, and endless sea.

The waiters wore tuxedos green at the lapels due to the natural forces of oxidation. Silently they brought food or drink, having resolved for themselves most questions concerning the meaning of life. With good Spanish, Mayan, Aztec breeding, they knew not to interfere with gringo thought.

A few blocks inland, Raoul Fernandez, a gregarious Mexican who had done time at the University of California at Berkeley and with Hunter Thompson in Big Sur, ran an American library. He accepted donations. He accepted the mission to interfere with gringo thought. Although he had majored in . . . the subject varied as he warmed to new visitors . . . he pronounced his favorite variety of beer "seek-pak." To make yourself welcome when you dropped by for an informal seminar, you brought him a six-pack of Dos Equis, Bohemia, Carta Blanca, Corona—yours to manifest Spinoza's freedom of the will by making the choice. Raoul supplied the avocados, tacos, onions, chili, the fiery dips that someone else had supplied to him. He supplied the jokes. He supplied the hostly affability. Raoul was a helper of others.

The patio of his combination library, hacienda, and tax-exempt foundation was dappled with Vietnam veterans on various sorts of disabilities, druggies on the lam, alkies nursing injured livers, artists who may have intended to go to Ibiza or Bali but had bought the wrong ticket. We sat in the sun or the shade, once again our decision to make, another exercise in the freedom of will, draped across a cozy collection of chairs, boxes, and jugs.

There was a gray-leaved tree dropping dusty leaves in a planter. There was a cat staring straight ahead, trying to hypnotize the sun under the illusion that it was a giant orange mouse. Whoever felt inspired to do so contributed supplemental food, drink, or used paperbacks. Six-packs disappeared fast.

The tree in its wooden planter needed more soil, but Raoul wanted to test how long it would survive in a planter. He compared it to a traffic blinker he had liberated in Berkeley and kept winking in his apartment until it faded out—glorious memories of research in the States. When I told him I knew a novelist who had done that in the East Village, he clapped me on the back. "Good friend of mine! Good friend of mine!"

The subject of our seminar that day concerned the necessity to repeat such experiments in order to confirm the findings of other researchers.

Then we talked about Henry Miller, the bookshops of Berkeley, and the sunsets of La Paz. We talked about Dr. Timothy Leary and the Brotherhood of God, which was one of the doctor's troubled LSD connections. We talked about ecology (too bad people drape toilet paper on the giant cactuses on the road to Cabo San Lucas—we deplored that). Some of the veterans were writing about their wars while living on their military pensions. Our host, who also supplied the salty nuts, was living fairly well on the books accumulating in his tax-exempt, cross-cultural, educational project (want to buy a novel to go?). It was hot. We finished the beer. We went home for siestas. Later, in the blessed cool of the evening, we returned to discuss the day's production of sunset. We had a farewell beer. We stumbled homeward.

There was a very tall Vietnam veteran who skipped along on aluminum crutches. I admired his agility. He said he knew the writer of *Born on the Fourth of July* and when his own book came out, as soon as he wrote it, Tom Cruise would be taking crutch lessons to play the role. "I'm not some Person Living with Disability," he said; "I'm Supercrip. I'm blowing the lid off this thing."

My handwriting in the notebook I kept grew more and more scrawled. The outside world retreated to the environs of La Paz, giant cactuses, dry ravines, lizards with unblinking eyes like

Raoul's cat. Supercrip liked to show me tricks he could do, hopping over ruts, proud of his broad jumping. "These lightweight jobs are an improvement over anything they had in World War Two," he said. "But nothing else is."

Finally, one more sunset and I returned to San Francisco before something dire (I didn't know what) might happen. Raoul asked me to send his greetings to a few friends in Berkeley and remind them of the need for new books in La Paz.

VENICE (WEST), CALIFORNIA, U.S.A.

During the fifties, one of the fall-off-America destinations for hitchhiking beatniks was Venice, California, at the Pacific Ocean end of Los Angeles. The deliquescent remains of a failed real estate promotion included brackish canals, rotting piers, tropical strolling along the beach. As a concept, it was a little like peace on earth and goodwill toward men—it hadn't worked. The canals were silted over. Monstrous flowers and tubular vines flourished amid the algae. The bars were dangerous. The housing was decrepit. The piers smelled of fish and neglect.

On the other hand, musclemen, bikers, leather fetishists, babbling social rejects found that Venice worked pretty well. There was charm and cheap lodging. Desires could be displayed and gratified. An old gentleman, Lawrence Lipton, wrote a book in which he seemed to be inviting recognition as president of the Beatnik Republic, but he asked his subjects not to come to Venice and bother him. They heard the rumor and came. As gracious tavern owners rose to the challenge, I attended blabbermouth nights for poets who sometimes read along with wailing saxophones.

"Hart Crane was a poet," one young artist chanted:

> *Hart Crane was a poet*
> *Who committed sigh-a-sude,*
> *That's more better by far*
> *Than su-i-cide. . . .*

It's said that those who remember the sixties weren't there. I don't remember every moment of the late fifties, early sixties in Venice, but the rhythm of things lingers on. Black tights, black sweaters, and aboriginal Zen—ride with the flow. Later Zen had a rival, "ecology," which meant that you respected the godliness in all creatures, plus picked up your own trash. Soon Richard Brautigan would discover a primitive form of xerography and stand on street corners handing out his poetry about girls with the kind of hair he liked.

Marijuana softened voices; tobacco made them rasp. The muted sounds of mimeograph machines reproducing poetry echoed over the blocked, mosquito-breeding canals. Some people were still "into print." The streets with their barefoot runaways and intense skinny poets looked a little like those of North Beach in San Francisco. Venice was on the route which also included Denver, Austin, Chicago; a western terminus where you could rest at the feet of Lawrence Lipton.

Potters, graphic artists, and sculptors also found the large spaces and good light they treasured. It became a beat and then a hip artists' community, troubled by more drugs than any community needed. Crime and street violence drove some of the sweetness from the air; the intentions of the love generation weren't enough when methamphetamine, heroin, and cocaine crowded the scene. "It's just like New Orleans," someone said. "It's just like San Francisco," someone else said. "It'll turn into Malibu," someone else, a better prophet, said, and then grinned: "Honi soit qui mal i bu." It was a literary generation down there.

The self-medication movement flourished in the beatnik coffeehouses of Venice. A young woman who had almost finished her first semester in pharmacy school whispered to me, "Hey, if you chew willow bark, you don't need aspirin."

"But aspirin is so cheap."

"Yeah, but suppose you haven't got the bread? You got a boss hangover, say? You find yourself a willow?"

"It might be in someone's yard."

"Trees belong to the People! Thousands of years ago, before the invention of drugstores, there was this tree they accidentally chewed on when they had a headache . . . it was called the Bayer tree . . . this acid in the bark goes straight to the source of the pain, man."

From the beating of the bongos, the pounding of the poetry, the jug wine and the next-morning scratchy throats due to what we smoked, many of us needed willow bark before breakfast. Now the beatniks are gone (not quite), the hippies have disappeared (almost), the yuppies are fading along with the banking system. There is a retro tendency toward high-fiving, peace signs, treasuring the canals and the tradition. Venice rapidly gentrified, partly because of the fifties and sixties people, nostalgic for the tradition of protesting the Vietnam war by getting high. Mellow rock survives. Some artists remain; the sushi bars attract visitors from the film community, and my friend the sculptor says he can get along with only one guard dog now. He squints and recalls his earlier career, hanging out easy, seeking grace by strolling, talking, arguing, and not sparing his body. Once a friend of Neal Cassady's slept on his floor, wouldn't leave, ripped off his black-light projector. And then it turned out he wasn't really a friend of Neal's. The fifties and sixties were a rose garden with brambles. "So now I'm careful with my space. I've turned into the working artistic proletariat," says the sculptor. "Is that what happens when you notice dying isn't just a concept?"

Since he asks the question, he must know the answer. Although dying is ecologically sound Zen behavior, he wants to leave his mark and memory behind him. He works at his art.

MAURITIUS

In Mauritius I met a multitalented, Cambridge-educated, much-traveled cabinet minister, a Tamil, who expressed his flight from ethnic Tamil village roots by marrying a woman of Chinese origin. This is not usual among the fierce Tamil people. He was a rebel, a Tamil dropout, although his Left Bank student and Third World revolutionary days had been succeeded, in the normal Third World course of events, by precarious high office and careful tailoring.

One evening he insisted on driving across the island to introduce me to the best Chinese restaurant in Mauritius. He waved his arms hospitably to brush away my protest that I had not flown from the edge of Chinatown in San Francisco to the middle of the Indian Ocean (to find Mauritius, go to Sri Lanka and make a sharp right or to Kenya and turn left) in order to eat out on Chinese food. "You will enjoy, I shall enjoy," he responded briskly, changing verbs to indicate he was giving orders to me but expressing simple futurity in his own case.

We were served a fairly routine Chinese dinner with stainless-steel utensils and a side order of what looked and tasted like Wonder Bread with a pat of butter. When I asked the proprietor if they didn't normally use chopsticks, he bowed—"Ah! San Francisco!"—and returned to our table with *one* chopstick.

My friend and I discussed the breakup of ancient traditions. What I had known about the Tamils was mostly that one of their ceremonies includes walking on fiery coals. I had an adventurous friend, a San Francisco doctor, who severely burned his feet trying to follow a group of Tamils in a fire ceremony. I asked my Mauritian friend if he walked on fire. He looked regretful. He composed his lips. He said in his precise Oxbridge accent, "Ek-shully, so busy, rilly don't have the time, y'know?"

He took pity as I attempted to spear a piece of roast pork with my single chopstick.

"But my father still does," he said. "Feel better now?"

While he still considered himself a member of the Tamil people, he described his ethnicity as more Soho, more Left Bank, more devoted to his student and revolutionary years than to his father's faith. "I have been to San Francisco," he said, "and I regret to report that I stopped at the Huntington Hotel."

I must have looked surprised at the word "regret." The Huntington, a distinguished Nob Hill hotel, is a place of quiet elegance and no conventioners with stick-it badges. He shrugged and gracefully apologized. His government was paying for the trip. He had no choice. If it were not for this irresistible fate, he would surely have stopped at the Swiss-American Hotel, the hotsheet junkie resort upstairs near Enrico's Coffee House, where Lenny Bruce tried to fly like a bird out the second-story window and found it isn't as easy as it sometimes seems in dreamland.

"All my time, all my strength, all my devotion was to our dear North Beach. City Lights Bookstore! The Jazz Workshop! And oh dear, give my regards to a certain young person with flashing eyes . . ."

His own eyes shone with the memory like the eyes of my fire-walking proctologist friend. Although the Mauritian diplomat and cabinet minister had achieved high rank in his island nation, his allegiance to the state of Bohemia was constant. He hoped to retain dual citizenship.

Mauritius was home to both my friend the Tamil and a more traditional dawdler on life's way. During my daily walks at the water margin, I noticed a tall, skinny, pipe-smoking old geezer, a European with a tangled iron-gray mop, who reminded me of Popeye the Sailor. He wasn't bald, but there was a resemblance— biceps, eyes, and that short pipe. He wore white sailor pants and a Libya Peoples Information Office tee shirt. Eventually—well, the second time we met on the beach—we began to talk. He was a Scot, a retired merchant seaman and poet. He knew Alex Trocchi, author of *Cain's Book*, a Scottish writer of Italian descent who lived in Paris and New York during the late forties, early fifties, and then fled home to Glasgow after drug troubles in the States. The Libyan tee shirt was one he had found on the beach where a submarine had landed or perhaps not.

"Are you still writing?" I asked Popeye.

"What's the use?" he responded cheerfully.

"Why are you here? Why Mauritius?"

"Came for the spearfishing and the women. The spearfishing is illegal now, and I'm too old for the women." He laughed heartily.

"But you stay anyway?"

"Well, can't understand a blessed word people say. You know how we Scots are—not too much talk. Suits me fine."

I took the hint. We trudged in silence on the sand, tying our shoes together by the laces and dangling them around our necks. He rolled up his pants. I rolled up my pants. Finally he said, "Come for dinner tonight. Meet this wee lass shares my kip, I call her my darling black Sri Lankan wife. Grill you a fish so soft and sweet you can spread it on bread with a butter knife."

We talked about Alex Trocchi; we talked about getting away

from Glasgow. Popeye did the cooking, the cleaning, the washing
up, but his wife did the smiling. It was a good deal for everyone.

Popeye was still writing. He was still spearfishing. He still had
a bulging sunwashed blue eye for the women of Mauritius. What
he had said to me about being too old (he was in his late seventies)
was merely Scottish modesty. When I pointed this out, he burst
into rolling gusts of nonunderstated, pipe-flavored laughter. His
consort beamed with quiet pride. She padded barefoot to a cabinet to pick up a battered old camera and take a picture of Popeye
and me laughing. Click. Then she handed me the camera,
perched herself in his lap, and patted the swelling in her belly.
Click. She needed a snapshot of the three of them.

BUDAPEST, MOST BOHEMIAN: Yuba City, Least

Hungary, or at least the lovely Budapest of it, was a natural home
to Bohemia. The floating islands of Bohemia have not suffered the
tragic vicissitudes of the landlocked geographic nation of Hungary, woebegone, glorious, separated by language from the rest of
Europe. Perhaps strict logic should have given the name Hungarian to what came to be known as Bohemian, since it was more in
the Hungarian style than the style of the province of literal Bohemia. The accidents of naming are not bound by logic; American
Indians are not from India and Hispanics are often not Spanish
by origin.

If ever a city deserved Bohemia, it was Budapest at the turn of
the century. Jews, gypsies, European tourists, even native Hun-
garians thronged the cafés which presided over a flowering of the
arts. Visitors sought sexual pleasure; Hungarian men were beautiful (sometimes officers wore corsets) and the women were handsome; things got mixed up, with a little wildness that came out of
the mists of Magyar history.

John Lukacs writes that Budapest circa 1990 had "no particular
vie de bohème restricted to artists and writers . . . no artists'
quarter—no Bloomsbury or Soho, no Montmartre or Montparnasse, no Munich Schwabing." He remembers, or his Hungarian

soul remembers, that the city entire of itself was Bohemian. Senti-
ment, expatriation, and the passage of time will do that to a
person—skim the fat off the goulash, intensify the glow of lamps,
the smiles and teeth, the smoky weather of a golden age.

I visited Yuba City, California, shortly after it was named by
Rand McNally as the least livable community in the United
States. Patriotic Yubans took this as an insult, and a literature of
bumper stickers, tee shirts, and motel marquees sprang up to
answer the allegation. While my first day was spent buying bargain coat hangers at the Goodwill Store, I quickly learned of
another, richer life—herbal gardeners, sketch classes, intense car
hobbyists, a welding sculptor who used the intersection of junked
plumbing with the furious visions in his head to fill his days with
esthetic intention. I found both Hindus and Hindu converts. I
found Strange.

Bohemianism, the yearning to break out into art, exists everywhere in America as a willed exceptionality of the soul. In Yuba
City—more a few roads and unzoned intersections than a metropolitan area—the artists meet in the Mom's Places of a small and
gritty business strip, not far from the bargain coat hangers and the
senior citizens' discount sales. I joined the debate in a coffeeshop
about which phrase shows greater respect for elders, "Senior
Citizen" or "Golden Ager." One of the discussants took us all the
way back to the story of Abraham, who lived into great antiquity,
siring children along the way, and to the respect owed the wise
and elderly among Indians and Greeks. This rapt lecturer was
countered by a friend who evoked exposure on mountaintops of
the uselessly retired.

"They did that to babies, too," someone else countered.

"Only girls."

There was a sharp rap on the Formica top by a self-appointed
chairperson calling us to order. He had a practical insight to offer.
"There would be a special discount in the Rialto early show for
over sixty-five," he declared with venom in his voice, "if only there
was still a thee-aytre on this goddamn dead strip. We live in a
Rand McNally ratstink."

"I think you mean rat-sink."

"Picky-picky. You know goddamn well what I goddamn mean."

The thing about this encounter in some Formica Mom's Place with a group of Yuba City codgers is how aesthetically fulfilling their non-Bohemianism seemed. The basic ingredients were not far from discussions in, say, the Plaza Gomila in Palma: coffee, plenty of time, opinions, metaphysical plaints about the passing of time, economic negotiations, marginal convictions, lecturing and hectoring about both linguistic and moral distinctions, laughter. Both groups buy clothes in yard sales and thrift shops, even if the labels in Yuba City tend to say Sears or J. C. Penney and those in more traditional locales say anything but.

The art forms in Yuba City questers tend more to the garage and basement crafts. But like those of the conventional Bohemian enclaves, these folks do not dwindle into that good night with all passion spent. They also need to talk about it.

One of the codgers shyly asked if I'd like to see a poem. Although he had later gotten into seeds and farm equipment, his early training was at Berkeley, where he had contributed to a forties-era little magazine. His verse was ahead of its time, a poem which began:

> We sat under the full moon,
> Clarissa and I,
> She English I Berkeley
> And the trains went by.
> As we sat under the full moon
> And she squeezed my zits.

Since he had used her real name, he had never published the poem. But now, since he had recently visited her at the Willows Retirement Home, where she spent most of her time watching television test patterns, he wondered if it would be okay to give the poem to the world. *Circle* magazine hasn't existed for about forty-five or fifty years. Did I know of any other markets for love lyrics? Since I came from a major center of verse production?

NEVADA

I drove through a desert moonscape. Sagebrush blew across the road, and dirt roads led back into the hills to hidden mining shacks and freestanding clapboard houses. The nearest metropolitan center was Tonopah. In Tonopah, Nevada—a former silver-mining town now eking out its economy with truck stops, gritty casinos, one optimistically restored silver-boom hotel, slag heaps all around—I found a blackjack dealer in the casino who whispered, "I have a subscription to the *New York Review of Books*. Come to my place for a drink tonight."

At her house, a former silver baron's Romanesque stone castle, I met a little circle of like-minded Nevadans—readers, writers, artists, astrologers. They kept in touch with the outside world and occasionally visited it. One of them was doing a census of the buildings in the desert. "I like counting empty structures—anything historical," she said.

With easy laws, no speed limit, and wide-open inexpensive spaces, Nevada has gradually accumulated a scattering of sun-dried former beatniks and hippies. A former beatnik beauty queen of San Francisco now reads tarot cards and, for extra cash and sociability, deals blackjack in Reno. She has put on a few pounds and a lot of wisdom since she was carried in triumph on a float down Upper Grant, followed by a happy black-clad throng sucking on flutes, kazoos, and marijuana cigarettes. Years ago she read her tarot deck and informed the woman I was about to marry: "A tall red-haired man will turn out to be very important in your life." A year later, after I married the lady, I reproached our friend the tarot reader for nonprophet activity. I'm neither tall nor red-haired. "Ah, Herb," she said, "those are mere details."

Years later, my sons turn out to be both tall and somewhat reddish-haired. So perhaps it was prophetic behavior after all.

Desert rats and freeway hermits, living in the generous interstices of Nevada society, help to support the good music FM stations of Reno and Las Vegas. The glitz psychedelic substrata of Las

Vegas, the Space Daisys and Magnolia Thunderpussies, found Los Angeles and San Francisco too crowded and official as Bohemias. "I keep the sixties alive right here," one Space Daisy told me. *Right here,* as she patted it, was her heavily freckled bosom, beneath which the heart of a flower child throbbed well into middle age.

I had attended her first wedding at the Avalon Auditorium and danced with the bridesmaid, her five-year-old daughter. "Oh, that one," she said. "She's a gynecologist or some damn thing by now. Dig for things. Hey, that's it—a *geologist!* Wants to know when her mom's gonna grow up and you know what I tell her?"

I had a few ideas.

"When rock'n'roll grows up, I'll be there too," she said, "pla-yin' on my tambourine."

When I came to Reno to stay in a Bide-Away House for folks seeking a quick turn at the gaming tables or the divorce laws, it was filled with people imitating the manners of beatniks, hippies, dropouts. Some may have been permanent recruits; others were temporary visitors. Sheryl, a lovely vegetarian mother of three, sitting out a divorce from her Christian Science practitioner hus-band, used to tell her children, "Don't walk on the nice grass. You'll hurt the nice grass. Can't you hear the nice grass crying when you walk on it?"

I worried that she might be frightening her kiddies.

"All living creatures are sacred to me," she said, "including my kids."

"Grass is a living creature?"

"Even as you and I, Herb." Since I was composed largely of protein, bone, and self-doubt instead of chlorophyll and fiber, I seemed to be guilty of American meatism. Sheryl had a point about the nice grass, but my own approach would be different. At night, after she put her children to bed, I could hear her sobbing for her perished marriage.

I also visited a smoky box of an engineer's chambers in Reno which broadcast talk and rock music through FM equipment greened over by condensed marijuana fumes. Women in tie-dyed tee shirts, bellbottoms, tired eyes, showed up to snap their fingers

in silent appreciation of the tirades against the CIA which filled
the spaces between Bob Dylan oldies and Van Morrison relative
newies. This was a free-form radio, stereophonically dissenting
from AmeriKKKa. It was also fun because it provided the rallying
point for a group of once and future hippies who frolicked in
God's brown desert during their off-air times. "Hey!" said Space
Daisy. "Doesn't surprise me at all, see you here!" I came to think
of the FM stations of Nevada as equivalent to the cafés of Paris,
uniting the secret societies of dissent, clear-channel, statewide.

After our friend's gig, had this been a Greek film with Melina
Mercouri, we would all have gone to the seashore. Since it was
Reno, we went on a picnic in the desert—a flatbed truck serving
as our table—threw frisbees in the sun, drank and smoked too
much, swore undying friendship. This was the tailgate Toyota
version of the Dôme, the Coupole, the Café de Flore, the Deux
Magots, the Select with its amber skylight admitting the filtered
winter sun of Montparnasse.

The Bohemians of Nevada seemed to have been left overlong
in the desert sun and dry air. The lack of a state income tax did
not entirely compensate for the paucity of strolling, hangout,
pedestrian places. Blackjack was not an art form in my economy,
but of course that's a value judgment, and who am I to have
values?

In another pickup truck wandering the desert between Reno
and Las Vegas, Minden and Donner, there still lives an old man,
father of a friend, who dwells in his vehicle while he finishes his
novel. Since he has no phone or stable mailing address, we were
not able to meet and discuss the problem of being a mirror on the
moonscape of Spaceship Earth.

SOME SOUTHERN ISLANDS

One helpful resource for Bohemia in the South is Senator Jesse
Helms (Fundamentalist, North Carolina) who has declared that
instead of spending money on a state zoo, they need only install
a fence around Chapel Hill. He was referring to the University of

North Carolina, with its graceful Berkeley, Boulder, Austin loose-limbed student tribes in permanent temporary residence. During my stay, I absorbed the normal pleasures of university revelry—rock music, herbal fumes, laughter and shouts amid the frisbee playing and bicycle riding, with regional variations in the form of grits for breakfast and the occasional unblinking stare of a native for a Yankee. There were artists, literateurs, food experimental-ists, would-bees hiving—a lot of shaking going on. In the cafés, white-bearded oldsters clipped from their copies of *Le monde* and ogled the young folks of whichever sex happened to interest whichever white-bearded oldster. Healthy emeritus status tends to renew admiration for the springtime of life. A graduate student gave me her rare copy of The Band's *Big Pink* album because she noticed the rapt nostalgia on my face when we listened to it. She also played Bob Dylan's "One More Cup of Coffee (Before We Go)" and asked if now it would be Our Song.

Jesse Helms's zoo would have to enlarge itself to include Duke University, Durham, Raleigh, the high-tech triangle of this part of the advanced South. I met a couple, call them the Lees, who believed that paper furniture and disposable clothing, using pine sawmill dust, would not only save the economy of the former Confederacy but also cut down on cleaning bills. They kept a Confederate flag in their vestibule, woven of cloth, not paper, along with a sign that said: JUST KIDDING. They referred to the Civil War as the War of Northern Aggression, but they were enthusiastic about including the entire nation, as presently illegiti-mately constituted, in their plan to paper the world with paper.

They had a dream. It kept their marriage together. All the forms of fiber which grow in humid climates can be turned into paper, paper can be turned into underwear, soon they would be rich beyond the dreams of avarice. The hemp normally used for marijuana could be recycled into fashion accessories and fuel. Vision sustained them. For the Lees, eating aspirin and drinking Cokes along with their grits at breakfast (the night's celebrations ended unjustly in an hour of dull morning headache), was part of normal southern dreamers' lives. Their discovery of the universal terrifickness of paper—eventually for building, too, properly water- and wind-proofed, glue replacing nails—was the natural

outcome of a search for specialness. If it never happened, not yet
at least, well, it surely would sometime. As sure as the Confederacy
would rise again.

In Nashville the questers intersect with the spangles and boots
of country-western urban cowpersons to produce odd flavors, a
whisky and spearmint art community. If the love poetry runs to

> *Mah baby done left me*
> *So I went downstairs*
> *And cooked me up some fried chicken,*

it's still love poetry. Where there is a university or where there is
music, or where both are vigorous, as in Nashville, Tennessee, or
Austin, Texas, there you have the contemporary American version of the life of Mimi and Rodolfo, tragically entertained for fun
and games. Atlanta, Charleston, San Antonio, Santa Fe, and Key
West also attract refugees from the work ethic, the sexual-con-
formity ethic, the pressures of family. Oddly enough, the refugees
take comfort in attaching themselves to established communities—the stately traditions of Charleston, the Hispanic energy of
San Antonio, the Indian legends of New Mexico, the conch fi-
sherfolk past of a Key West which has receded into tee-shirt and
postcard remembrances. As long as it's someone else's tradition,
the All-American, good old boy and girl Bohemian can sip from
it as happily as he drinks someone else's wine.

In the South and Texas, Bohemia tends toward eccentric dis-
cretion. When I visited the white-bearded scion of an old Charleston family who was said to be a Gullah speaker—I was investigat-
ing the connections between the Gullah dialect and Haitian
Creole—we sat in his little cottage in a garden and he confessed
anxiously that he waited till sundown to take his first drink of the
day. He also never cruised gay bars or performed any act which
was illegal in South Carolina before sundown. "But I can ride a
bicycle," he said, "whenever I feel like it."

I kept asking him to say something in Gullah and he kept
glancing through the wisteria at his window to see if the sun had
descended below the horizon.

Finally I persuaded him to speak to me in what he described as

Gullah. He downed his drink, his white goatee bobbled, he threw back his head, and he bellowed: "COME ERE BOY WIN AH CALL YEW!"

Perhaps south Florida should not be counted as the South— more like a mixture of New York and Cuba on a peninsula stuck onto the South because there seemed to be noplace else to put it; God trying to create another daring offbeat happening, like the nose, but not thinking it all the way through. New Orleans, with the French Quarter, Dixieland, and the traditional Carnival, provides one of the early legends of American Bohemia. Faulkner came there, and Sherwood Anderson, fleeing small-town Ohio, passed through. In Moscow I met a painter who wanted to set up an easel and be a street artist in front of Creole iron grillwork. People still loiter in cafés, eating blackened fish and seeking adventurous sex lives.

Seth Morgan, whom I knew as a child in Manhattan and later as a reckless young dropout in San Francisco—refugee from a Park Avenue family, declared to be the last male lover of Janice Joplin, a North Beach girl-show barker with a trust fund, a speed-freak and psychedelic dabbler, convicted of useless crimes—was finally sentenced to a term in Vacaville, the California state prison for the seriously disturbed. He seemed to benefit from the discipline. The institution also housed, when I visited its creative writing seminar, members of a well-known rock group who had combined dope scams with murder; a man with a genius IQ who had killed his mother, his grandmother, and a few others in the Santa Cruz mountains; and a former air traffic controller who got off work early one day to find his wife in bed with his best friend (shot them both). Some of the cells looked like college dorm rooms— posters, books, fuzzy animals, and ceramics from the Vacaville workshop. I felt right at home. Seth worked at the novel he had always talked about writing. He was released and managed to finish the book, entitled *Home Boy*, and it was published to some acclaim.

He moved to New Orleans to start a new life, a new novel, and occasionally would telephone in the middle of the night to announce that he was not drinking, not doing drugs; he was seriously writing. These were all serious and difficult matters to accomplish—the not doing of the drugs and alcohol, the doing of the book. He wanted me to know he was cared for, although he had left San Francisco for the innocent temptations of the gentle South. He clung to reminders of meeting me at dinner in his father's apartment on Park Avenue when we were all much younger. But life was good now, he had straightened up, New Orleans was a sweet place, a little worn at the edges; why don't I come to visit? The long middle-of-the-night telephone calls, announcing that he was clean, organized, productive, working away with discipline at his new book, and reconciled with life, had a self-canceling pathos.

Then one day he was stopped for dangerous drunken driving of his motorcycle. Somehow the tolerant New Orleans police understood—writer still celebrating publication of his first book—and they didn't take him in. Seth had a big easy smile and charm.

Later the same day he ran his motorcycle off the road, killing himself and a young woman he was entertaining on the jump seat.

SLACKER ASTEROIDS ORBITING A HECK OF A LOT OF COLLEGE TOWNS

The slacking asteroids, experimental space stations on earth, are mostly located in the back neighborhoods of university communities such as Ann Arbor, Ithaca, Berkeley, Austin, or Columbus, where the colonists can continue their desultory college careers with a desultory postcollege one. Laundromats, garage sales, street stands offering crafts provide social life, economic support, and a familiar environment. Students trade their bicycles, vans, books, clothes, and furniture for other bicycles, vans, etc., or concert tickets. The hustling of meals, musical goods, and company has a rich history. There is both the thrill of novelty and the security of tradition. In the active universe of night, people sleep where they crash, pick up bread from the trucks unloading in the lot of the Safeway or the A&P. The stale loaves in the dumpsters can be magicked into a bread-pudding treat. Scrambling into a dumpster is the slacker's version of rock climbing or hiking in Nepal. A handful of raisins hijacked from the Real Foods bulk display adds a festive sweet speckling to the pudding.

The difference between a slacker and the wandering hobo or homeless dropout is the lower octane of slacker desperation. Why deal in negative emotions? Does not good, gets no sympathy, makes no mark. "What we're looking for is a good dead end," the slacker explains. "No exit? Hey, so where is it?"

Slackers drew closer to traditional Bohemia by becoming anti-Bohemians. Where Bohemians dream of art and bliss, slackers seek *no* bliss except the patience to live without it. "The important thing is to lose desire," said a Berkeley philosopher in the Mediterraneum Café, flipping the single long hair growing out of the mole on his nose. Sometimes the hair tickled and he treated it like an annoying fly.

Actually, there were three hairs, two short, one long. "You have this habit," I commented, "when you say something you want to write in your notebook later, when you have the time, you flip a finger against your nose."

"Right, right, caught me, didn't you? The important thing is to lose that habit out of here."

He didn't hate me for my nagging. Hatred was a desire he had already ducked. In return, I decided it was indiscreet to mention the nose mole hairs (well-mannered Herb). He didn't need hate; quiet contempt would suffice.

If you have enough lack of promise in your youth, the slacker believes, maybe someday you can become a rock critic for the local free shopping weekly. If you find the time. If somebody lends you his old word processor. If you develop that do-gooding desire to share the fruits of your lack of experience. When you're an old guy (half Herb's age, say).

Garage-sale clothes, dumpster French bread, bragging about the immense effort required *not* to create (so many traditional faculty Bohemians put pressure on you to be some kind of great artist or something). . . . "Hell no, I have less important things to do."

Don't even need to bother to point out the sheer oppression of history—the excess of music, the overflow of paintings in museums, the forests cut down to produce books which have their covers ripped off before they join the landfill on the outskirts of great cities. Okay, hippies and beatniks liked music and poetry. Let 'em; that was their thing. Slackers just let other people's things happen. They give anomie a nice gloss: what's wrong with melancholy and despair? In the age of AIDS and herpes and reduced food stamps, it pays better to sit around. Talk is expensive if you factor in the cost of good coffee, but it's not Kaposi's sarcoma.

A fine upstanding investment banker from Boston visited his daughter in Ann Arbor and asked her consort, who enjoyed a small trust fund: "Tell me, when you get up in the morning, what do you do? How does the day pass for you?"

The couple lived in a dark basement apartment, so "morning" was an abstract term. The morning seldom came to their dwelling. But the young man understood the question and answered his non-father-in-law while the young woman sat with her hands demurely folded, hiding her marijuana stash. "Well, first—after breakfast, of course, a couple of health pop-toasts from Quaker Oats—I go through my boxes and look at my socks and jockey shorts. If any of them need darning, I darn them."

"Darn," murmured the investment banker.

"Then Linda gets organized; her hair is dried—"

The daughter interrupted. "I have to wash my hair every other day, Dad. Remember when Mom had healthy hair with a lot of oil from her scalp? Take after how she used to be before she ruined her hair with perms and the Change of Life."

"—and then we grab our bikes and head down to the Bent Can Store to buy our beans or whatever they've got on special—"

"The Bent Can Store?"

The daughter explained patiently. "Long as it isn't swole up, Dad, noxious gasses or something, it's just as healthy as any other can. You can get fresh cans of tuna sometimes, if you're careful it wasn't dolphin-trapping tuna, where the basement of a warehouse was flooded and the label got a little mooshy so they had to ship it to the Bent Can Store—"

"We call it. It's actually Surplus and Overstock and Good Deals—"

"So then sometimes, Dad, we can also buy Commodity milk or

honey or rice from the Indians still lurk around here in Jackson or Detroit, they get it from the BIA—"

"Bureau of Indian Affairs."

This couple was so close that they finished each other's thoughts with no sense of interruption. They survived as a team, happily practicing anomie together. Only the father from Boston seemed to swivel his head from one to the other with a certain gracious puzzlement.

"Trouble is, the Indians get all this Commodity stuff, honey, rice, beans, more'n they can use, but no cash for tobacco or alcohol they really need for their rituals. So they sell it to us and we share the benefit, the honey is really sweet, all bee honey, and then they can buy the stuff *they* need—"

"You ought to taste their fried flat bread, Dad. It's really real. We got invited to a first menstruation ritual one time, this cute little fattie, looked just like an Eskimo—"

Dad had attended Princeton, then a year of sketch classes at the Léger Academy in Paris, then married a pretty woman with glossy hair who happened to be off shopping during this discussion years later in the Ann Arbor basement. He didn't understand his daughter and her companion. But then he wasn't supposed to.

A Santa Cruz mall philosopher, who used to teach at Foothill College before he turned on, was named Boron—"because I give gas the Power."

Now he gave air the smog.

Boron had taken up slacking after a brief term as a near-Ph.D. teacher, then as a French-intensive gardener, then as a dealer in psychoactive substances. He ran into trouble with the Ph.D. dissertation. French-intensive was hard on his back, all that hoeing. With his first bust for magic mushrooms, he realized his mom wouldn't like to know he had—was heading toward—a felony drug-dealing conviction.

Mom died, but slacking turned out to be what he had been looking for. Other people could do art, scholarship, agriculture, commerce. He had tried them all and found them lacking. Renaming himself Boron, on the advice of his Subud master, represented his last burst of individualism. The Subud master had gone away, but Boron remained.

"You don't get bored doing the same nothing day after day?"

"Hey," said the philosopher—*hey* serves the same rhetorical purpose as the older Ah, O, or the ancient quaint Harken ye. "Hey, you listen to music?"

Cautiously, sensing a logic trap: "Ye-ess."

"So you like a piece less after you already heard it once?"

I saw the point and I would have hit my forehead with the flat of my hand, had it been easily available. Great music gets better, richer, deeper, more engrossing, the more often it's heard. The same Mozart aria or long Corelli violin melody can break our hearts, exalt our spirits, with regularity, forever and ever, and even more than the first time when we were dewy children. I could stipulate the fact for more than purposes of argument. "La Folia," the César Franck Violin Sonata in A Major, Mozart's *Requiem* . . .

"So it's like sitting zazen, man. Only I'm sitting here at a table with a nice caffeine jag, the appestat on high, thinking can I stand another oat bran muffin with raisins and apple crunch."

He could. I went to the counter to get it. He bartered recompense for this tribute with a long anecdote about how he had spent a weekend in southern California once and the lightning struck so close he could smell it—like ice, like battery fluid, like a worn-out stick of deodorant, man—and ever since he had like this sacred Native American vision. "I don't use underarm death sticks and I don't plan for the future. *The lightning can strike at any moment.*" He leaned close. He didn't use anything like a toothbrush, either. "Only next time they might call it Desert Storm."

During the Gulf War he informed me that the Israelis would definitely, absolutely, drop a hydrogen bomb on Baghdad within the week and I had better prep up for Armageddon. I reminded him of the time Natalie Wood announced her plan for the film *Arma Geddon,* herself playing the title role as Arma.

"I'm way past putdowns, fella," Boron said. "So what I'm gonna do, I'm gonna gas up my bus, head down to Big Sur with the ladyfriend and plenty of supplies, rice, beans, my oat bran for anticholesterol, six-packs—"

The prevailing winds, he believed, swirled the fallout away from

Big Sur. They could stay in this cozy little cabin at Dietgen's Big Sur Inn, look out over the cliffs, take comfort from the sea lions and whales. In his enthusiasm he seemed to have forgotten the ex-wife and the two ex-kids living in the well-radiated ex-house in Oakland.

6

Israel

Many years ago, in a coffeehouse in that Greenwich Village attic of New York, the Upper West Side, I fell into conversation with a jovial Israeli veteran of the elite Palmach Corps in the 1948 War for Independence. Now Haim Hefer was practicing his hanging-out skills after the struggles of life in the desert. He was in the process of turning into the Israeli Bob Dylan, songwriter and performer, and also into a comedy director and actor, and also into a poet, journalist, and sometime cultural attaché in the Israeli consulate in Los Angeles. Along the way he married a Yemenite artist and art dealer, wrote movies, produced festivals, spent his lazy life in eating, drinking, and devoted hanging out—a kaleidoscope kind of guy. "It's a small country," he explained, "so we have to do many things."

Haim was especially good at what beatniks called digging the scene (in French, "diggink ze scene"), and over the years we have managed to do a lot of it together, watching black stockings come in, go out, and then back into fashion again, irrespective of their intrinsic value.

We shared, among other historically validated habits, an addiction to the warmth, manners, energy, and fellowship of cafés. We both like to sit with our notebooks, encased in the writer's mumbling and fumbling, while the social facts flow underfoot. The hiss of an espresso machine sings like Mozart in our ears. We can always hurl a sullen word at anyone who interrupts the train of thought when the pen, following its own rules, begins to wiggle like a straw between the fingers.

Recently I sat with Haim Hefer in Rosebud, a café on Dizeng-off Street in Tel Aviv, named for that famous sled of Citizen Kane's childhood and also for the legendary intimate babytalk between William Randolph Hearst and his mistress. Earlier we strolled past another café, nicknamed "White Collar Crime Café" because of the demon police commissioner who visited there every day to do some relentless observing. "So is *this* the right place?" I asked, and we both began to laugh. Upon my arrival in Israel on the fourth day of the October War of 1973, when things were still going bad, I had telephoned my old friend.

"Herb," he said, "you're a Tampax."

"What?"

"You're in the right place at the wrong time."

Then, on the fifth and sixth days, the war turned around; the Israelis stopped the Syrians. The whole country seemed to tip on its side as armored brigades rushed from the Syrian to the Egyptian front. I watched the columns of half-tracks, trucks, and tanks, grim and weary soldiers sitting on top of armor, their eyes invisible behind their sunglasses, heading into the battle an hour away. A few days later Haim, attached to a high-ranking general, reached me to ask, "Herb, now would you like to go to Africa?"

"Pardon"

"Just a little picnic—in Africa, Herb?"

So I knew the Israelis would be making an effort to break through on the Egyptian front. In "Africa" they surrounded an Egyptian army near "China Lake." Playful names for slaughter fields; teasing questions from the Israeli Bob Dylan with his rhymes and riddles.

It's not easy to be moon people, making poetry of unforgiving reality, in a small country afflicted with perpetual crisis. Folks create little enclaves for teasing, fun, flirtation, laziness, and invention. Jews have become the people of many books. Back from "Africa," a paratroop colonel complained that history was forcing Israelis to make their fame as soldiers rather than artists. "They don't give Nobel Prizes for lightning strikes," he said. "It's not what we were meant to do."

But I noticed that this rust-haired young kibbutznik, with his boots and his rakehell rusty handlebar mustache, looking like the South African he had once been, didn't really approve of the felafel-eating city people who surrounded us.

During the Gulf War, when the Scud missiles were landing on Tel Aviv, forty-two "long-haired members of the Los Angeles Bikers-for-Jesus motorcycle gang"—as they were described by the Jerusalem *Post*—arrived in their black leather jackets and stomper boots to show solidarity with Israel. These rebels of the freeways, brain-jolted, starry-eyed, came to stand guard by glowering. They were accustomed to frowning menace away; I couldn't see them patrolling the skies like Guardian Angels.

I also met a Canadian fundamentalist of Scottish descent doing a fire watch with a copy of Robert Burns's poetry in his pocket, something to occupy his mind in case no Scuds landed to keep him otherwise occupied. One of the L.A. bikers explained that he was just paying back the Israelis for the help they'd given him. "The Bible got me off speed, man," he said. "I was whacked, but I read that Book. Used to be nothing but an outlaw. Now I'm an inlaw."

Heroically his eyes scanned the horizon, looking for an incoming Scud. His lips were moving. He was reading portents in the sky.

On previous visits to Israel I used to call Dizengoff Street Goose-and-Geese Boulevard because of the strutting and parading of Tel Aviv Bohemia, the *jeunesse dorée* of Israel, the white-haired remnants translated from Warsaw, Bucharest, Budapest, Vienna, the narrow-hipped prowlers from North Africa on the daily lookout. The air of languor and dreaminess was modified in the cafés by the sight of poets, actors, and painters carrying their weapons because talk of art and philosophy filled an interlude between tours of duty. Politics here took precedence over Picasso and nonlinear prose. Earnest discussions of historical contingencies were grounded in the dangers of hard duty in reality. Discourse was deconstructed by risk. But there were still plenty of what a young woman with a shiny helmet of straight dark hair called "no-hip creeps" among the guitar strummers and pickup artists in pursuit of young women with interesting hair.

She fixed her pale gray-blue eyes on me. She had learned at Habima, the national theater where she was in training, how important it was to use the gifts God had generously granted her; she easily won arguments with her stare and her hair.

Haim Hefer asked to be caught up on the news of the Upper West Side, and I told him people were talking to their plants to help them grow. He sighed. He wanted to know if they grew, and I said yes, if they were talked to nicely, plus water and sunlight and not too much steam heat. He dreamed of romantic Manhattan here on Dizengoff Street. In Manhattan I had dreamed of romantic Dizengoff Street.

It was very late now. Catching up with things in 1991 under a trellis in a café garden on Dizengoff, taking our supper at something after midnight on a humid Tel Aviv evening, Haim tried to explain about eternal youth. "In my case it's not vitamins. I don't like rabbis, gurus, those big leaguers. I'm never satisfied, never. Nothing is ever proven, so I have to keep playing. . . . Maybe," he added compassionately, "in your case vitamins are proven. Do the plants talk back?"

He was busy writing his column in verse, promoting a concert, preparing a film. His old and clear eyes, at once eager and perplexed, crinkled with the joy of teasing an old friend. This was better than following big-league gurus. "Do you try singing to the plants?" His boyish grin lightened the late evening.

Someone nearby was playing a flute from a window. I didn't see cows and violins floating over the eaves, but the spirit of Chagall presided over the Tel Aviv midnight. In the alley where Ailanthus, the tree of heaven, would grow if this were Cleveland or New York, there was bamboo grass growing, and listening to flutesong, if bamboo grass listens.

For years, the man called Rafi Nelson because he had one eye, like Admiral Nelson, and maybe was a naval hero, and maybe his name was Rafi, ran a motley encampment in the desert near a spring not far from Eilat. He sold barbecued lamb and cold beer, a major factor in the desert barbecued lamb and cold beer business. It was a continuous picnic, almost as old as the state of Israel, he said, and as precarious. He exaggerated everything. He welcomed the young, the formerly and would-be young, those who liked fun under the sun and in waters fresh from underground streams. The camp was decorated with sets from a Hollywood biblical epic shot nearby, including a Noah's ark in which bikinied animals occasionally still entered, hand in hand, two by two.

Rafi dressed in cowboy clothes, plus eye patch, like the Marlboro plus Hathaway shirt man. He was lanky and tall and more of a pirate captain than an admiral of a fleet. He was a tale spinner. When I came by, he took a liking to me, or at least to my snap-button shirt—shiny agate snaps—and so we exchanged vows of undying friendship and shirts. With my shirt and his beard and ponytail, he now looked like a giant eye-patched Willie Nelson. When he asked where he could find more shirts like mine, I recommended the Sausalito flea market.

Rafi Nelson's southern camp in a desert oasis was a resort for the sort of people who go to hot springs in the gold-rush country of California. It was a hideout for lovers. I met a half-Haitian, half-Jewish Israeli army captain with his starlet friend and we talked about whatever it is that people talk about under the influence of wine, sun, desert, heat, Noah's ark, and memories of Port-au-Prince. There were dust, mud, and palm trees to make us feel at home. Maybe this was what Shirley MacLaine should have meant about past lives. I had known the captain's father, a Magnum photographer who found his way to Port-au-Prince, married a Creole beauty he met on a fashion shoot, and for a time ran the Grand Hotel Oloffson. Then, as life in Haiti seemed insecure, the restless Russian-French-Jewish photographer and the Creole beauty moved to the calm and peace of Israel with their sons. What they were looking for was home. I told the captain that his family should be considered elders of the secret nation of Bohemia and he answered, "What the hell are you talking about?"

A good answer, I thought.

Rafi loomed overhead, summoning us to lamb on skewers, with peppers, onions, roasted tomatoes, and an assortment of Middle Eastern yogurts. The ice chests with beer were flung open. Food and drink took precedence over analysis of the ineffable.

Danish beer. String bikinis. A formation of three skinny fighter planes far overhead, swooping like hawks over the desert and the Red Sea, except that hawks don't break the sound barrier.

Nearby there was a young woman who noticed that the Haitian Israeli captain and I were staring at her, so she pushed in her cheeks with her index fingers to communicate the idea that she was aesthetic, could easily be a hollow-cheeked model. The art for art's sake effect was augmented by the fact that she was wearing only the bottom part of her bikini.

"Herb!" Rafi cried. "Ever since I wear your shirt, I am happy cowboy!"

The Jerusalem telephone directory may have wilder listings in the spectrum of academies, institutes, fellowships, mystic world head-quarters, and save-the-universe foundations than any other city. *Luftmenschen* float easily in the thin dry air of the world's central holy place. Dreamers seem to soar, like Chagall's violinists and cows, above the rooftops and walls of that ancient orangeish Jerusalem stone, borne by their robes, braids, embroidery, wide black hats, pointy red ones with tassels, beards. They clutch their sanctified books and commentaries of three great religions, includ-ing the warring subdivisions of each. They keep their eyes on the cobblestones or on the sky or on the fatal imprinting in their hearts. Each of them is *right;* each follows a clear command from heaven.

Many Jerusalemites carry guns or hide rocks on their persons; that's the reality of this city devoted to eternal peace. Yet better visions, a paradise or paradises which do not exist in history, are more real here than mall shopping, temporary marriages, more real even than the permanent impatient taking of lives which seems to accompany exclusive landlordship of the Truth. In this place blessed by the dreams of God, there are even anarchist associations and an institute to treat dyslexia, defending it as a choice about language. The air people of Jerusalem dwell in ethereal realms, firmly drifting in fantasies of salvation, and some even include others in the plan.

For poets, God is still in the details. Grounded in reality, they too find the ancient city beautiful and congenial. Austere is relieved by vines, flowers, fountains, courtyards with laundry and voices singing, walls covered with green, the thin sunlight of winter and spring. Strolling with my ten-year-old son in the restored quarter near the Moses Montefiore windmill, I happened to encounter the great Hebrew poet Yehuda Amichai, also strolling hand in hand with his daughter, and perhaps because of the magic, verb-crazed air of Jerusalem, I recognized him although I could not recall seeing his photograph. I had read his poems. I knew this must be Amichai. He had written a poem about divorce which I recalled as:

> *Our marriage is like a severed snake*
> *The head is dead*
> *But the tail twists at night.*

Blocking his way, I began to recite, beginning politely with his name: "Mr. Amichai, our marriage is like . . ." I quoted inaccurately, but the image had shaken a divorced husband and father when I read it in San Francisco.

He smiled with the gratification of a poet who, out of his own pain, has managed to speak truly about something and therefore transformed the pain into something else, a partial mastery. I suppose he recognized the fellowship of those who wake in this way at night. He invited my son and me back to his house. He made tea, we ate cookies from a box. We talked about love, marriage, and the end of marriage while our children stared at each other. Quite properly, they were bored with their fathers' griefs. The cookies were okay, though.

I remembered visiting Fink's Bar in Jerusalem, a few days after the Six Day War, with the woman who was to become my wife, the mother of our three children, and then my ex-wife. We were in love in 1967; our hands touched, our foreheads touched in the Jerusalem night, we whispered to each other. Nobody slept in that aftermath of a war which was a triumph except for those who died, their families, their friends. The tragedy contained in this glory and victory made everyone crazy, heedless. The lady and I danced on captured Soviet tanks and visited an Egyptian officer's tank complete with carpets, a samovar, a tea service. We lay awake in the King David Hotel and heard Israeli soldiers playing tennis at dawn. Sleep seemed to have been abolished. The war had ended so fast; the blood was still running on air-raid emergency. But it seemed that survival would continue awhile longer. We listened to a folk-rock group called The High Windows swinging a Mamas and Papas-like tune to words taken from the Book of Isaiah. It was Old Testament rock, greedy for life and tragic.

In Fink's Bar an officer with an eye patch and sharp planes in his face took a table alone near ours. I was flattered that General Dayan happened to turn up near my companion, wherever she happened to be. We learned the deep truth about flirtation that a man with one eye cannot eye a woman unobtrusively.

Other men in uniform sat with their girlfriends or families at other tables, respecting the privacy of the architect of victory. Later, when it seemed evident that I was not going to invite the general to sit with us and then disappear myself, like the Arab armies, General Dayan graciously passed from table to table, chatting with the soldiers.

Later, during that visit to Israel, we encountered an actress whom I had first met in Florida when she was making an American film called *Wind Across the Everglades*. First I saw her among flamingos, alligators, Klansmen, swamp creatures; then among ancient holy places. "What are you doing here?" I asked.

"In Jerusalem?" she said. "I'm not really here. I'm in Tel Aviv."

Yet I could see her with my own eyes standing and pouting in front of me, no doubt about it. But many expect the Messiah to come soon and all Jews to return, perhaps next year, to Jerusalem. So why couldn't the actress in all her humid sultriness, who recently played a barefoot swamp waif with mascara like algae trailing from her eyelashes, have been part of the advance party, scouting locations for a production bigger than any by Cecil B. De Mille?

There was also reasonable expectation in the heart of the sleek and handsome one-eyed general that the spoils of victory should come sit in his lap. He had organized the defeat of combined Arab armies; one coltish American girl shouldn't have been able to resist. In the celebration of release from dread, both tennis at dawn and dazed hunting of pleasure at night seemed part of liberation. The griefs of loss darkened festival at its edges. We could also hear lamentations from windows.

Old women stopped us on the street to ask if we would come home to meet their families. *"My son lived. My grandson lived."* We picnicked on Mount Scopus with another young couple we just happened to meet. There was an epidemic of goofy and dazed. I saw the entire country, in a revolt against historical dreads, taking on free and easy ways. Such euphorias, of course, do not last; in due course both history and the human body tend to level things out.

Later, in the 1970s, I met a chain-smoking Russian film director who had come to Israel because of Soviet anti-Semitism. They would not let him do his work. They let him go to film school, but as a Jew he could not make the films he wanted to make; and then he couldn't make any films at all. Now, as he sat with other Soviet émigré artists at cafés on Dizengoff Street, Israel's rive gauche corridor, he complained bitterly about the paradox that Israel wanted him, welcomed him, but then perversely refused to give him a few million dollars to make his film. "Perhaps," he suggested, "you could tell American millionaire?"

Mobilize, perhaps, the revolutionary American millionaire masses.

In a bar in Jerusalem near the pedestrian Ben Yehuda Street, a sergeant in uniform, cappuccino in his hand, gleaming Uzi leaning against his chair, argued with me about deconstructionism. It felt odd to be speaking from the patronizing heights of my great age (this was 1991) to this young man enrolled as an English major at Hebrew University when he wasn't wrestling with the nonacademic distinctions of rock-throwing boys and the occasional knife-bearing terrorist. The jargonizing of semiotics, the remasticated, instant clichés of deconstructionism, the used-baggage of postmodernism seemed like rejects from contemporary academic garage sales, but the quest for a new and truer sense of language and the mortal struggle for existence were real to Amos. For him, they were not unlinked. His decision-searching was a commitment to finding a fate. His life was on the line, as everyone's is, but in a way different from the English majors I was used to. He intended to make "prose narrative," leaving me to ask whether he meant story, novel, history, or confession. For me the phrase "prose narrative" was associated with indulgence and self-display, but this young man was modest, earnest, committed to Truth. At his age the word was still capitalized. His ambition to enlist in the outposts of Israeli Bohemianism and the life of Art, leaving war behind, making war no more, was infinitely moving. He said "the Truth," but then amended it: "the Truths." He already had the idea of plurality.

In Amos, an Israel Defense Forces sergeant, I saw the struggle of the Bohemian nation to survive in a world of continual mortal event, where history was a bad breath leaning close. While he did his duty as a soldier, Amos also sought to reconcile a young artist's need for love, and the pain of birth, fear of death, dread of war, hatred of injustice. His way was to look for the meaning of meaning. As a non-saint and a young man, he probably also wouldn't mind a little fame, riches, and love of beautiful women through a franchise in the beauty and truth trade.

We drank too much coffee. I tried to buy, and he consented, so long as he could buy the felafel. While we ate the spicy mixture of chick-peas, sesame seeds, oils, and spices in pockets of pita bread, I asked what he would do when he could go back to school full time, his army service finished. "Never done," he said. "Not till I'm fifty-five."

"Or there's peace."

"Maybe when I'm fifty-five," he said. "That would be the miracle, wouldn't it?"

With his dark sharp features, body that of a wiry boy, shoulders jutting in a khaki shirt which seemed slightly too large for him, Amos could have passed for one of the haunted poets of Berkeley, Havana, the East Village. Ease in the world would contradict his brooding stare, but he consented to confuse matters with a sudden flashing grin, leaning back so that his shoulders briefly filled the shirt under its epaulets. He was a boy-man with that inconsistent lyrical softness within lean, a gleaming eye, the bridge of his nose sunburned. Surely he took time out from toting the burdens of history to break a few hearts; didn't brag about his conquests. I wanted to do something for him, compose a letter of recommendation of his entire being. And I wondered if this boy would ever reach the age when he no longer had army service to do. The age of fifty-five seemed an eternity away, like the Messiah's coming.

Later we sat on another humid terrace in an ancient city not far from the Mediterranean and catastrophe and waited to see if the conflict over deconstructionism would be resolved, if the gum-chomping actress/waitress would waltz over with our bottle of mineral water. She was busy being discovered by a squat hammer of a man, middle-aged, who might have been a producer from Los Angeles or Tel Aviv; he was, of contemporary dance plays. "I dance, I dance!" she assured him, dancing—whatever was right.

Middle-aged, but not a hammer of a man and not a producer, I could wait for my mineral water.

Amos called her sharply, asking in Hebrew, "Ma'im b'vaka-sha." Water, please! He was used to waiting, both for peace in Israel and to be served. In his uniform, his weapon nearby, it was evident he could do nothing for the lady's career as she hastily remolded it as waitress, actress, *and* dancer, sucking in her already tight little belly. She was so clever she could do two things at once, suck in both stomach and cheeks. There were also eyes in the back of her head, taking inventory of the producer, as she brought us our bottle of water. She didn't stay to chat. We could open it ourselves. She didn't want to miss her future.

This could have been a café on Second Avenue in New York; it could have been the Café de Tournon in Paris; it could have been the Puccini in San Francisco. It was the holiest of cities.

David Hume said that reason is—and ought to be—the slave of

the passions. The disorderliness of Bohemian loafing and need reflects this subservience of efficiency to desire. A scientist for whom I worked during my early scuffling would-be-writer years shocked me by describing personality as "the index of inefficiency." In other words, in a rational world, we would all fit neatly and noiselessly. I admired my employer's strictness, and forgave him because I noticed how he doodled intricate weird patterns, complicated his romantic life, married a teasing, taunting, lazy, dangerous young woman. He had the saving grace of inefficiency, although he didn't understand how his failings to fit made him an interesting scientist. The Bohemian is openly not neat, unfitting. What seems like mere inefficiency may end as a vivid abstention and strangeness, a contorted mastery of the flux whose pattern is not yet revealed.

Not yet ever to be revealed. As long as the mouth hungers (and the rest of the body does, too), we will use reason to get what we crave. And whatever trouble craving yields, in our time on earth we will treasure both passions and the memory of them. We're not usually nostalgic for the times in history when we efficiently carried out our routines; rather, for the time of exalted love or even for the time we lay in wait in the bushes for a glimpse of the loved one who has given us pain and asked us to be gone. We are out of her sight. We smell the bushes and the fertilizer, feel the ache in our bones, as she comes home laughing with someone else.

William James thought humankind could be divided into two sorts, the once-born and the twice-born. The once-born live in the here and now, suffering no regrets except for their ambitions or failures in a life with recent beginning and limited span. They may be intelligent, but alas, they are efficiently so. The twice-born twist and squirm under the certain dream that there was and will be another life, the soul in permanence, no matter about the body in this temporary place. The metaphor of a soul struggling to harken back to a previous life evokes the artist's need to remake the universe in some pattern he cannot exactly recall, must keep reshaping, though no image will ever fit the idea. Celebrating sensuality, claiming that life is a festival and they will live for today, the nation of Bohemia struggles to reconcile itself with the suspicion that there must be More. More, even for the successful artist or the gratified pleasure-lover, is never enough. In the Garden of Imagined Delights there can be no final satisfaction of appetite. "When the mouth dies," Yeats asked, "what is there?"

Amos told how his first year at the university was a release from family, politics, army obligation, history, as new friends suddenly discovered that they were all great poets, all intending to tell the story of the times, whether they came from the kibbutz, the cities, the moshav, or the Arab villages; and yes, the Arabs needed poetry even more, because they were struggling to reconcile two languages, cultures, and several loyalties. Because the Israeli Jews had to do their military service first, they were older than their Arab classmates.

"I had an Arab friend at the university, maybe I still do. He used to want to write the epic of the Arab nation. I used to say that was too big for a subject. Now he sits at the American Colony Café, near the fig trees, and sells interviews to foreign journalists. That's too small a subject."

"You're not happy with him."

"He used to be a poet. Used to be a *good* poet."

"You speak Arabic?"

"Gnugh." Enough. "The reporter from *Newsweek* leaves him a big tip, so he talks about Intifada, he talks about stone-throwers and tells the man from *Le monde* they are his brothers. . . ."

It seemed to me he was angry with the reporters from *Newsweek* and *Le monde,* not his friend the former poet.

Amos was greedy for news of the outside world of deconstructionism, modernism, postmodernism, and—the dry Jerusalem air plus jet lag plus the current academic fashions was distracting me in this city touched by the holiness of words—*post* postmodernism. We debated the distinctions between signifier and signified. When Amos spoke, with a glance at his weapon, of the meaninglessness of language, I was more sympathetic than I might have been to the same conversation at the Mediterraneum Café on Telegraph Avenue in Berkeley. I taught him a French word, *fumisterie,* which refers to the smoke in the head which comes out in the form of smoke in the mouth: jargon, pretense, stylishness, this year's the-

ory. "The emperor was naked not because he was gender-typed,"
I said.

"His role is to be naked. I see. You're laughing at me."

"Please forgive me, Amos."

I was ready to hear him declare, "Descartes was wrong. It's not
I think, therefore I am; it's I think, therefore I think that I am
thinking but my expressed thoughts are only a strategy of domi-
nation by the old power structures."

"That's already complicated, and it's even a little more complicated than that." The visiting professor from Yale must have left
in a hurry. "Perhaps the implications of 'I am' need to be explored
through marination in the experience you are having even now,
as we speak—"

Amos waited till I shut up. He had a proposal. He was a young
man full of hope. He was saying, "When this goddamn war, these
goddamn fightings are finish, maybe I can get a fellowship to study
in New York? Only for a year or two, then I come back home. But
right now I need to breathe more air and not Gaza Streep. . . ."

I wondered if he was one of those being overtaken by the bone
weariness of decades of adrenalin alertness.

"No. *No.* But I regret God led Moses to a place where there was
no oil. He was thinking of something else, perhaps the sky and the
color of the hills of Jerusalem—the *rocks* on the hills. That was an
error. He was an artist distracted by Jerusalem stone."

He fell silent while we both contemplated that rough dull glow,
the hills reflecting the fruits of quarrying in the walls, houses, and
holy places of three religions. I remembered a courtyard with olive
trees, February flowers blooming, a village within the city, and a
young woman with whom I strolled. I remembered some of the
rocks moving on the hills as we gazed, miracle rocks that turned
out to be sheep.

Amos grinned. "He forbade us to worship things, but this entire
place is a golden calf."

I had spent part of a winter breathing the high dry air of
Jerusalem. The nights were chilled, and sometimes snow sanded
the hills, scraps of snow blew in the air, but the days were warm
and flowers bloomed. "There have always been three seasons in

Israel—spring, summer, and war." The young woman made the days of that winter into springtime, summertime, and no wartime; made the rocks seem to wander on the hills. She confessed to her astigmatic friend that the wandering clumps were grazing sheep.

I wasn't ready to argue with lopsidedly grinning Amos just because he was exaggerating a little. This was a café, after all, and in love I too had exaggerated.

"If we are to be born again and again," said Amos, "then we must die over and over—"

"That's not the Jewish way."

"So now I am in the first hour of one of my deaths."

The thought made me dizzy. I was reminded of Jack Sarfatti, Ph.D. physicist and reincarnation of the fourteenth-century mystic Rabbi Sarfatti, holding his permanent floating seminar at the Caffe Trieste in North Beach, San Francisco, with rapt descriptions of how events from the future cause events in the past. Eleven time zones away Amos took a pessimistic view of the doctrine of reincarnation, thinking of repeated dying rather than the promise of rebirth. I could see how a soldier on active duty a few kilometers from Jerusalem might think earnestly of death, even at his age, with all of life rightfully ahead of him.

Occasionally he fell into a disconcerting absence from our conversation, like a willful child, sleepy and sullen. It made me uneasy, as if I were intruding, and reminded me of what anthropologists in Haiti call the psychic's torpor—the dreamy abstraction and silence of a voodoo priest after possession by the gods. But Amos was a sinewy young Israeli noncom, not a psychic or a mystic. He was a secular Jew. Yet he imagined another life, had the imagination of a better fate for Israel and the world. He suffered the itch of philosophy which might, when he had time from his army duties, make him an artist.

I learned to accept his silences. They weren't really sullen. He was practicing sitting and doing nothing with me. I considered myself a master of that trade.

"Tell me about Paris in 1949," he said abruptly.

"There used to be lots of Israelis at the Select. I think I used to see Haim Hefer there."

"Tell me about *Paris*," he interrupted impatiently.

That rouged and terrible city, Victor Hugo said. A movable feast, Ernest Hemingway said. I always knew it would be like this, so many visitors cried out.

"And tell me, is it true?"

"About what?"

"The Trilateral Commission."

"Whatever you've heard, not," I said, "but have you heard about the International House of Pancakes?"

His dark eyes widened. "Is that what they're calling it now?"

In Berkeley the conspiracy theorist might be lanky and blond, with ten-thousand-dollar teeth for which he compensated by the proletarian backward wearing of his mesh Toyota truck baseball and barbecue cap. Here no visor shielded Amos's neck from sunburn. Where there was plenty of actual menace, imaginary menace helped in the continual rehearsal of disaster. As long as it was only a disaster, it wasn't the apocalypse.

Streaks of orange sunlight caught the shredded late-afternoon clouds over Jerusalem. The air was keen on this café terrace, keener for me with the smells of coffee, tobacco, felafel spices, people. I no longer saw rocks becoming sheep, browsing on the hills, but Jerusalem was still the golden city, city of promise and eternal renewal, towers, churches, minarets, and tombs, the center of faith. I wanted Amos to notice the smiling Ethiopian waitress with her high cheekbones and glittering black eyes. I wanted him to come back to the belief in life here and now on earth which was his birthright.

In adolescence, the biological tides sweep boys and girls into strangeness and rebellion, desires for the distantly imagined and, in their lonely beds, for the close and sweatily imagined. Teenagers are all potential artists, candidate Bohemians. Amos, caught in that turbulence, felt the artist's need to experience and create which was very like lust. Old age is wasted on the elderly: the young know what to do with it—insist on something different.

Tell me about Paris.

7

Paris

The life of a young artist here is the easiest, merriest, dirtiest existence possible. He comes to Paris, notably at sixteen . . . establishes himself in the Pays Latin . . . labors among a score of companions as merry and poor as himself. . . . The pictures are painted in the midst of a cloud of smoke, and a din of puns and choice French slang and a roar of choruses, of which no one can form an idea who has not been present at such an assembly.
—William Makepeace Thackeray, *Paris Sketchbook*, 1840

I could never be lonely.
—Ernest Hemingway, post World War I, taking charge of Paris, springtime, and literature

PARADISE OF MISERY, CAPITAL OF HOPE (1949–51)

In 1948, recently out of the army and fresh out of college, I promised my wife-to-be that we would go live in Paris, the cradle of new lives, the catacombs where old ones could be buried. Like Rastignac, I would stand in the Père Lachaise cemetery and raise my fist to challenge the City of Light: "It's between us now!"

Where my wife would stand was not so clear. Muse for writer was a vocation on its last legs.

In the Paradise of Misery and the Capital of Hope, I was ready for my portions of both. Existentialists and cold-war exiles were gathering together on the rive gauche; the coffee drinking was serious and the wine was better; forward, into pregnant wander-jahr. "As an artist, a man has no other home in Europe save Paris," Nietzsche said, and thus also spake a heck of a lot of recent GIs, college graduates, jazz exiles, artists, seekers of their own tropics of cancer, dreamers with pent-up visions glamoured by the war. For the French and a few others, Paris is still the measure of the rest of the world. Two generations earlier, the novelist Huysmans declared that "Paris is a sinister Chicago," a bit of French poetry which we can probably deconstruct to mean that Huysmans never traveled to Chicago. In his novel *À rebours*, he described the perfect room, every detail esthetically topnotch, but then discovered it had a certain static quality. A bit of lamentation was in order, and in due course the remedy. His hero installed a jewel-encrusted live turtle to lend the design the necessary kinetic element as the turtle slowly trundled across the carpet. Chicago was never like this.

Paris, for the good reason that it was Paris, had kept its dense concentration of human café tapestries, hangers-on, who did no work except the essential one of providing backdrop for those who played out visions of yearning. An audience and patrons are essential to the ecology, accompanying the big fish, feeding and cleaning them, necessary plankton although they occasionally may show a bit of temper themselves, just like a regular genius. Some of the shrewdest would-bees understood their role. Sometimes a person who seemed to be in training only for pleasure-seeking, an artist at evasion, emitted by contagion some sort of work, almost inadvertently, like a sneeze. Mason Hoffenberg, who made his living by selling hashish to snobbish French Bohemians—he called it marijuana, and with this packaging insight commanded a premium price because of the chic for all things American—slipped from perfect hustling to coauthor the cult book *Candy* with Terry Southern. It was published by Olympia Press, Henry Miller's Paris publisher, and eventually made its way to the U. S. and the movies. Mason sold out—became a writer. Somehow, my first day in Saint-Germain-des-Prés, I met him and he took me to Raffy's in the rue du Dragon, ordering a "jumbo omelet," by which he meant an omelette jambon, with ham.

Some months later I karmically repaid him by meeting another American on his first morning stroll in the neighborhood and taking him to Raffy's. Harry H. was busy publishing the magazine *Death* (the answer to *Life*) and had the encouragement and support of Orson Welles. I asked him to invite the next new arrival on the scene, to pass on the karma at Raffy's.

"How about Kiki?" he asked. She was the artist's model and career girlfriend emeritus, known as Kiki of Montparnasse, who still stared under her bangs out of her painted eyes from the terraces very late at night, looking like one of the madwomen of Chaillot.

"There are rules," I told him. "Doesn't qualify."

"Mason tells me this place serves a great jumbo omelet made with eggs," Harry said. "Orson loves a good omelet made with eggs."

"My treat," I said, "unless he wants to treat."

James Joyce went into Bohemian exile from Ireland in order to forge in his famous silence, exile, and cunning the uncreated conscience of his race. He committed long books and sang in his fluty tenor among his friends in Trieste and Paris—he was not silent. *Leave and learn* could have been his motto. Exile deepened and darkened his remembrance of home, of Dublin and Ireland. Live and learn; leave and yearn.

Some Bohemian geniuses cut themselves away from their roots in order to take the measure of their roots; others, like Vladimir Nabokov, are cut away by history. The greater number, less gifted, choose to separate from their home grounds and fall into the congenial café temptations of idea-mongering, flirtation, time-passing. It's hard to separate the congeniality from the mere frivolity, the depth and play from the mere showing off of notions; the risk of triviality is accepted. One afternoon I sat with a friend in the Select, a Montparnasse café from the time of the surrealists, Joyce, and Hemingway—now it's the time of folks with literary guidebooks. Without knowing its history, I had found my way here on my bicycle, had given up studying, began a novel under the warm amber skylight, sheltered from winter rains and the moldy damp of my unheated room.

My friend was from Marseilles and rolled his r's like an Italian. He felt himself an exile in Paris, like the meridional Denis Diderot. "Repression and exile squeeze the ideas," he said, "get the air out."

"And maybe the juice, too."

He shrugged, one of those Mediterranean shrugs that involve the shoulders, the corners of the mouth, and the eyebrows. "Sometimes you have to be hard when you leave your family, home, land, the place with nice bowls of hot milk for breakfast."

"With honey from your own hive."

"Without the good honey." He nodded bitterly (shoulders, mouth, eyebrows). He missed his mother's bouillabaisse.

Then he peered into the mirror on the café wall and grinned back at his image because *he got the joke.* He had chosen this trouble for himself. He had picked this fun. During icy winters he too wrote in the Select to the music of the stuttering espresso machines spitting their jets of steam.

Postwar Paris was still a village, few automobiles, food shortages, black market. I walked the streets trod southward by Roman legions, and listened for their footsteps; I searched the rue Saint-Jacques for the Pension Vauquer, where Vautrin challenged Rastignac to become a criminal cynic—I thought he might win me over to his creed; I studied French by reading Gide, Sartre, and Villon in the garden of the little Russian Orthodox church at the corner of the boulevard Saint-Germain and the rue des Saints-Pères. My wife and I took bread, cheese, wine, and our solemn selves to lunch in the public gardens of this town of which we were the newest natives. We had always known it would be like this.

Stunned and goofy, we practiced marriage and philosophy at the Sorbonne and in our little hotel, rue de Verneuil, where I set out to study France and the meaning of life. By reading, walking, bicycling, and keeping my eyes open a lot, I would become an artist-philosopher, a stroller on two banks, unlike other men but brother to them all. I developed strong leg muscles. At the *bains publiques* (there was no bath at the Hôtel de Verneuil), my wife and I met an old army buddy from the 100th Infantry Division at Fort Bragg, North Carolina, whose French was still in basic training: "Hey, it's so fucking great to be in fucking Paris, n'est-ce pas?"

My wife thought he had no culture. I explained that we had crouched in red sand with M-1 rifles, done KP together in forty-eight-hour stretches. As my muse, she considered this no excuse. Although the idea had previously occurred to me, I understood that I had a problem.

Saul Bellow winked at me, was kind; Lionel Abel explained the differences between Sartre and Heidegger while pieces of a croissant flew from the corners of his mouth; James Baldwin, called Jimmy by everyone, became a companion and neighbor in the next room at the Hôtel de Verneuil. Perhaps jewel-encrusted turtles were creeping across sealed perfect rooms on the Right Bank. Where we spent our time, the dream was more turbulent.

A swarthy little guy with bug eyes came calling at the hotel—consistent with the lack of bath, it also had no telephone—and asked for the painter on the fifth floor. "Not here," I said. "Who should I tell him was asking?"

The bug-eyed man seemed a bit surprised that I asked. "Mais c'est moi, Picasso."

My wife got a job running errands for Ella Winter, an American leftist, widow of Lincoln Steffens, wife of Donald Ogden Stewart, an exiled screenwriter. Ella used to whisper secret commands in the middle of her room because the walls had ears, the CIA was on her trail: "Go to the post office . . . buy stamps. . . ." Once, when I was summoned to an early-morning errand, she stood hissing into my ear something about cutting the pages of a book by the poet Paul Eluard and then asking him to sign it for her. Donald Stewart came toward us in his undershorts, put his head between ours, and whispered: "Anybody see my toothbrush?"

One of the founding surrealists, Philippe Soupault, then working as a UNESCO bureaucrat, gave my wife the benefit of his insight into my character: "Il est sadique." How many of my friends from Lakewood, Ohio, had been so nailed by a person mentioned in every significant history of Paris literary Bohemia between the two wars? And in French?

"I hadn't thought of that," the muse said.

"Oui, oui, sadique," firmly repeated this man who had traveled with Aragon, Breton, Eugene Jolas, since the beginning, and now, wise and weary after life's voyage, was resting his freckled, care-worn hand on my wife's thigh.

From our hotel room we could look out onto the street and see the little urn of painted clay placed against a wall at the corner with the words Ici est Tombé Pour La France . . . Roland LaPorte, age 17. A man had died in a pool of blood at that place only a few years ago. The *patron* at the hotel had seen it happen. Surely Roland LaPorte's family somewhere in these anonymous build-ings were the ones who replenished the flowers in the urn. I watched for hours, and the fresh flowers appeared, but I never saw who put them there.

We were busy defining ourselves at the Hôtel de Verneuil—artists, students, Bohemians—not children and not adults, either. I was not the only one who sometimes wished he could be Roland LaPorte, age 17. In the dramatic self-pity of the expatriate, sugar low in the blood, it was not part of the routine to observe our neighbors, the family LaPorte, creatures of habit, buying flowers on Saturday and watching them droop and scatter to the pave-ment after the weekend. I thought constantly about the war which I had passed in schools and training, crawling under fake bullets, while my cousins and friends died. The memory of Roland La-Porte was a distanced French image, like the baguettes swung home in the evenings, the little bouquets of flowers carried with the bread, the intensely nervy, cursing drivers who tried to run down my bicycle with their 4-CV Renaults, the bleary, aquiline sexuality of the girls at Saint-Germain-des-Prés who were imitat-ing Juliette Greco (one of them was Juliette Greco). We were another nation living among the French.

A THOUSAND YEARS OF VIRILITY

At the Salle de Géographie, near the church of Saint-Germain-des-Prés toward which a statue of Diderot across the boulevard raised a skeptical finger, I attended a lecture by a veteran lover of beautiful women concerning his revival of the medieval medical remedy called Sunamatism. "Not remedy—*cure!*" he said, spitting through his French false teeth, the clenching of logic unimpaired by inaccurate dentures. Although he was only eighty years old, perhaps a few more, he seemed elderly to me. I was in my early twenties.

I had met Doctor Sunamatique at one of his outdoor lectures at the corner of the boulevard Saint-Germain and the rue des Saint-Pères, across the street from the Café Le Rouquet, where Saul Bellow and visitors from *Partisan Review* used to repair for company and where medical students now hang out and where the poet Ted Joans still picks up his mail and messages when he's not tracking the muse in Mali or Berkeley. Docteur Sunamatique lectured daily, weather permitting, near the *vespasienne* on the walkway alongside the gardens of the little Russian church where I studied French by reading André Gide's *The Counterfeiters,* underlining the words I didn't know, relaxing to the pleasures of an outdoor pee and a fragment of explication by the tireless Docteur concerning why he was tireless. He said I was one of the few Americans in Paris to understand Science.

Since America was the land of eternal youth, he graciously accepted an American disciple. Further, I could apply to be his friend. My master had drooping tobacco-stained mustaches—it seemed like a collection of them, layered white, yellow, and white again—and the glint of a rogue in his eyes, which were also yellow and white due to the conjunctivitis to which he was as indifferent as if it were mere dandruff. He was a conqueror in theory and in fact. He was indomitable, his voice was hoarse, his finger shot into the Paris air, up and up, at climactic moments in his discourse at the Salle de Géographie. Since the subject was virility, his specialty, he attracted a crowd from which the steam rose. I leaned my rusty eight-dollar bicycle against an iron grille, not locking it because I believed the condition of the bike would discourage thieves—in Paris, reason prevails—and hurried inside to take a *strapontin,* a folding seat. The good seats were already claimed by ardent old men whose need was greater than mine.

Sunamatism restores absent vitality, energy, creativity, and the ability to get it up. Lots of folks are interested in that. The emperor Charlemagne, king of the Francs, son of Pepin the Short, conqueror of Italy, conqueror of selected portions of Spain, subduer of both Moors and Saxons, founder of the Holy Roman Empire, was one of them. The treatment worked for this good friend of some of the top popes of his time. His ultimate victory was to overcome—"par le moyen de Sunamatisme, mes amis!"—the debility of age.

Have I neglected to specify the treatment? The prescription is uncomplicated and, for most patients, agreeable. As Docteur Sunamatique described it, few could deny the combination of medicine with common sense.

It requires (a) going to bed . . . that's already a good start . . . with (b) two warm young women, not necessarily virgins, one on either side of the patient. So far, all is normal. But then comes the contribution of ninth-century scientific wisdom: (c) one must be blond and the other dark. So many men, in unseemly haste, neglect the details.

We returned to his imperial case study. The lecturer paused for historical and medical precisions. The event took place in A.D. 814, a year of turmoil. Docteur Sunamatique stood before us with arms extended, yellow and white mustaches vibrating, yellow and white eyes benevolent, smiling. We could predict the results.

The treatment absolutely brought back the virility of the emperor, according to the report of the two young women. A flanking movement like that which outwitted the Moors, a subtle attack like that which took the Spaniards by surprise, a double application of carrot and stick like the one which charmed the Lombards into submission—total victory was his!

A single unexpected difficulty perplexed ninth-century science.

When the three of them woke up in the morning, only two of them woke up. The emperor, Charles the Magnificent, was dead. "Alas, the triumph of His Highness came at a certain cost, which can be termed the price of majesty," explained Docteur Sunamatique. "Sirs, may I ask if the glory of a hero is diminished by his sacrifice of self on the field of battle?"

"Non! Non! Mille fois non!" answered the heartfelt croaks of the crowd.

Vive l'Empereur! (But my bicycle was stolen by someone who paid attention neither to rust nor to reason.)

A group of writers gathered to meet James T. Farrell, famous for his Studs Lonigan trilogy, who had just returned from a conference of the Committee for Cultural Freedom, where he had urged the dropping of an atom bomb on Moscow. "They don't have it, we do," he explained.

He had no doubts. His intentions were pure. Secure at our table on the outdoor terrace at the Deux Magots, we dared to argue with him.

Farrell replied in an irritable tenor, rasped with smoke, drink, too many meetings, too many disappointments. He was one of the great men of my boyhood; I had read his books in high school, and now here he sat, dandruff flecking his shoulders, flesh heaving and sweating through a nylon shirt, telling us that the Communists had let him down and he wanted to finish them off for it. I changed the subject. Paris was something we could agree on; how about Paris in his own time on the Left Bank—the time of Hemingway, Fitzgerald, Kay Boyle, Djuna Barnes, Robert McAlmon, James Joyce?

"There were pretty girls then," he said jovially. "And geniuses. I don't see the pretty girls." He stared severely past the three young writers gathered for a word from a master. "I don't see any geniuses. Nope, no geniuses; it's all gone dead."

Me! me! me! we wanted to cry. Your glasses are too thick, Warrior!

"Oh there really are some pretty girls," I said modestly.

"Nothing like it was. Nothing like it was, boy."

And in fact, for the onetime happy Marxist, whose monumental book had been deemed great by a generation, here in a new time nothing was as it had been, his former loves had disappeared; and as to the avid young writers sucking the air around him, their frayed faces turned toward him as toward the sun, he wanted only to make them wince. He was drinking sweet vermouth for his cough. He knew the remedy for his troubles, he was trying to strike a deal, and sweet vermouth for the cough was one which a corrupt world still provided. Other remedies—a great book, a great love— were now out of reach. He turned back to the atom bomb and its proper use; that is, as soon as possible.

I'm not sure I like the young man who looked at the older writer and saw only a fool. Perhaps he deserved no indulgence for the books I had admired. He wanted to murder the race of his enemies. But I'm not sure I like the young man who gave him no shrift in his decline.

The next morning a delegation of our colleagues in the Hôtel de Verneuil came to our room while I was supposed to be writing and my wife was out buying the cheese, bread, and tomatoes which we took to lunch with a bottle of wine in the Luxembourg or the Tuileries or the little garden of the Russian church. There was the Norwegian lesbian and the American filmmaker and Jimmy Baldwin and the Belgian painter, all knotted up with their high-level proposal. "Ve vill all cheep in," said the solemn Norwegian woman. "I arrange ex-hee-beeshn."

There was a moment when I thought she meant paintings.

"You will join us. You vill bring vife." It sounded more like *fife*. It was a command.

We had our marching orders. Having read Henry Miller, Villon, Francis Carco, and Henri Murger, having seen the Opéra-Comique version of *Les mamelles de Tirésias*, and the folk singers at the Lapin à Gilles, we had come to the time for more basic Paris stuff. We were too young for tourist sheepishness at the Lido. We were too shy to lurk about the White Russian doormen on the rue Notre-Dame-de-Lorette. We were too free, independent, and unfettered to do anything that wasn't advanced, artistic, and shared with our gang.

"I'd like to go to an orgy," I said, "but I'm not sure my wife will let me."

OUR PERSONS OF THE FLOWERS

Bernard Frechtman, who had just translated Jean Genet's book *Our Lady of the Flowers,* published in a limited edition in Paris, was devoting his life to bringing into English the work of the famous homosexual thief, blackmailer, lover of a Gestapo officer, poet. Frechtman had a heavy, mournful face; he was gentle and obsessed. When he told me that Simone de Beauvoir was the most beautiful woman he had ever seen, I had another vision of the impossibility of understanding how anybody else thinks. But I shared his admiration for the rich and turgid, concealing and confessing prose of Genêt, who was just at the beginning of his fame. He was also admired for stealing the money and belongings of his admirers. Of course I would be happy to meet him.

Formally invited to Frechtman's room in a little hotel on the rue de Vaugirard, I told Jean Genet that I liked his book, the illustrations, the binding, and (Frechtman signaling madly) the translation. Also that I had read his other books in French.

"Do you masturbate?" he asked.

"You said?"

He repeated the question.

"No, I'm married."

"Idiot," he said.

Despite this inauspicious smalltalk, he invited me to go with him to the Rose Rouge that evening to hear Juliette Greco sing her famous versions of "Feuilles mortes" and ballads by Sartre; the Frères Jacques would also perform, a quartet that wore white gloves and did comic turns with an existential twist to them, a kind of Kingston Trio of the Paris postwar years. I adored Greco from afar, seeing her about the "quarter"—long nose, long hair, long legs, black stockings, black turtleneck sweater, black look in the eye. I can't remember how I got permission from my wife, but somehow I must have managed on the grounds that . . . I wanted.

The Rose Rouge and the Tabou were the neighborhood existentialist cabarets, their clientele consisting of Sartre, de Beauvoir, Merleau-Ponty, Camus, Barrault, Jouvet, Marguerite Duras, Philippe Soupault, Nathalie Sarraute . . . oh, surely there must have been a few others. I recall that every table, and they were small ones, was filled. The numerous geniuses of the period couldn't breathe up all that air by themselves, replacing it with the acrid smoke of Gauloise Blue, Gitane, and blackmarket American Pall Malls. Also Fulbright and GI Bill Americans, leftover prewar expats, international Francophiliacs, selected celebrities like Eartha Kitt and Orson Welles, and prospering money changers descended into the caves for a dose of culture, satire, and yearning. A favorite subject was *le cafard*—that special French melancholy, the Paris blues, named after the cockroach. True existentialists headed out at night to proclaim their doomed loneliness, a public no-exitnicity, *le cafard,* because it was cold and damp in their rooms.

I was in my early twenties. This wasn't mere history I was passing through; this was what Paris was supposed to be. Languidly Harry H., editor of *Death,* waved to me from the table where he sat with Kitt and Welles. Soon he might allow me to buy him another omelet with eggs.

Jean Genet reached for my knee; I removed my knee. It was a first draft on the part of Jean Genet which was doomed to fail despite all attempts at revision. The arms of Jean Genet were too short to reach across disposition; the American from Cleveland, Ohio, was pigheaded. I listened, rapt, to "La vie en rose" and a song about asparagus, divine asparagus, and kept my knees out of range, shifting whenever necessary.

"Tu m'énerves," said Jean Genet—you make me nervous. I was giving the great poet, thief, blackmailer, and lover of a Gestapo officer a case of *le cafard,* the existential blues.

Even after the performance, when we left the nightclub—the French words for it seemed right, *boîte de nuit,* box of night—no angry words could tarnish my joy in the occasion. Jean Genet wanted me to continue the evening with him; I was determined to go home to my wife. Jean Genet insisted; I insisted. He said all I had done was promise her to come home; betrayal would deepen me. I said I *wanted* to go back to her.

I began walking down the darkened streets of Saint-Germain-des-Prés while the distinguished writer followed, shouting angry words, not forgetting to be existential and paradoxical. I was deserting him at 1:00 A.M., leaving him to his own devices. Literature did not deserve such mistreatment.

Our brief friendship expired. A few days later I saw Genet sitting on the terrace of the Royale Saint-Germain, a café situated where Le Drugstore is now, with a young American would-be, tall and good-looking and dewy out of Harvard, who had come to Europe with the idea of writing about his meetings with the great old men. He managed to do so; André Gide invited him to tea. What did you think of Gide? I asked. "Gide liked me and I liked him." What did you think of Santayana? (George Santayana, reclusive, cared for by nuns in Rome, had responded with a "neat" letter granting an audience.) "Santayana liked me and I liked him."

I knew what he would tell me about Genet. Well, I had liked and not liked Genet, and been liked and not liked in return.

Juliette Gréco became friends with an American producer, starred in an American movie, shortened her nose, seemed to shorten her nose *twice*, still sings now and then. (Maybe her nose shrank from being washed in hot water.) The Frères Jacques performed with their white gloves, their choreographed mime and patter, their comic ballads, then disappeared into Rive Gauche memory. Jean Genet, an international success with his plays, *The Balcony* and *The Maids*, visited the U.S. in a leather coat as an official emissary to the Black Panthers, turned silent, died. The Rose Rouge and the Tabou closed. Bernard Frechtman, who served as agent, translator, business manager, and errand runner for Genet, committed suicide when Genet ended their partnership.

MY DINNER WITH WILLIAM S. BURROUGHS AND THE GENERAL'S DAUGHTER

At the origins of William Burroughs's career as drug addict, collector of boys, Bohemian wanderer, and loyal accountant of his dreads, there seemed to be a midwestern American moroseness, a passion to relieve boredom, find something to do, manage to fill the hours of his time on earth. It was appropriate that he was a son of the manufacturer of Burroughs calculating machines. Thanks to the good equipment he had inherited, and hard work, he tinkered with the controls until he opened the locks into his nightmares. He won a partial victory. It wasn't easy. The morose mask became permanent, even in his peaceful and rewarded last years.

During a filmed interview, Allen Ginsberg said that everyone needs love, everyone wants love, a speaking from the heart, that's what we're all after—love—"Isn't that what you want, Bill?"

Staring coolly into the camera, Burroughs muttered through his teeth: "Not really."

The little hotel on the Left Bank alley called the rue Gît-le-Coeur, which surely means Here-Lies-the-Heart Street, now advertises itself as "le Beat Hôtel" and is decorated with photographs of Burroughs, Ginsberg, and Gregory Corso where snow scenes and retirement sunsets might be hung in similar lobbies elsewhere. I first visited the premises in the late fifties. My dinner with William Burroughs, who was then finishing *Naked Lunch*, came along with the complex good luck of returning to Paris for the first time after my postwar years as a Fulbright scholar, when I had tried to be a writer and a husband while getting a graduate degree in philosophy. At age thirty-three, seasick on my bargain Dutch transport across the wintry Atlantic, deep in divorce miseries among the mile-high waves, I had wondered not only if my life was over but also if Paris would no longer be Paris.

It turned out that Paris was still Paris, maybe even more so because of the occasional *plastique* explosions that supplemented political argument in those times. On my first day, revisiting Le Mistral bookshop on the rue de la Bûcherie, I met a young woman who consented to stroll with me. She understood that I was nervous. "Just do what pleases you," she said, "and I will do what pleases me."

Life was not over.

Françoise lifted burdens of doubt, gloom, and leftover existential angst from my battered spirit. Her giggles blew care away. She was not too beautiful; she was merely lovely—round face, pointy chin, a Flemish pink in her cheeks and soul. Her father was a general, she had a Peugeot 405 with a sunroof, and she was happy to offer George Whitman, proprietor of Le Mistral, the satisfaction of doing a good deed for me and, it seemed to my amazement, for herself. (Soon George would change the name of Le Mistral to Shakespeare & Company.) Since Françoise was angry with her father, we spent part of our second day together returning the birthday presents he had given her—returning them not to him, but for refund to Cartier in a cobblestoned square. She was practical in her gesture of revenge.

Then she asked if I wanted to play badd-ming-tonne at her club. Chasing feathered birdies wasn't why I had come to Paris. She laughed and the inside of her throat was pink, too. Perhaps the offer of badminton was still another test of my preferences for the end of a long May afternoon. The song we heard on her Blaupunkt car radio—one of those keening French ballads—had clearly been written in honor of our friendship:

You took my arm as if you loved me . . .

During the same season of reacquaintance with Paris, I renewed my college friendship with Allen Ginsberg, traveling with silent Peter Orlovsky, his spouse equivalent, and Gregory Corso, whom he praised with his customary generosity as the Shelley of the beat generation. During one café meeting the waiter made the mistake of putting the plate with the bill near Gregory. Before I could reach the check, Gregory slapped his hand over it. "I'm going to pay it! I'm going to pay it!" he cried.

"Don't be silly," Allen said.

"Allen! I've never paid a check before! I'm going to pay it!"

Reproachfully Allen shook his head. Firmly Allen removed Gregory's soft fingers. Generously Allen handed me the check.

In the normal evolution of beat-generation diplomacy, Gregory took a powerful dislike to me. He assured me that I would never know happiness in love because (he explained) my feet smelled.

He was half right. I have experienced love miseries despite undiseased feet. When I complained to Allen, he consoled me in his gentle baritone, "Oh, that's just something Gregory says." The beat Shelley was having difficulties and couldn't be held to rigid standards about the lovelives and feet of others.

Françoise, the general's daughter, assured me that my feet smelled about average for the French army.

Generous in building a community of congenial spirits, Allen took me to meet William S. Burroughs in his hotel room. Burroughs had liked one of my novels, *The Man Who Was Not With It*, which describes heroin addiction in a traveling carnival and a young man making his way through the runaway world. He offered me a cool hand of welcome. The masklike face reminded me of André Gide. Stern, lofty, and slow moving, he explained why he had been an addict so long: It gave life some routines. Now that he was finishing his book, he was less bored. When he fell from grace, there was a doctor in England who helped. In the meantime, writing *Naked Lunch* filled the idle hours.

Despite his imposing formality, he seemed pleased to have company. He invited us all to dinner, which he would cook in his room on a battery of alcohol stoves. "Beat cuisine," he said, a little notch suddenly appearing at the corner of his mouth. It could have been a smile, and then it was gone.

My stupidity turned out to be drastic. Without thinking that I shouldn't bring another guest, I invited the French general's daughter. I was infatuated and grateful, and thought everyone would like her as much as I did.

Holding my arm, Françoise arrived to find a small hotel room filled with young men and our host. Burrough's eyes blinked very slowly when he saw her. There was no notching that could be taken for a smile at the corner of his mouth.

She sat demurely by my side on the bed. Burroughs seemed inclined to forgive, and began a description of life in Tangiers, Times Square, and Mexico before he had settled down to pull together the scattered pages of his hallucinatory novel. He stood by the sink in which the lettuce for our dinner was being washed. The leaves were spread along the sides of the bowl. Like a good mother, he believed in salad, especially with a simple meal. Still talking, he opened his fly and prepared to pee in the sink. The lettuce leaves glistened. He paid attention and took care to avoid the salad, aiming directly into the drain, which was rusty and brown.

Of course, the john was down the hall. Of course, it would be inconvenient to interrupt his anecdote. Of course, he didn't want to desert his guests. Of course, he was making a statement about my bringing a female companion.

The steaks were served. The wine was poured. The salad was consumed. There was a tangy vinaigrette dressing and I hoped Françoise would not be distressed by Gregory's pronunciation: "vinegar-ette."

Françoise and I were the first to leave. She said her good-byes with the normal politeness of a well-brought-up general's daughter, but as we crossed the place Saint-André-des-Arts, the blocked emotions came pouring out: "Oh que c'est dégoûtant! Oh que c'est dégoûtant! Oh que c'est dégoûtant!"

Oh how disgusting—in a turbulent stream of repetition.

I tried to explain about this group of beat writers, and the special corners of American Bohemia, and probably, in my eagerness, the history of humankind since the origins of Cro-Magnon or perhaps the Neanderthal personality. American literary history is a hard job; suddenly there I was, minding the store. My French seems not to have been sufficient unto the task, because she kept cheerfully repeating, "Oh disgusting, oh how disgusting, oh disgusting."

My lovely general's daughter with the Peugeot 405, sunroof, the proper French rearing, the credit at Cartier.

William Burroughs had expressed his disapproval with a gesture that required no cutting words. He remained charming, gracious, and suave. One could learn from this. His aim was precise.

Gregory Corso, on the other hand, is relentless in his criticism. Many years later he informed me that I would always be unhappy in love because—I waited, toes clawing my socks, while he groped for the familiar words—"God doesn't listen to your prayers." I'm not sure if the beat Shelley had forgotten about my feet or if this represented a critical escalation.

My friend Françoise has put the incident to rest. Every year she sends a Christmas card from Lyons.

RENAISSANCE ROGUE (C'ÉTAIT NORMALE)

Love, he knew he had it; at least from the most important bestower of love. The long life of Emmanuel d'Astier de la Vigerie was charmed and lucky, validated by others, but more important, by himself; it was played for real in the way a good game is taken seriously by the player. D'Astier enlisted for the highest stakes, gracefully risking his body—this gallantry not too difficult for a French aristocrat of his breeding—but also risking his integrity and reputation. His pride was impregnable. Unlike William Burroughs, he never needed the mask of American cool. He had no use for the morality of others, either. His most earnest concern was to keep the pleasures going. His heedlessness enraged right-thinkers, and it surely was intended to do so. It was all part of the privilege which appetite, family, and history had come together to offer a favored son. It was normal. No point in questioning justice when fate has brought a person good luck. If the person has good teeth, they must be for biting. This is only logical.

It seemed that d'Astier inherited from his ancient lineage—sliding on his bum down the family tree—a dispensation to play, treating life as that experiment which later, in times of advanced computers, *ordinateurs,* came to be known as "virtual reality." In his time, the tragedy of Europe offered a sporting field for a dandy, a player. He breathed happily in disaster, he served himself heaping portions of adrenalin, he was unafraid. He sped through seven decades with an ironic smile notching his lean face. It was all "pour le sport," "le high-life" (pronounced "hig-leef" in French, "I-laif" in his English). If eventually, like so many others, even he would be obliged by mortality, knocked over by a bubble in his veins, d'Astier remained a winner. Mere death could not take that away from him. He had already danced through graveyards.

My friend Claude Roy introduced me to Emmanuel d'Astier de la Vigerie, describing him as another "paysan de Paris," peasant of Paris, an expert at sniffing the air of cafés. In addition, he was a duke and heir to one of the great French names, a poet, editor, and publisher, Communist, Gaullist, Résistance hero, aquiline-nosed pursuer of women who for a moment seemed beautiful and the bewitching center of the unknown world; or at least there was something he liked in her style. Some of his careers, such as Communist and Gaullist, were mutually exclusive. The elegant juggler had time to adjust the pins he kept in the air. His love of the word and of women persisted unchanged through shifting responsibilities.

I tried unsuccessfully to persuade American publishers to bring out his reminiscences of the war and the Résistance, *Sept fois sept jours (Seven Times Seven Days),* in which he played swashbuckling roles. During the fifties, he was a trophy fellow traveler for a period, founding a newspaper secretly subsidized by the Soviet Union, but left this allegiance when they cut the subsidy. "Herb, you understand, don't you? They took away my money! Without even asking me!"

This dandy duke knew no shame. I saw no reason to know shame for him.

In late life, vexed by Comintern rudeness, dissatisfied with the limits of his previous incarnations, he became an information officer in de Gaulle's government. He was a popular television broadcaster, an ardent spokesman for de Gaulle, the anti-Communist. C'était normal.

Since the seat of government is in Paris, and also the seat of Upper, Middle, and Lower Bohemia, d'Astier's chores as a minister and public explainer didn't conflict with his duties as a *flâneur* of the cafés and brasseries on both sides of the Seine. When I arrived in Paris and telephoned him, he would consult his carnet and say: "Hmm, let's consider, I seem to recall a little corner on the rue de Bac—today at one o'clock?"

The little corner had tiny lamps at every table, like a London idea of a Paris restaurant. As a bow to assassination threats, he reserved a table near the back, on the assumption that gunmen would expect him on the terrace. In the dark, the lines etched in his cheeks, an elegant calligraphy wrought by the years, twitched with laughter. No angelic indifference came with his good manners and age. Just like any other writer, he was exasperated that American publishers didn't take his book, but—breeding is worth something—it didn't interfere with lunch or clear-eyed delight in whatever seemed pretty in the immediate environment. Books are mere objects, even if ones with spectral shadows, while good digestion and a graceful chin or habit of tossing the hair are something in which a man can take permanent comfort. Especially if it's nearby, at the next table. C'était normal.

I told him *Seven Times Seven Days* should have a sequel, *Seven Times Seven Decades*.

"Mademoiselle," he asked the person at the next table, "since you are lunching alone, which in your case means you only esteem the best company—and I have the most profound respect for your judgment—might you consider honoring by joining a visiting American and a . . . Tell me, Airb, what am I?"

"No," said the young woman.

"Tant pis." (So much the worse for us.) "But I salute your decision. A refreshing collation alone in the shadows gives one time to gather strength for the afternoon."

She paused a moment between the pâté campagne and toast. "Aren't you the d'Astier who published *Libération?*"

"I used to be. Now I'm the d'Astier who was justly called to order at lunch by a beautiful young woman."

"Well, maybe since I've come to the salad . . ."

He was able to arrange these negotiations, surrounding the young person without crowding her, in a particular way which I've seen in other successful layabouts at the Crystal Palace in St. Louis, at Cyrano's in Los Angeles, at Lanciani in Greenwich Village—a practice of active charm as a vocation which has nothing to do with ordinary pickup invasiveness. Those of us who observe the art learn nothing from it except to feel awe. It has something to do with caring more about style than the supposed goal. It has something to do with genuine admiration. Even the grief of rejection offers a reward—feelings are stirred. It's the play of biology and history, and it is fate. When the mouth dies, what is there? The play's the thing.

When she came to the salad and waited for her chair to be moved to our table, he entertained her, he pleased her, he flattered her, he called forth her repertoire of smiles, he elicited her own terrific Left Bank moves, he inquired about her job (antique dealing), he recommended other restaurants in the quarter—especially one that specialized in rabbit—and he let her go without protest. In a shy gesture, when she extended her hand in good-bye, he didn't kiss it, he bowed his head, he touched her elbow with his hand. "We are both close to heaven," he said, "you by beauty and me by age."

She blushed.

He walked with her to the door.

"You didn't ask for her card," I said when he returned, "and why make a point of your age? What were you quoting?"

"Ah, as you say in English, my friend, the truth shall make ye free. And there is plenty of time. There are only a few dozen antiquaires in the neighborhood. I'll find her."

And he would, even if he had to eat rabbit three days running.

"I was quoting," he said, "to my shame, Goethe or George Bernard Shaw, a writer who was not even French. We are all one now, are we not?"

Not quite. Some of us would not go patiently onto a diet of rabbit until we achieve the goal.

Later I asked Claude Roy why it's always the long-nosed French women, like Juliette Gréco, or beaky French men, like d'Astier, who seem most vividly present to me. Claude thought maybe it was a personal quirk. But he, on the other hand, happened to agree with me. Almost everyone on the rue Dauphine had a strong nose when the light was right. "Maybe it's the optique," he suggested. "This demands inquiry."

I told d'Astier about the young French singer in San Francisco (she has a brave and flagrant nose with flaring nostrils) who performs a love anthem which seemed as touching as the ballads of Jean Ferrat or Leo Ferré:

You're lying on a cloud,
My lipstick on your ass . . .

"I must absolutely visit San Francisco," he said. "I must make a note to do so. And you say she writes her songs in *English*?"

What sealed the definition of Emmanuel d'Astier de la Vigerie as a Bohemian was his account of parachuting into occupied France as an emissary from General de Gaulle and the Free French forces, bringing instructions to the Résistance. He wandered through gray, defeated, silent Paris, patrolled by the Wehrmacht, that evil clank of armor in the streets. The city was filled with collaborators and he feared he would be recognized and denounced. He needed to find his contact in the Underground as soon as possible and then slip away into the countryside. He decided not to take time to eat, drink, shit, piss, or look for his mother. So far, just another patriot. But then first he made his way to the bookstore Le Divan at Saint-German-des-Prés in order to confirm that his books were in their usual place on the shelves. After all, this was his quarter. C'est tout à fait normal.

Long-nosed d'Astier was a terrific duke. Best duke I've ever known.

FOR A GOOD TIME IN PARIS, CALL . . .

Jim Haynes seems to have bracketed Paris for an epoch or more, although he is too young and mortal to have done so. Perhaps it's only that long-shot reign, the Aquarian Age, which he is leading through the future. Writer, publisher, high-liver, and friend of John Lennon, about whom he wrote a book, he is an American in downtown Europe, making his way courteously and smilingly by living off the land. This pied piper, this street busker from the Milky Way, this old-time Bohemian in Paris makes out okay. It works! There is a look of gentle surprise on his large, fair face.

Sunday nights, at 83 rue de la Tombe Issoire, not too far from Montparnasse, not too far from the Latin Quarter, not too far from where Gertrude Stein offered to crush her enemies by falling upon them, he conducts an enterprising seminar and benefit feed. Volunteer cooks and shoppers make sure the food and wine are worthy of the causes he has in mind. Jim supplies his apartment, his outdoor alley garden, and his abundant downhomy goodwill. He has reinvented the rent party. This event is to the rent party as the mighty computer is to the abacus.

The procedure has followed strict rituals since its origins in 1980. A person who wishes to apply as a guest must telephone in advance. Credentials and references are discussed. Do you know somebody? Are you the friend of a friend? Hints of charm are mutually exchanged; promises implied. Artists are preferred. Folks of cultural bent are preferred. Students are preferred. Americans, Poles, and French are preferred, along with representatives of any other delightful nationality. If Jim decides the applicant has passed the test, he or she is invited to appear, handing Jim an envelope containing the sum, periodically adjusted for inflation, which compensates for the expenses of the evening, plus, of course, a margin to support Jim Haynes's publishing, journals, audio labors, causes, and tastes. Minimal solvency hurts nobody.

Bringing the envelope is definitely preferred. The exchange is discreet. No reasonable person can object to the companionship of a carefully screened collection of Hungarian actresses, Russian writers, English painters. It's hard work and a whole bunch of us have got to do it. Jim Haynes is our filter in the drain, catching the good parts.

When I telephone for my invitation, it doesn't matter if a few years have rolled by. The instant friendship of a decade or two ago is still valid. Jim is still writing, hosting, performing, indefatigably entreprenurial. Dinner evokes something old-time and easy, bar-becue or picnic, plus a whiff of singles networking. "Hey, man," says Jim, "how you been keeping?"

In the fall of 1991, I asked if I could bring two friends, a journalist from Marin County and her husband, a painter. I listened to myself and realized that a few years ago I might have said a painter from Marin and his wife, a journalist. Times change. A person can learn from listening to him/herself; this is a truth practiced by Bohemians. Jim said: "Put seventy-five francs per person in the envelope and make sure you introduce them to me."

The evening was crisp and autumnal. Most of Jim's guests wandered into the alley garden, exchanging the things people exchange before they exchange telephone numbers and addresses, remarks, glances, inventories, net worth: You're a painter . . . A sculptor . . . Where did you get those green eyes? Are they contacts? . . . My father had them . . . So why are you in Paris?

In New York, the question might have been, Do you come here often? Here it was, Why Paris, why now? In yuppie Manhattan this might have been singles avidly networking, business cards shuffled from hand to hand in a sport intended to bring love and fortune. I found myself trying to explain to an earnest French student of American culture what San Francisco Gay Freedom Day Parade politics were about, and why young activists were trying to overthrow the older leadership of the festival organizing committee by charging the last parade with "insufficient fabulosity."

"Pardon?"

I could deconstruct it in French, but since I didn't really understand the matter, we reached a rapid point of each needing to go search elsewhere for conversation. Particle physics follows the same ruthless haphazard rules; accidental collisions lead to new accidental collisions. The verbal delirium of café effusion was replaced in Jim Haynes's garden by Cartesian precision, a mutual technical knockout. The Vincennes deconstructionist and I ended precisely as ignorant as we had begun. Out of the corners of our eyes we warily watched for the dreaded reapproach of the other.

The Jim Haynes Fun-Raising Feed recalls both the psychedelic sixties in its earnestly carefree insouciance and the beatnik fifties in its rent-party subtext. With nineties efficiency, one doesn't need to offer wine or a casserole; one brings cash in an envelope. Cost effectiveness and menu planning contribute; unencumbered by shopping bags—my friends and I walked up the gentle slope from the Quartier Latin to Montparnasse—free spirits can keep their eyes on the sparrow. There were finches chattering in the eaves overhead, excited by the human activity below. The Silent Spring doesn't apply here.

Our happy host, mid-southern grace honed by his years in England and France, presides with warm handshakes and toothy smiles. He is running for senator from the Left Bank, and can be elected if we all vote early and often, bringing our sealed envelopes.

A lanky American, blond, with the rangy look of an athletic Texan, stood with her hip cocked and her hand leaning on it. A few years ago I might have guessed that she was recently a model, then manager of a modeling agency, but now—wait—she was a lawyer in the Paris office of an American firm. "Georgetown," she explained, "French major, then law school." She answered my questions with the crisp precision of a woman who charges by the hour. In the same spirit, she added, "You're okay, but you're leaving in a few days," and slipped away before I could ask for her telephone number in case I returned to Paris. I was ready to promise an early return. . . . She was gone.

Tonight the star hot dish was a risotto, nice black French mushrooms, cooked by an Italian mime who used to work at the Piccolo Teatro in Milan. After she brought the risotto to the table, she did a terrific imitation of the Leaning Tower of Pisa without tipping over. I was concerned that her makeup might run onto the rice.

There was also ratatouille. There were vegetables, cute and small and tasty, unlike their American cousins. There were string beans in a pot, haricots verts, and I heard a painter resident in Paris since my years there imitating a tourist, pronouncing them "hairy cots." If you have no humor of your own, you can at least make fun of people who don't speak the language. Humor isn't required of remittance men.

I chatted with two other Americans, a musician and a journalist, who said their friendship was based on both having a French wife (not the same one). "Sometimes I want to qualify for the problems you share," I said, and they looked at me as if I had lost my mind. Then the musician clapped me on the back and said, "Hey, you ought to meet Howard Hesseman; he's got a French wife he *likes.*"

I knew Howard Hesseman, who played the stoned deejay in the television series *WKRP Cincinnati,* when he was named Don Sturdy and a member of the improvisational theater group The Committee, in North Beach, San Francisco. Inside, deep in his soul, where it counts, he says he is still Don Sturdy, alive and well and married to a French wife in Paris.

Ted Joans, my old friend from the Village and beyond, who used to be confused with LeRoi Jones–Imamu Baraka, now lives in Mali, Paris, and, sometimes in rooms provided by his various children all over the world. When they get old enough, they establish a Ted Joans Room in their dwellings. None of them confuses him with Baraka. Ted is a troubador poet and gabber of genius. I told him about my adventures with Gregory Corso; he imitated the Corso tough-kid whine. Then he asked if I could arrange an evening for him in San Francisco or Berkeley. People would pay ten dollars each, more if they really love poetry, but it wasn't really about money. He could stay with one of his kids; kind of liked visiting northern California.

I have no space in my flat, no university connection.

"That's fine," he said. "I'm just grateful for the thought."

I told him about the time, on my way to Dakar, when my bags went to Mali. The airline promised to return them, but it had been eight years now, so perhaps, next time he was home in Mali, he could keep an eye out for a blue canvas duffle with black nylon straps and notes for a novel about growing up in Cleveland. The baggage handlers in Mali couldn't have much use for them unless they were plagiarists in search of an exotic locale.

We arranged to meet the next day at Le Rouquet, the café where he picks up his mail in Paris. He would buy some tunafish and a cucumber, I could bring the beverage, and we would picnic together in the garden of the little Russian church across the street, catching up on this and that. Ted is sometimes a vegetarian, counts tunafish as a vegetable. As an urban poet, why should he judge what grows in the sea? That's Herman Melville's field.

A New Yorker, voice pitched for subway penetration, was telling the world about his new "good baby;" temperature, humidity, general storminess—she was being recommended as a meteorological phenomenon.

After a while, his friend happened to ask, "How old is she?"

The lover man considered the question. "Put it this way. Unlike my last wife, the young one, she never said I'm a premature you-know."

"Ejaculator?"

"You're just like that bitch, use all the long words." A rising rasp; the Number One line was pulling into an express station.

"So this new person in your life, she's a grown woman?"

"Okay, put it another way. Short words. She's grateful for anything I do."

His friend reared up like a heat-seeking missile. His mouth made a whistling sound, though no whistle emerged. "Wow. *That* ugly."

A very pretty green-skinned creation—the kind of unhealthy Parisian beauty I treasured from coffee and cigarette years in the Quartier Latin and Saint-Germain-des-Prés—corrected my French reflexively, repeating what I said with an improved accent. Perhaps seeking a level playing field, I retaliated by asking her not to blow her smoke in my face; but then, being a man of northern California courtesy, and also liking her bony, high-bridged nose, I explained that I'm from San Francisco where people think a lot about health. So please blow it elsewhere.

To my surprise, she nodded, seeming to understand. She transferred her cigarette from one hand to the other. However, she continued to blow smoke in my face.

I tried to compose the French for *unclear on the concept.*

She explained that, in French culture, such a concept did not exist.

I prepared to make that run for the buffet or bar which people use to explain abrupt departure, as if the lifeboat is about to depart. Despite her nose, I felt unwanted. Seeming to sense my state of mind, her smile curving under a nose of genius, she held me for a moment by remarking suddenly: "I love my mother more than anyone in the world, more than I will ever love anyone, and because she will never know my children, I will never have any. So I can do what I want."

"Never see your children?"

"Jamais. Dying soon, dead soon." She smiled her wistful smile with that twist at the corner which indicates dramatic irony and how odd it is. She didn't have to say lung cancer. ". . . but I like it. I like to smoke. That's what I like." Courteously this time she averted her head to exhale. And turned back to me to say, in French which has an easy English equivalent: "So fuck off."

I did so.

A man I had earlier noted for his bravery, and also avoided for it, wearing both orange makeup and a toupee from the Smithsonian Institution, offered me a rest from flirtation. He had heard that I knew something about Haiti, and spoke those words dreaded by every writer: "I'd like to read your book. . . ." This tentative yearning suggests that the writer should reach into his sleeve and pull out a copy. The normal answer goes something like: You're welcome to do so.

He added: "Something I wonder."

"Yes."

"Could I find what I like there? Ah-ee-tee?"

What did he mean? Drugs? Boys? Beautiful sunsets? Rice and beans? Peace and quiet? A new toupee?

"I'm not sure what you like," I said.

He sighed. "I suffer from anhedonia. Inability to feel pleasure. As a writer, one wants to express oneself, but one is blocked. I can't write, never have. For an author, that's a tragedy. One hates to explain—need one? Sometimes I can talk, such as now, when I meet someone congenial, like yourself—"

People who use the word *author* are almost never writers. A rule of thumb, a law of vocabulary.

He was unstoppable. ". . . have something to say, a whole lot, meditations nurtured through a lifetime of, of, of meditations, since I haven't wasted them through trivial use." (Like some people I meet. One knows who.) "Yet people don't appreciate anhedonia. One doesn't get sympathy or understanding. So what do you think?

"About what?" I asked the man with the askew rug.

"Is Haiti the place for me?"

If I turned, he would have the chance to slide his toupee back into place, and so for his sake, I turned. One did one's best to escape.

"You know what I like about him?" It was a woman having woman talk with another woman. She was speaking of a rock musician they both admired. They were wearing his Grand Tour 1991 tee shirts. "He doesn't just have a big dick. He has a big heart, too."

"Did you let him know?"

"I mentioned about the dick, but that's all. I don't want him to get a big head."

Lots of men might take being told they have big hearts with modesty; I would, for example, but I wasn't invited to contribute. I was invited—judging from how they raised their voices, gave each other high fives at the appropriate moment—only to eavesdrop. They went on to discuss the rock star's skill with the guitar and the synthesizer and I drifted away to a quiet discussion of the disappearance of Sartre and de Beauvoir from the intellectual scene. Death seems to speed up the procedures of fashion. In the nineties it was old-fashioned and passé even to talk about the *absence* of existentialism; that's how far out of fashion it was. I appreciated these defiant archeologists of Paris style and told them I had learned from Sartre's essays collected in *Situations* and from the earnestness of Simone de beauvoir's discussions at the Deux Magots and the Flore. Sartre on the vocation of writer in *The Words,* de Beauvoir on the dilemmas of women and the shipwrecks of old age were wonderful, would endure. We didn't give each other high fives, but there was a moment of congeniality and community. It was getting late; Metro shut down; time to walk back down the gentle slope toward my hotel on the rue de Seine.

I didn't like to leave without a goodbye to Jim Haynes, Ted Joans, the two American men with French wives, and a few other old friends and colleagues. There had been yearning and comedy here, good food and drinkable drink, encounters that did not lack importance even if they lacked consequence. People warmed themselves by the twig fires of banter and insult and perhaps, some of them, by an exchanging of sincere wishes, hopes, confidences, griefs. It was not a business meeting. It was an orchestration of the yearning to make contact with other yearnings. Even the Brillo-headed book-beggar could come out of his terrible isolation and longing into an hour of random warmth and confession. And since there had been a couple of Polish filmmakers and a Hungarian literary critic, there was also a meeting of East and West.

Jim Haynes took my hand, tirelessly beaming. He may have done his share of drinking, doping, and leaving places in a hurry. At this stage in his life he is hanging out, not in a hurry to go, and this nice savoring of the world is something he is gifted at sharing with others. I wanted to tell him he was a good and useful citizen, supreme governor and prefect of an atoll of the Bohemian archipelago.

The finches sang under the eaves. They didn't care if they had to begin again tomorrow.

L'ENVOI

In the twenties, survivors of the pre–World War I Paris Bohemia tended to complain about the invasion of typewriters, Bolshevism, Americans, and cocktails, although they were willing to drink the new drink and touch money from the new soft touches. The rich daughters and widows who filed off the great ships were sometimes willing to settle for an artist if they couldn't find a Georgian prince among the White Russian taxi drivers. "Cocktails!" exclaimed Sisley Huddleston, a chronicler of this period. "That is the real discovery of the age." He accepted the innovation but lamented the retreat of the bellyish, mustachioed, heavily dressed male ideal (himself) in favor of "willowy" tennis-playing young men, Freudians, Citroëns, divorces—the flood of novelties which meant his Paris was no longer the actual Paris. Those who wish to own Paris always claim that the real Paris has disappeared and only a ghost remains. I have caught myself at George Whitman's Shakespeare & Company lamenting to young visitors that things aren't the same since the shop stopped being called Le Mistral and I rode my rusty bicycle and had a first wife and wrote a first novel and *then* the City of Light, Capital of Hope, Paradise of Misery, was dense with youthful genius. I try to remember James T. Farrell.

"The present Paris . . ." Sisley Huddleston declared in 1928 in his *Bohemian Literary and Social Life in Paris—Salons, Cafés, Studios,* "I am not to be understood as flatly condemning it." Yet he thought it "meretricious. I like all classes, but I do not want them shaken together—orange juice and gin, butter merchants and nobles, actresses and princesses. . . . The former Paris satisfied one's sense of order."

So as I slouched in an armchair at one of Shakespeare & Company's Sunday-afternoon teas, nattering about my student days, I reminded myself of Sisley Huddleston's fragrant disdain. Nostalgia is a dangerous drug, increasingly detaching the addict from the life of the time. The reality is that actresses and princesses stirred together make for good fun, and there is even an argument for orange juice and gin, marijuana and bananas, whoever and whatever else is nice. Even the willowiness he deplored works for some, so why not be graceful, too?

Circulating among such writers as James Joyce, Hemingway, and Gertrude Stein, Sisley Huddleston reserved his serious praise for Henri Béraud, "the cleanest writer in France . . . sincere, honest, means no harm."

Yet Huddleston manages to evoke the necessary legend of this garden of musettes, opera dancers, cobblestones, plane trees, ghosts, and free spirits. He praises the prankster who raised money for a statue to the memory of Hégésippe Simon, an imaginary philosopher. He remembers the prewar fat men who celebrated wine by toasting each other with beer, the jokesters and loafers of Montmartre and the Procope in the Latin Quarter, the ancient tippler who "has written more verses than Ronsard and Victor Hugo put together." When he recalls those he loved, I can forgive his disdain for those he meets first only in stagnant age. The permanent Bohemian runs the risk of pursuing the ghosts of his youth after he has stopped pursuing anything of serious flesh and blood today. But that lumbering Latin Quarter chronicler still cried "Bravo!" to something, a dream carried intact in his soul, while those younger than Sisley Huddleston only heard an old guy with a bad liver tottering in his patent-leather pumps and crying, "Bis! Bis!"

Play it again, Sisley.

. . .

The equivalents of all these figures from the past still exist. When I revisited Paris a few years ago with my twin sons, I was sure I recognized myself in their enraptured thirst for the capital of *le cafard*. At Vavin-Montparnasse I showed them the statue of Balzac with his cloak and his triumphant belly, riding down the world. We paused at the monument to Diderot, that pioneer Bohemian, giving the finger to the church of Saint-Germain-des-Prés across the boulevard where Korean street buskers sang classic Beatles songs and fire-eaters spewed forth their lighted fuel. It was the summer of my sons' seventeenth year and their minds were so fine they could hold at least several ideas at once—Rodin's implacable Balzac, the grin on Diderot's stone face, healthy parisiennes strolling past in the season of the wiggle, and their dad telling them about what used to be.

8

Miller and Nin

MY LIFE ON ANAÏS NIN'S HOUSEBOAT IN HOBOKEN

At age seventeen, fresh from Lakewood, Ohio (go to Cleveland
and keep on hiking westward), I thought New York City and
Columbia College, fog-shrouded ramparts of the east, were just
the places to bring me into contact with the great world of truth,
beauty, poetry, and girls. Like a greedy picker from the menu at
a Chinese restaurant, I wanted all four of the above.

In high school I had taken to sending poems to a little magazine
printed in New York on thick brown butcher paper. Amazingly,
some of them were published. I announced my arrival; rough poet
slouches into town from the Ohio frontier—neglecting to mention
that I was a pimply goggle-eyed college freshman. The cordial
voice of the editor, whose voice reflected years of cigarettes and
blackberry cordiality, invited me to a party of poets, nothing but
poets, in his apartment downtown. It turned out to be five flights
above Mott Street, Chinatown, in what would now be called a
loft, probably called an attic or (by poets) a garret in 1943. Randolph Van Trochaic (not his real name) was the author of a book
printed on the familiar brown butcher paper by his own press. He
asked if I had read *Ho, Watchman of the Night!* I told him I had just
bought my copy. He said to come early, say nine o'clock, after
dinner, because there were so many poets eager to make contact
with a leader of the Cleveland imagist scene.

I prepared a little warm-up conversation in advance so I wouldn't be caught short. "Saw the whole universe yesterday. Like an epiphany, you know? The whole universe in a drop of water. Pretty fascinating."

I scrubbed and got ready for lyrical repartee.

If the middle-aged poets already gathered, dinner plates piled in the kitchen, were surprised to see a skinny adolescent, they courteously kept their counsel. Some of the women wore long skirts to their ankles. Fat legs didn't occur to me; what occurred to me was sexy, European, depraved. I could smell the ruins of spaghetti and tomato sauce. Open bottles added to the sophistication.

I didn't realize I was supposed to bring a bottle with me, but this circle of true artists was inclined to mercy and forgiveness. Would Rimbaud, age seventeen, be asked to contribute to Verlaine's liquor stock? Not even expected to supply the mix or pretzels.

I sat at the feet of a middle-aged woman—late twenties—with a brown cigarette dangling from her lips. There, in that position on the carpet, I hoped to peek at her legs; no such luck. Long skirt, ends tucked under feet in some kind of backless flimsy sandals. In my memory she had a furrowed and ravaged face, nicotined teeth, but that must be an extrapolation from the chain of cigarillos poking out of and into her mouth. Surely the ravaging was yet to come. Midwestern baby plumpness, cashmere sweaters, brown and white saddle shoes, teenie-tiny unformed parochial school noses were all I had known. Vivid nasal cartilege lay someplace in the future of erotic experience.

"You write blank verse?" she asked.

"Free," I said, establishing a finicky distinction, although I wasn't sure what it was. "Lyrics mostly. Tried a sonnet sequence. Don't see my way, all the homework I have to do, branching into an epic."

She nodded sympathetically, dropping live ashes onto her blouse. Of its own accord, my hand rose up to brush them off, but the fabric seemed to extinguish the little glow, leaving brown spots on rayon like the liver spots to come, dermatologically speaking. I couldn't be expected to grope for the Homeric mode at my age.

I wasn't blind, didn't yet know war or Aegean voyages separated from my beloved, had a shitload of term paper requirements. Oh could my pen but glean my teaming brain . . . I meant teeming. Plenty to moan about already without getting into the epic verse hassle.

If I remember the name right, this long-skirted person later became the widow of a famous southern agrarian.

Our host, Ichabod Von Iambic, long and emaciated, seized me by the elbow, saying, "So many burning to make your acquaintance. . . . You found my book where? Up on Morningside Heights?"

"At Publix Book Mart on Huron Road in Cleveland."

He sighed. "I'm penetrating. I'm penetrating the heartland."

I was passed from hand to hand, dazed and exalted by so much genius gathered together above Chinatown. There was even an Asian poet, although he turned out to be Filipino, not Chinese, named José Garcia Villa (his real name). In keeping with macrobiotic principles, the furnishings of the loft reflected its Mott Street location—a brass Confucius, big-bellied laughing Buddhas, tea cups with eclectic advertisement for restaurants, piano scarves used as wall hangings, a pair of ivory chopsticks crossed like swords and framed on the wall. As part of my voyage of discovery into Manhattan I had already tried using chopsticks and discovered that chow mein and chop suey slid off the slippery ivory onto my shirts. These new shirts were ones my mother didn't buy me. Establishing the maturity of a young poet, I had taken to buying my own shirts, learning to eat with chopsticks, suffering the consequences. Let's not discuss the problems of egg foo yong.

Spencer Ter Strophe, genial author of *Ho, Watchman of the Night!* kept his hand cupped under my elbow until I shook it free, like a gear disengaging from a ratchet, and he deposited me with a dainty dark person who sat in a corner with a hat, a veil, and an embroidered notebook in addition to the usual haberdashery of elderly ladies. Elderly: I mean more than twice my age: in her late thirties. She was also, judging from how the others deferred to her, the most important. It seemed logical that the poet from Cleveland, green and Rimbaud-like, should be left in the care of the most veteran of the artists. "A-nass" was how I heard her name.

"Herbert. My friends call me Herb."

"A-na-ïs."

We sat for a while. We sipped for a while. We mumbled for a while. Her accent was mysterioso, strangely vivid yet gauzy. The sentences sprouted, waved in the breezes, disappeared without coming to flower . . . trailing . . . off . . . There were lots of . . . 's. Suddenly she murmured, "Houseboat . . . Hoboken."

"Pardon, ma'm?"

"Would you like to pay a visit . . . houseboat . . . Hoboken? Flowers . . . my trellis . . . the looming, phosphorescent, spectral sea. . . ."

Heat flooded my chest. At age seventeen I had room for little in my mind because the one big idea took all available space: sex. This invitation meant sex. The odd little Portuguese (actually Spanish and Danish) old woman was not like the Barnard girls I was learning to covet or the Wellesley girl from Lakewood I dated by canoeing on the Charles, ordering fish at Durgin Park in Boston, returning by night train to New York, exhausted, dirty, sweaty, and unabatedly horny.

Here, out of the mists above Mott Street, emerged a magic lady of intergalactic class, uttering hypnotic soft fragments; and then those eyes, those mesmerizing eyes, and those knobby elbows poking through some sort of expensive crumpled fabric—mesmerizing elbows, too—and mesmerizing knobby knees shadowed under another dark mottled fabric—mesmerizing waif joints and tiny limbs, cheekbones, a toy forehead under hat, beneath a patterned veil! "Paris," she said, evidently a woman of dependent means, "Lisbon . . . Havana . . . Edmundo . . ."

Edmundo? Or was it Edouardo? Hugo?

The eyes penetrated and saw me through and through. Was that a smile behind them? No, worse than a smile, a judgment of my soul. She must have known something I didn't know. After all, she was thirty-nine years old (I looked it up later). She was measuring me and finding me wanting. (What I was wanting at the time was the pleasure of a certain Donna's light kisses.)

I had/didn't have Donna and she had/maybe didn't have Edmundo-Edouardo-Enrico-Hugo.

The oval eyes took cool inventory. She was a flamenco moon person and I was a lunatic from Cleveland, O. Stark seventeen-year-old monomania wrestled with stark seventeen-year-old terror. To the victor would belong the spoiling.

The offer was so unreal it had to be real. Hoboken, houseboat, harbor, the salt and smell of the Atlantic, the Azores out there someplace beyond the Statue of Liberty, the history of lust and lyric poetry, all that was surely due a Rimbaud (only straight), a Byron (without the club foot or the noble breeding), a Hart Crane (also from Cleveland but not a suicide).

She stood up—not very far, however. She was dainty. She tucked her notebook into an embroidered pouch. She took my arm. I burned with desire. No salivation; lips, mouth, and throat were dry with terror.

We must have said good-bye. Her antennae waved a soft, fragile, dominating farewell.

Silence fell over the gathering. The veteran heroine, the near-virginal lyricmeister from Cleveland, together on an evening of early wartime above Mott Street, departed. She liked to ensorcell (her word) more than she liked to hang out. So many myths, but so little paper in her diary.

Anaïs was the name; Illumination's the game.

I was ready for whatever came next. I had already given proof of courage by refusing to go clothes shopping anymore with my mother. We descended the long winding staircase toward Chinatown. She held my finger and, birdlike, seemed to hop from step to step in a peculiar irregular gliding—she *glid*—like a creature with wings she was choosing not to use. I trudged behind. With her fist she kept a firm grip around my finger.

The sorceress even breathed daintily. I could hear the timid panting. I felt her breath. I was magicked to the max.

And then, near the bottom of the stairwell, she spoke the fateful words which abruptly altered my fate. "You remind me . . ." she whispered. "Remind me . . . of my . . . remind me of my father."

Ma'm?

The echo reverberated around my crewcut, slightly jug-eared skull. I remind Anaïs of her . . . *father?*

It was the most terrifying declaration she could have uttered.

The words slipped a flamenco shiv into my pants. It was so out of touch with my own picture of her, of me, of what we were supposed to be heading for in Hoboken, on her houseboat . . . trellises . . . water lapping . . . instructional passion . . . that I simply pinwheeled into panic.

"Here's my nickel, there's the subway!"

Ow, ouch, oh, I'm only seventeen! Hoped for glamorous initiation into fancy grownup sex by heavily accented mysterioso veiled Lilith from the Azores! Instead, hip, hop, back onto the Oedipal box. . . . I remind her of her *father?*

O Pallas Athene, get me back to the freshman dorm.

"Lots of homework, paper due Monday morning, Hartley Hall gets locked if you come back too late!"

"Oh god! I hope the subway is still running!"

"Got my nickel right here! Good-bye!"

This was not the lyrical love poet wailing. This was a requiem for lust. I was breathless before I fled, showing her my nickel, proving I had the fare ready, and breathless all the way back to safe harbor on Morningside Heights. In my memory she still stands on the bottom rung of a long staircase on Mott Street, her tiny face under the hat, behind the veil, showing elegant Spanish incomprehension. Pale. Wondering. Hoboken-bound without company.

There may have been a spectral moon. There may have been a phosphorescent glow of incest in the dimmed lamps of a wartime college dorm. But how would I know? The blankets were pulled over my head back up at Columbia in Hartley Hall.

Within a few months I was learning how to jump out of airplanes, learning Russian for the U.S. Army, thinking about possibilities which made my mouth even more dry than being smooshed into the ghostly father of Anaïs Nin. It's fifty years now. Not long ago I looked in her published diaries to see if she had any comment on that evening of poetic interaction high above Mott Street.

Ah, the vanity. Ho, watchman of the Chinatown-to-Hoboken ensorcelled path not taken.

. . .

In the early sixties, a bookseller in San Rafael was busted for selling *Tropic of Cancer,* Henry Miller's masterpiece about Bohemians in Paris. Barney Rosset, publisher of Grove Press, ferocious and money-disregarding, a laughing sleepless millionaire from Chicago—a toothy, frequently married, high-living, radical Upper Bohemian—crisscrossed the U.S.A. to do battle with lubricious post office officials and smarmy district attorneys.

A priest and a minister testified to the high moral importance of Henry Miller for Marin County. Along with Mark Schorer, distinguished literary critic and professor at the University of California at Berkeley, I testified about Miller's literary place. The DA nagged us with questions about the blasphemy and immorality of such foreign—*French!*—words as *bidet.* He asked if I would like my mother to read such a word.

Keenly the DA insisted that conversation among characters in the book were in fact statements by Henry Miller. ("I refer the witness to page 226. . . . Please read aloud to the jury.") I found myself explaining the function of the literary signal called "Quotation Marks." With exasperation trained at Notre Dame, the district attorney asked why an author would allow his characters to say things he didn't believe. He asked the jury if this meant the author was a liar. The mind boggled, the flies buzzed, the eyelids dropped. A lovely Eurasian artist made sketches.

I explained to my mother what a bidet is and she said, "Oh, nice for washing string beans." The priest took up this theme with the DA and corrected his pronunciation: bee-*day,* not bee-*debt.* I was kept on the stand so long my car was towed away.

In the end, the bookseller was acquitted of both obscenity and pornography charges and the jurors came to the victory celebration to eat Barney Rosset's food, drink his wine. A spokesman for the jury explained that, well, they acquitted the bookseller, oh, uh . . . not on the grounds of "redeeming social value" . . . not because of the testimony of the eminent theologians, the literary critic, and the novelist . . . but because the poor bookseller said he thought *Tropic of Cancer* was a book about astrology. A normal error. Even in the early sixties, this was already Marin County.

We're still wriggling to get something very simple through our patriotic American skulls. Henry Miller was a funny, charming, life-enhancing, amoral, dirty writer.

Henry Miller would be a hundred years old by now. When his most important books were published in Paris in the early thirties, the U.S. was perishing in isolationism, depression, and Prohibition. In France, despite the gathering political darkness, folks wore berets, danced the can-can, prescribed red wine against *le cafard,* washed everything but their string beans in the bidets, and took multiple simultaneous triangulated love affairs as part of the deal, now that the Garden of Eden had been closed down for lease violations. The geometry of love was neither plane nor solid: it was a subject for debate, it was talkative, demanded constant attention.

Tropic of Cancer, Tropic of Capricorn, and Miller's rambunctious celebrations of life in Big Sur and many beds declared loud and hot, with dash, brio, careless grammar, and bawdy self-centeredness, that idleness, drunkenness, and sexual complications were essential to a proper life. Miller looked in the mirror to find the model for this life. When asked to identify himself, he said, "Yup, it's me all right." He was Everyman before there was an Everyperson. He couldn't even escape jealousy. Partington Ridge in Big Sur rang with cries of pain and shifting sublets due to conjugal revolutions. Although a small volcano of crude macho, Miller really seemed to like women. He was honest about his dependence upon them, even his abjectness, his miseries. There was what you could call *regard.* Despite his nonstop rambles and howlings, there was a kind of courtesy in him—perhaps not old-country but old-Brooklyn, mush-faced courtliness.

The complications made for terrific prose. The tradition was that wild one of Mark Twain, Walt Whitman, and carnival barkers. The American GIs and tourists who smuggled Miller's books home from Paris in their blue barracks bags had learned from the censorship, which told readers this guy was important, not just dirty; else why would the customs officers pore so earnestly through used underwear in search of blue or green Olympia Press volumes? Those who bought the later Grove Press editions after reading about yahoo prosecutions learned the same lesson without having to get seasick in the process. And the old geezer, settling down with his last epidemic of wives and lovers in southern California, kept on chuckling as he approached the age of ninety.

Earlier, sleepless in Paris, escaping Brooklyn and German rectitude, sleepless in the whole world, broke and desperate and frolicking, he poured out confessions that people took for pornography. If they kept their hands in their laps and concentrated on the thought of the U.S. Customs Service, they might have become aroused while reading. But actually what Henry Miller was in the business of doing was reinventing American Bohemia, reinventing the American rogue and urban slave, mapping the road away from a massified society, lighting out for the territory ahead— doing what Mark Twain did earlier, and William Saroyan later, and the beatnik esthetes still later. It was his business with the American lingo: to demonstrate the possibilities for fun in verbs and adjectives while depicting the fun in beds and cheap restaurants. He swam along in the belly of Jonah's whale, shameless about his free ride.

What gave him depth was the wistfulness in a story like "Dieppe-Newhaven" and the longing in his doomed pursuit (it was more like evasion) of willful women. It wasn't all just fun, red wine, and hangovers. It was *meaningful* hangovers, too.

Later, a celebrity in southern California, very old, he painted watercolors—I have one—and coasted, basked, tried to get used to being accepted. For *Esquire* he posed for a photograph in bed with Erica Jong. I don't have a copy, but it's all too clear in my memory. He no longer asked people to send him postage. His family quarreled over his new money. He died full of years, still writing, still painting—"to paint is to love again"—still in love, undefeated by the creaks and squeaks of his well-used body. He was a Charles Bukowsky with irony, a Jack Kerouac who really liked sex, a bourgeois gentleman with an Asian dancer on his arm and a proper middle-American wife giggling in the closet. He was a fine ancient party who never forgot that he was once both a wolf and a jackal.

. . .

"Henry Miller. Wanna play Ping-Pong?"

The small bald old guy was grinning. The Brooklyn accent was intact despite all the years in many exiles. It was 1963 in Formentor, Mallorca, at an international publishers' boondoggle, and he had accepted a free trip as a member of the American delegation because of old Bohemian habits of accepting anything that cost nothing if it promised drink, food, bed, and the options of idle minds. He preferred blonds, brunettes, redheads—any woman who could breathe. I'm sure he preferred bald women, too. He may have excluded necrophilia.

We played Ping-Pong, I forget who won (probably he did), and then he took to his room for a nap. The nap lasted for the rest of the week. He was not in the business of wasting his time with international writer prize chat when he could spend it profitably with a fast game of Ping-Pong followed by gracious audiences in his hotel room.

I am of that generation which went to Paris to buy books by Henry Miller, smuggling them back past the U.S. Customs. That's what a summer or a year in Europe meant—strolling Montmartre and Montparnasse, reading about the adventures of this scavenger of lust, this bullheaded experimenter of sex, this shameless hustler who answered fan letters with requests to send a little money or at least a few spare postage stamps. Until late middle age, he was broke, busted, banned, and afflicted with sore complications in his marital and antimarital adventures. In old age he grew rich and celebrated—finally Grove Press broke the ban and made him a bestseller in this country—but the pyramid scheme of his sex life never ceased.

Once at dinner in southern California, I sat near this icon of American letters while a charming, bawdy starlet perched between us. She was employed in movies designed for Debbie Reynolds but so low budget they couldn't even afford to hire Debra Paget. She knew her place. Her décolletage was disconcerting, inviting, as she intended it to be. So as not to waste the precious moments while waiting for the salad course to be removed, the icon reached down the front of her dress and grabbed. "Henry!" cried the lady.

He removed his hand, shrugged, and consoled himself with shrimps on baby lettuce. What can an old boy do but live up to his reputation? The starlet, all rosy, has been telling the story ever since.

9

Upper Bohemia in America

MIAMI

Thirty-five years ago, as a skinnied-down divorce pauper, I used to load my typewriter and my chagrin into a salt-eaten old Ford convertible and head south toward Miami during the black midwestern winter. It was cold inside and out. The idea was to write myself up from the negative-worth pit while enjoying hibiscus, palm, seawater, and a hospitable community. I found Coconut Grove, its sun and damp, its green and verdant subtropical smells. I found graceful companionship. If I hadn't been so miserable, I'd have been in heaven.

I settled into a room at 6th and Collins, one block from the beach, for two dollars a day. I didn't intend to hibernate. The prospect of hanging wonderfully concentrates the mind; a negative net worth has some of the same astringent quality. I opened a factory with my typewriter, writing stories under several names, including my own, for magazines that paid actual money. I swam in order to wake up and fell into conversation on the deserted morning beach with another dropout swimmer, a woman with long legs and sad eyes who said she used to type for a writer in North Carolina named Thomas Wolfe. I took her to the Big Dollar Steak Dinner (with shrimp cocktail, $1.10) at a Cuban restaurant a few blocks south and got her to talk about the Old Days of American literature.

The next winter, when I returned, driving down Route 1 in my hundred-dollar Ford convertible, the price at the hotel had soared to $2.50, inflation taking its toll, and Thomas Wolfe's typist had vanished from her furnished room on Washington. A neighbor said she had gone for her morning swim and continued straight out toward heaven. I wrote an essay called "Death in Miami Beach" about the old Jews warehoused by their families, the Georgia country folks and the blacks, the Cubans, the jerking street crazies, the mind-split dropouts, and the soft-voiced swimmer who knew Thomas Wolfe, author of *You Can't Go Home Again.*

This bruised southernmost end of the South Beach was a kind of purgatory, which is better than hell but not as good as heaven. I wrote, swam, cleared my throat for enough voice to ask for coffee or a newspaper. In its long decrepitude, you could say the South Beach with its unfashionable, unclean art deco hotels seemed ugly. I liked ugliness. It fit my mood.

Even earlier, as a teenage runaway from Cleveland, I had hitchhiked to the beach and met an ancient vegetarian codger who lived up a winding cast-iron stairway in a stucco tower he named Eagle's Roost. He asked if I was hungry (I was) and took me home to feed me apricots and raisins. He lectured me about Spinoza. He did not make a pass at me, or if he did, I was too dumb to notice and he was too shy to insist.

So the South Beach and I go way back. Ugliness may be superior to beauty because it lasts longer, as Serge Gainsbourg said, but here the process is confounded. The Art Deco District has become beautiful again; perhaps, after its early neon tubing and later decay, really beautiful for the first time—fervency has done it. It has been youthified by a combination of Latin joie de vivre, antiquing nostalgia, and (grant the point) imaginative real estate speculation making the best of what the law allows.

Upper, even uppity Bohemia makes an offer we can't resist—a no-risk adventure in consumership while the senses are legitimately delighted by tastes of art, culture, history, and attractive bodies. The Bohemian folks of Coconut Grove love life because, after all, the predeath experience is all we've got on hand. They can add a little love to the recipe, the palazzo Viscaya, one of the

Seven Wonders of the Florida Tourist Bureau, botanical gardens nearby, a church with a 400-year-old door, parks, marinas, trails, and steady, year-round good taste. In the fifties, if you happened to mention art in the South Beach, only a few minutes drive distant across the causeway, people would say, "Art Who? The zipper man from Canal Street?" Now even in South Beach the life of art has become an accepted preoccupation.

But in Coconut Grove, invited to a house that amazed my cement-sated soul with its tropical orchids, all the luxury, calm, and voluptuousness money could buy, I made valiant efforts to live up to the promises of paradise. The olfactory bulb, that part of the brain which distinguishes some ten thousand different scents, broadcast nothing but sweet signals into the back lanes and southernmost portions of the psyche. A young woman looked deeply, consentingly, into my eyes, but said, "No, not until I know you better—maybe tomorrow."

There are lawyers in my family. I suspected this was only an oral contract.

Then, as I walked on a dock, calming myself in friendly Atlantic breezes, I heard high heels chasing after me. I turned. There was no one. Again I walked, and again that ghostly clicking. At last I caught the source of the seductive sound—a land crab high on its claws.

This wandering beatnik emeritus, now a middle-aged graybeard, returned to find the promised tomorrow of that dark-eyed young woman and the descendants of the land crab passionately clacking near the fiberglass hulls of yachts and sailboats. How old would I be if I didn't know how old I am?

Michael Genden, a lawyer who grew up in the Grove, remembers folk music, guitars, the acoustic metaphysical rapping of the fifties; he remembers the protest, hope, and heads filled with wild surmise of the Aquarian sixties, when the herd of independent minds discovered "the Grove." There were little cafés and little bookstores and easy loafing in the mists of his boyhood. "Gone, all gone," he sighed, uttering a truth which can be uttered about so much.

But since nothing ever really dies, the young of Coconut Grove find new cafés (larger ones), new guitars (electric), and the Monty's mall, beerhall, restaurant, video store, bakery, and boatyard to replace the old and funkier Monty's. Hey, it's still Monty's, and the South Seas–Caribbean style of sloshing beer around still attracts heavily tanned fun crusaders, those unintimidated by melanoma. I watched a waiter (ripped clothes from Air-Conditioned Jeans) approach a contrasting couple of young women, one straw blond, the other henna dark, both triumphs of minimalism in masterful skimp of dress. "Two gentlemen over there want to buy you a drink."

They peered. One shook her head at the other. The dark spokesperson spoke up: "Tell them maybe when hell freezes over."

The Grove's period as Miami's Haight-Ashbury, like Venice in Los Angeles and the East Village in Manhattan, is over. Venice is now a yuppie-condo-sushi resort; the East Village has started on the way there. This is America. And yet the sun still shines over Coconut Grove, the green shimmers, a certain grace which attracted poets and dreamers still works its wiles.

Only now the dreamers had better be the heirs to well-managed trust funds or cocaine dealerships. Things have gotten expensive. Crowned heads, such as Prince, take up residence with their show dogs, just as if they were headed for Coral Gables. The Grove is a dreamland of luxury, *aesthetic* luxury, in which the fine-tuning of life-style approaches what actual, desirable real life might be. Plus a Latin flavor. With the young women parading on Commodore Plaza in hip-and-thigh–hugging miniskirts and high heels, making the act of strolling to the multiplex moviehouse in CocoWalk a demonstration of emergency metabolic mobilization. The skirt hikes up, the hands tug down, this is the mother of voyeurism. The café umbrellas in the streets shelter folks who give thanks to the snake which brought the knowledge of good and evil into Eden. The street scene recalls the Prado in Havana before the revolution, another gift Cuba has offered Miami.

Carmel-like traditional Bohemia has evaporated from the Grove under the hot wind of development (it's gone from Carmel, too)—or so the former artists, beatniks, and hippies assured me in their law offices and condos. And yet, in the apartment complex where I bivouacked, I found a dropout professor editing a collection of contemporary German poetry, a filmmakers' collective, and a man who described his profession as "blocked novelist." The dropout prof writes for little literary magazines, dreams of Paris in the twenties. I treated the blocked novelist with the compassionate healing words, "Write! Just write!"

One of those larks that sing too early in the morning, I found the bakery at Monty's not open yet. I hiked into downtown Grove, world headquarters, past runners, bicyclists, and other dawn dreamers. A middle-aged runner, wrists burdened with lead weights, a Grove version of the self-flagellating God-seekers of New Mexico, panted out an answer to my question about a place for breakfast: "That one! Greasy but good! Or the La Petite Pâtisserie opens at eight!"

Many a mile, arms hefting, before he could rest. I didn't have the heart to tell him he didn't have to say "the" before "La" when he's citing a French name.

It seemed important to perform my morning carbo loading with muffins and coffee at outdoor tables. Strolled through Mayfair, an eerie Arabian Nights Plus Balinese Temple Caprice Mall. Strolled through the adjacent CocoWalk with its instant traditional Caribbean Spanish decor, tee-shirt shops, Banana Republic, Victoria's Secret, and a joy-pak assortment of frozen yogurt, beer, pizza, and even full-course dinner opportunities. Mayfair, fountains splashing, seemed deserted at all hours. CocoWalk has captured the youthy appetites of modern malldom. The contrast of market-sensitive triumph and idealistic failure carries on one of the persistent patterns of Coconut Grove, the performance-art tradition of real estate speculation.

At La Petite Pâtisserie I chose French bread instead of muffins. When I asked the server behind the counter if she was French, she said, "Don't have to be to make fresh-squeezed juice, do I? Unless you want Tropicana, it's cheaper."

A little group of Brazilians with designer backpacks was taking an hour to see the Grove between planes. Their stretch limousine waited. They were on their way to New York, but thought Coconut Grove was magnifico, might deserve more than an hour, especially with all the shopping options.

As the morning parade thickened, young mothers in pickups stopped for coffee, ferrying kids to school. A photographer, headed for the Keys, used his cordless phone to make a series of short calls (cordless interrupted). A budget sport in that tippy Japanese jeep, the Suzuki, came by to read his *Wall Street Journal* and ogle the other oglers. Not only high heels with hip-and-thigh–hugging miniskirts display the Cuban influence on fashion hereabouts. When the skirts were looser, for variety, there were fringes—fringes dappled the knees. The man with the Japanese jeep, living dangerously, according to *Consumer Reports,* seemed worried about the sudden decline in IBM, encouraged by the rise in biotechs, and reassured by free coffee refills. Life requires art because it's a series of mixed signals.

In San Francisco there are fewer high heels, fewer fringes, rare free coffee refills in cafés.

At the Grove Bookworm in the nearby Old Bank Building, an inviting hangout bookshop, I wallowed in a jumble of non-top-forty books. The proprietors seem to be proud to make room for the few contemporary novels which are not by Danielle Steele.

The neighborhood bulletin board in Deli Lane hasn't changed much through the eons. My friend George Shelley, photographer, tennis player, sometime model, actor, and real estate owner, who spent his college years in the Grove, grew sentimental over the invitation to a Hare Krishna feast ("Anyone can do it! Just chant HARE KRISHNA and be happy!"). We wondered if those who used to visit the Virginia Street Hare Krishna headquarters in his day, when the Grove was funky, are still happy. We wondered if the Harry Kirschner chant would do just as well. The Libertarian party didn't offer happiness, but instead, Freedom from Taxes, which may be more enticing than perpetual bliss in the Coconut Grove of today. Another notice was headed DO YOU KNOW THIS GUY? with a computer portrait drawing:

> His name is Danny Finley and he recently played music with Kinky Friedman and the Texas Jewboys and also Montezumas Revenge

with Panama Red. . . . He did live on Main Highway about 20 years ago. We were both in a band called Bethlehem Asylum. I was the roadie. My name is Lee and he can find my last name by looking on the second Asylum album and call me.

Lost Rock-'n'-Roller Alert! Someone had scrawled in pencil on the notice: *Doing carpentry around the Grove.*

One evening, taking my forward observation post at La Petite Pâtisserie, I saw a scuffle outside the Bookworm. Two thieves, one a young woman with a razor, were captured and held by a heroic book clerk until the police arrived. The clerk broke a finger, the thieves had long records, and this is not Eden but real life we've sometimes got here.

Denise Chardiet, a history student at the University of Miami, comes to lunch in the cluster of outdoor cafés on Commodore Plaza for a taste of Europe without actually leaving home. "When I was a kid," she recalled nostalgically, *"then* it was flower children in the Grove." A Cadillac cruised on by, emphasizing her comment with a front license plate that read: RETIRED No Address No Phone No Clock No Money.

The driver in his Eisenhower-style golf cap made a wide U-turn, calling out, "Waitin' for anybody, miss?"

Retired No Class.

The Cosmic Connection on this Saint-Germain-des-Prés stretch of Commodore Plaza has been there little more than a year. The proprietor hasn't lost her Long Island accent. Yet it expresses Full Sixties Chic, mandala designs, New Age books, crystals, natural foods, including Natural Junk Foods, and the latest news on the tarot, astrology, and Touch of Peace Massage fronts. Perhaps the dining area shouldn't be named the Garden of Eat'in. In the sixties it would have been something like Karmic Kuisine or Stop-the-War Head Munchies.

An organic foods store nearby, Oak Feed, has been on the Grove forever. "Come back sometime for our natural-food juices," advised a glum clerk with that health-food pallor in his cheeks. "Unrivaled for twenty-odd years. Soon's the man come in to fix the machine." He directed me to the Healing Support

Group and the Macrobiotic Foundation of Florida if I wanted to run amuck in the Grove's counterculture.

During my stay, arguments were still raging about the annual Coconut Grove Arts Festival. Was the art up to snuff? Too much beer on the streets? Were the logo tee shirts boring? "Skyooz me," cried a defender of the festival, cutting straight to the heart of the matter. "Excuse me! My macrame sold real good."

Carrying on the tradition of craftspersonship year-round is the shop called Om, finely worked jewelry, operated by a pony-tailed sixties veteran named Wayne; Leathery, the sandal-making resort which has moved with the times, now does actual shoes, including laces; Athene, a New Age books and crystals conglomerate, three outlets. I have friends who survive without an automobile in this mid-Miami, mid-metropolis strolling village, where they can walk to work, play, exercise, swim, and visit their friends under banyan and eucalyptus trees, observing fellow creatures who don't require the infernal combustion engine for locomotion, such as the lizard and the landcrab. Of course, unlike the lizard and the clacking land crab, my friends' children own automobiles. And, Upper Bohemians, they do have a nice little sailboat. Mankind has got to fish, doesn't it? In the best bay for sailing in America?

Bob Hardin has worked many times for the same newspaper—always managing through talent to get himself rehired—and lived on a houseboat. Now he is both a freelance writer and, in a new Bohemian tradition, an aspirant real estate promoter. The long commotion of the sixties has taken some surprising turns. He has this vision of a lease on a boatyard where folks can put their feet up, kick back with a beer and view of the sunset. He still plans to write his great book.

"I'll be in a beat-up old white Cadillac," he said, and sure enough, there it was. We drove for breakfast to a greasy spoon near Route 1 with a waitress named Rosie, ordered eggs and grits, greeted Bob's fellow questers. When it came time to begin the morning's questing, his car mysteriously wouldn't start. He confiscated the Toyota of a nearby friend, "from the motor vehicle pool." After all, we're in this thing together. That's the spirit of

Auld Coconut Grove. Otherwise you might as well just get on Route One and drive north to nowhere or south to Key West.

After breakfast, on a day of skies like a baby's eyes, later clouding over to the color of eyes buried in a chic Cuban lady's tumble of hair—small face, big hair, threatened storm—I set out to explore the cottages among the peeling trees of the back streets of the Grove. Many For Rent signs. I moved into them all with my imaginary boat, my dream Karman-Ghia convertible, my actual Olivetti Lettera 32 typewriter, and the curse of optimism rediscovered here in the Grove of my dream, those clacking land-crab claws on a deck, so many years ago.

BOHEMIA IN BEIGE (RETRO REAL ESTATE)

Two fashion models are eating frozen yogurt and sitting at the curb because they have wearied of their table on the sidewalk at the News Café. They stretch out their miracle legs. "You want a ride?" asks a man in a Japanese red power convertible with a Zen nameplate ending in -i, stretch financing.

"You take us back to Stockholm," replies one giant beauty, "but first we stay in the Bitch." He looks startled. She means Miami and South Bitch, of course.

Someplace an earnest anthropology doctoral candidate is working on his thesis, "Art Deco District Religious Rituals: The Mating Dances of Six-Foot High Swedish Models and Love-Crazed Real Estate Speculators at the News Café in South Miami Beach, USA." Despite five years of public relations, that beige-infested, streamline-modern Retroland which succeeded the alcohol and crack slum preying on the Cuban and Jewish old-folks warehousing ghetto—which in turn evolved over the years from the early resort explosion on a spit of fill, a refuge from New York, Cleveland, Chicago, and other places of Siberian winter—is still terra barely cognita. Today, a complex phenomenon of Eurotrash and beauty ruck, preservationist salvationism, "Soho-by-the-Sea," a palimpsest of money and style coexists along with Marielitos and old folks with sunburnt knees clinging to the interstices on their aluminum lawn chairs. The crack houses are mostly gone, although there may have been a few ghosts in the hotel where I stayed. A unique American Bohemia has been willed into being in the famous tired resort.

I settled into a hotel that goes for many times the rent circa 1956–60. The conversation is similarly inflated. Where folks used to rock in their chairs pulled out onto the sidewalk, playing canasta and murmuring about Social Security or their son the doctor in Buffalo, I now heard a young man say, "I can't make it for brunch because I got a date to wax my legs and chest. But I hear their brunch is delish."

His friend, a decorator with Nautilus knots in his muscles, strode about a lobby with litigious intensity, gritting his perfect teeth. Having lived in California with teenage kids, I know how expensive are perfect teeth. He said: "Until I get paid for this restoration, final completion, I've made a solemn vow. I'm not buying myself one more earring."

Gypsy encampments of fashion-shoot vans cluster in the alleys and sidestreets, filled with photographers, coordinators, makeup experts, coffee-seeking support staff. The air conditioning throbs. In their catalogue clothes, spring, summer, and fall—prop tennis racquets, prop riding equipment, prop babies—the stony-faced models sit, waiting. With their stilt legs and collagened lips they look like captured Scandinavian Ubangi girls, victims of a war fought with cameras, light reflectors, and crash diets. Sometimes Miami Beach police in uniform shorts lounge nearby, protective, hoping to be discovered by a sharp-eyed director. This is major business for the South Beach. Art deco backdrops are big. The action brings tourists, frozen-yogurt vendors, significant others.

George Shelley, photographer, connoisseur of Florida Bohemian scenes, took me to the temple of anorexia called . . . Well, how about calling it the Temple of Anorexia? It was also an outpatient clinic for women suffering from henna dependency. Like a foreign correspondent in the art deco wars, I studied a young man in a vested white linen suit with a watchchain draped across his middle. If you pulled the chain, it would more likely chime than tell the time. He was sitting with an older woman, sharing the pangs of life in the nineties. "My father died." "Did you have to go to the funeral?" "No, I did it all by credit card." And I guess they could fax her the ashes.

The free-living style includes a freedom from self-censoring, although it allows judgment of others and the ability to take. Respect for self easily sags into what might be named narcissism. Let's name it that, and there's a lot to be found in the art deco universe, which has some of the heroic style of prewar Mussolini futurist architecture, decor, and armor against reality.

A roller blader glides by, swooping across the wide walks along the beach, a fashion statement in muscles, knee pads, and Day-Glo Spandex, all the while earnestly conversing on his porta-phone. "What's he talking about?" "Owns property on Collins. Thinking of putting in a pool . . ."

Remnants survive of the decayed and funky South Beach of recent times, the widows in old-lady butterfly glasses, spangled and glittery with totally unfestive results, the widowers methodically munching their chow in the cafeterias on Collins Avenue or Lincoln Boulevard. Here counterinsurgency recapturing of a never-was past, not so much preserving as lacquering it up to a high gleam to make a Walt Decoland attraction, is disorienting. The alternatives, of course, razing the South Beach to make condos and malls, or letting it rot with crack and crime, are worse. I've seen the same antiquing impulse at work in such places as Saint-Paul-de-Vence, the medieval walled town in the south of France, where costumed peasants wax and buff the cobblestones outside their ancient, we-take-American-Express inns and students are hired to stroll the alleys where Crusaders paraded, with the message I SPEAK ENGLISH TALK TO ME printed on their ancient quaint fourteenth-century tee shirts.

A visiting fashion journalist from Manhattan confessed at the News Café, Eighth and Ocean: "People speak of my so-called Edwardian beauty, but I don't think I'm a drop-dead knockout, do you?"

"Uh . . ."

"I think it's more like an art deco loveliness I've got—beige overhand, nice cantilevers, don't you think?"

Great cantilevers, ma'am, and you hold up both ends of the conversation.

She was temporarily a journalist to put gruel on her breakfast table. As soon as she runs out of Edwardian beauty, she plans to retire to South Beach (has bought a condo) and write the great American novel about a woman whose cheekbones and style were seriously misunderstood by everyone.

A certain amount of what we're dealing with here is men who wear one set of jewelry before sundown, another for evening; skip over the toupee period and go right into hair transplants; exercise when the grease starts to accumulate into love handles, that stuff around the belt which is so embarrassing when you're in lounging pajamas with your significant other pro tem. They are forward-looking, scientifically minded, and use money for personal productivity. They seriously consider liposuction for a rapid fix. ("Hector, you fit your pants again," says the Sharon who wishes Hector were Oliver North or someone more patriotic, although Hector must be more fun than Ollie ever was.)

I sat with a Miami criminal lawyer at an outdoor table at the News Café, discussing the difference between beautiful young women in California and those parading the sidewalk in front of our Greek salads. A brilliant antagonist before juries, he cuts straight to the heart of the matter: "High heels," he pronounced. "It's the Cuban connection—even my wife is Cuban."

In San Francisco they don't wear high heels for daytime ambling with those hip-and-thigh–hugging tight minilike skirts. While discussing the coke trade—under the American system of jurisprudence, every well-off criminal deserves a defense—we also noticed flights of six-foot-high angels wearing tennies, speaking their foreign languages, Swedish, German, Chelsea English, turning the blank fashion-model stare on each other, ardently inhaling their cigarettes. Our waitress was French and monosyllabic. A lively young woman at the next table was speaking with an accent I recognized. When I spoke Creole to her, she grew even more lively, repeating incredulously, "Ou vieux habitant?" after I said I had lived in Haiti.

My friend the lawyer pointed out, "You notice we're hearing other languages?"

Including Swahili. Although a graduate of Yale Law, he too is alert to new traditions, wishing our Haitian neighbor a Merry Kwanzaa, since Joyeux Noël is not in their shared west African ancestry. Nicole, the Haitian beauty, was more into dancing and her modeling career than Swahili activism. "That's cool, man," she declared with her entrancing Creole lilt.

This is a cosmopolitan sample world around Ocean Drive and Eighth. The News Café sells a few books, foreign newspapers and magazines, in addition to café food and heaping portions of Euro-surplus charm. The sidewalk parade includes gawking families huddling together for protection, Asians marching smartly to the click of a different camera, hefty collegiate beer drinkers in shorts and no socks, like the ones at Monty's in Coconut Grove—in fact, the folks you might find at a normal pedestrian mall in Copenhagen or Nice, too. But this is *South Florida*. What lends the scene its grounding is the persistence of a traditional culture. Nextdoor to restored art deco hotels in all their proud pastelness are the worn-out prerestored ones, lobbies crowded with ancient codgers, wives in aluminum lawn chairs, their puckered and sun-bruised knees spread to catch the vitamin D in the air. The old folks discuss their blood pressure, prostates, and children while the fashion shoots carry on a bagel's throw away. The codgers and codgerettes make contact with the South Beach of my well-misspent youth.

A real estate guess is that all these hotel rooms can never be uniformly gentrified into a mile-square fashion shoot and international pickup mall. Old folks from New York still need the balm of heat, sand, and sea; some of the real estate will devote itself to them and their budgets. The twenty-four-hour cafeterias on Collins will feed them. The study groups upstairs of graffiti'd walls on the side streets and on Collins and Washington will educate them about technocracy, homeopathy, Sholem Aleichem, and the problems of the Middle East. The native beach bunnies with the tastefully shredded jeans, the Jacksonville Hell's Angels motorcycle assault troops traveling on ego and speed, the honking death-call ambulances (I saw one seeming to *return* a body on a gurney to the Starlite Hotel), the gay men who emerge blinking from hotel-motels and apt-short-terms at 11:00 P.M. when the underground clubs open for their AIDS defiance rituals, the dropout surplus beatniks and hippies and old-time punk Bohemians seeking an American alternative to Nashville, New York, San Francisco, and Los Angeles—there is a place for all of them in this unique tapestry. But I wondered if the apparent corpse carried back into the Starlite hadn't come up to the mortician's aesthetic standards. And if tomorrow it would be spreading its knees to take the rays in a lawn chair on the terrace.

It used to be that a person could count on ugliness, but beauty passed. Now it seems even ugliness is temporary when clever people come calling. What *Newsweek* named "Soho by the Sea" turns out to be lively, energetic, and disco-delightful while London's faded Soho lives mostly in legend. (Would *Newsweek* call it Carnaby-by-the-Canyons if it were L.A.?) The Playhouse on Ocean Drive, "Happening Underground," welcomes everyone who can claim to be cute, whatever the sex, "Sat. nite from 11 P.M. 'til ?." The Cameo Theater on Washington offers open mike, open mind, poetry readings on Wednesday evenings, weeklong beatnik revival sports. And in the afternoon, on the Lincoln Road pedestrial mall—no traffic, strollers, an art center, lots of the vacant stores which invite low-rent innovation—a Cuban street band played "Guantanamera," followed by "Bei mir bist du schön." Coins and a few bills drifted into their guitar cases. A preacher in a shiny black wig lectured about how Mohammad Ali wasn't brain damaged at all. "Mr. Ali is takin' his time before he make his new move, float like a butterfly, sting like a bee. . . ."

At Botanica La Caridad, "Consulta Espiritual," they sold Santeria Good Luck Candles, blue-and-white Star of David candles, and twisted Haitian voodoo ropes. I asked the proprietor where he got the statue of Papa Legba, Guardian of the Crossroads, an important Haitian god, and he said, "Friend."

"So what does it all mean?" I asked an artist in Cordozo's, one of the hyperdecor'd new bars.

"Meaning is fascist," he replied. He meant that the idea of meaning implies a hierarchy of values, therefore someone deciding what the values should be, therefore fascism.

I answered: "Fascism is fascist."

"That's phallocentric hegenomism."

Nailed again.

For refreshment after this conversation, I stopped by the unrestored Starlite, next door to the Boulevard Hotel with its many-star Italian restaurant, and asked the price of a room. The desk clerk looked me up and down and said, "You wouldn't want to stay here, mister."

"But if I did?"

"You wouldn't."

I proceeded to a rock-'n'-roll street fair in Espaniola Way, balloons and laser display, music by Warsaw and E.S.P., and a load of sand on the pavement, celebrating spring break for the benefit of AIDS patients. There were motorcycles without mufflers, Social Security gawkers on walkers, swivel-hipped Latins, and of course the fully muscled, the in drag with lace and parasols to protect themselves from the moonlight, a variety-pak of the Miami gay community. "We're ecumenical, man," one of the organizers explained. "Some dynamite lesbians from Chicago— accepted just like brothers. We're cool."

A Miami Beach cop, with soft blond mustache, saw me taking notes. "You a journalist? Write down the cops are cool long as folks behave theirself."

A plump entrepreneur parades down the Art Deco Strip of Ocean Drive with a Burmese python tastefully draped around his shoulders. "Pet it! Pet it!" he commands, and the models shriek, but sometimes a brave escort-to-models or tourist shows he's a real man by being photographed with the python wrapped around his neck. ("You're such a wild and crazy guy, Freddy.") The Burmese python never strangles the wild and crazy guys. "Pet it, you can, touch it, just touch it," begs the python artiste in front of the News Café, where blasé world travelers barely look up from their copies of *Le monde, Politikken,* and *People.*

Upper Bohemians are not disabled by their lack of the vital element of poverty and struggle. They are differently abled. It's okay to have money. They still have to get some paint on that canvas and their names up front in the Passport Café or printed in *Antenna.* They fight to fill the ozone holes yawning above in the bone-warming, unforgiving sky. This is melanoma country. Life is a single mother and then you die.

The major political movement during my stay seemed to be the HELP STOP MUSIC CENSORSHIP—Fight for Your Right to Rock! campaign. The young woman from Colorado who gave me the poster said she was also working on abortion rights, rain forest, and ozone-layer matters but hoped to get home for a little skiing before everything melted. She invited me to an organizational meeting at the Career Institute, Twelfth and Washington.

At an oceanfront party, a kindly elderly gentleman wearing a foulard introduced me to his other guests, saying, "Do you happen to know my ex-wife, Tansie?"

"Is that all the identification I have?" she demanded indignantly. "I'm a shaman! I'm a Santeria mystic! I'm not just your ex-wife!"

Another woman explained that she was working as a star of stage, screen, and dinner theater only until she gets her series on cable. Her walker whispered to me: ". . . or a good paying position as a manicurist."

I've been to such parties, with the same kindly elderly gentlemen, serpent-tongued walkers, and ambitious young would-bees in Ibiza, Saint-Germain-des-Prés, Malibu and Venice (California), the Hamptons, Chelsea—wherever the pretty would-bees of any sex buzz and the enchanted folks who take care of them seek Aura, Attitude, and Strange. What South Beach demonstrates is that America in the post Flower Age has become user-friendly to the Bohemian nation. Places like Sausalito and Mill Valley, South Beach and Coconut Grove, Venice and Malibu, or the Wood-stock-Hamptons axis show how Upper Bohemia attaches itself to great American metropolises. Similar Upper Bohemian encampments have taken root in Oklahoma City, Cleveland, Detroit, Chicago, Nashville (where it adopts a country-western CD accent), Charleston, New Orleans, even Reno, Nevada—more faintly than in Miami, but there, too.

Americans seem to need that throb of accident, art, and adven-

ture in the relentless dailiness of our lives. We look for love in
strange places, coffeehouses, bookshops, the street parade of
dreamers with hope on their minds and the jingle of a few coins
in their pockets. Amid familiar rhythms, Upper Bohemia offers a
syncopated stroke of Strange.

McFadden's Law, named for Cyra McFadden, the San Francisco social history expert, is that any storefront with the words
"Karma" or ". . . A-Go-Go" on it also wears a For Sale sign. On
Washington Avenue the Studio A-Go-Go building was boarded
up, but I found nearby a thriving clean-air, vegetarian, women-
run café, Our Place, also selling its vegan recipes in *The How to
Overthrow Any Gov't without Violence Cookbook*. There's a photograph
of James Baldwin in the men's room. The founder and minister
of All-Veggie Meaning, Amani Ayers, was a friend of Jimmy's;
knew him, or maybe didn't (I asked twice).

On Collins at Fifth, the first all-natural bakery in south Florida
was founded in 1966, during that ancient moment of Aquarian
optimism which linked whole grains with the ending of war in
Vietnam. At Chow, "Big Healthy Food, indoor-outdoor cafeteria
dining," they are not pushy about politically correct eating. Sugar
has been known to occur in the desserts. Sweeping up to Collins
Avenue from Ocean Drive, two ravenous Swedish models were
engaging in a vigorous recreational tongue-lashing of their agencies and handlers while enjoying a yogurt, chocolate, and honey
power confection. The gravitational pull of time and chagrin had
not yet lowered their metabolisms. They were healthy young
women with world-class appetites, big eyes staring down the sidewalk oglers.

One evening at the Passport Café on Collins, which offers
books, magazines, and chatchkas in an atmosphere of beatnik
funk, a short block from the pastel and pink neon seaside boulevard, I met a young woman called Slim, a singer, dancer, model,
and seeker, sitting with her pita bread and salad, her glass of red
wine, her cigarette, and her copy of *Antenna*, countercultural bi-
weekly. She was nicknamed for Slim Keith, the much-married
beauty, Paris, London, and New York star of the prewar "lost
generation," who finished her life as a photographer. She was

giggling about a nasty dance review in *Antenna*, and then the Collins Avenue Slim invited me to her going-away party. After a lifetime in Miami Beach, she was moving to Milwaukee, where the people are said to be normal—that is, exotic.

I told her about Benjamin Two, a café in Milwaukee which served bagels, wine, and acoustic music to models, actors, photographers, and dropout artists, and her eyes glowed with disappointment. "Oh, *no!*" Surely Milwaukee wouldn't let her down by being another Bohemian colony.

LA JOLLA: "They Smile, They're Tanned, They Love the Arts."

My good buddy Jarod lives in a condo near the beach, races a motorcycle, runs barefoot on the sand every morning and then plunges into the salt before breakfast. Briefly he made his living as a radio call-in talkshow host. Now, although young for retirement, he has no job, due to the youth fanaticism of the media. His favorite song is Bob Dylan's "Forever Young."

Jarod has developed theories about living a long time; eternal life, in fact, thanks to a diet which mixes grains and nuts in proportions guaranteed to reverse the effects of cancer, heart disease, and memory loss. When I ate this morning's gruel, after a grueling workout, some nut or seed in the formula caused me to break out in orange blotches. I felt orange and green itching within.

"I'm allergic!" I cried, being a normal coddled citizen.

"Poor Herb," he said compassionately, "what poisons your body is riddled with. The poisons are coming out now."

Jarod supports life, culture, and theory in the little community of La Jolla, California, an upper-income district of San Diego. He nourishes it with the help of small trust funds from his father, his mother, plus a tiny one, hardly worth mentioning, from a maternal grandparent. (In her honor, the BMW motorcycle is named Granny.) La Jolla turns out to be both a place and a state of temper where an Upper Bohemian like Jarod can thrive in a friendly year-round climate for running, swimming, and theorizing. And he does so.

• • •

A typical La Jolla Upper Bohemian was Jack Vietor, General Foods heir, wine lover, writer, magazine publisher. As a very young man, he had been one of the few American volunteers for Franco. Then he fought in the U.S. Army, became a prisoner of the Germans, wrote a book about his adventures. It was a sporting time for him. He emerged from the war as a left-liberal bon vivant, ironic about his childish sympathy for fascism, which he never tried to hide. It had been one of life's jokes on a favored son. When someone mentioned the comedian Jack Benny, Jack Vietor said, "Oh yes, an employee of my Jell-O division." When his wife complained that all he had given her for Christmas was a terry-cloth bathrobe, he made up for it by adding a Rolls-Royce to her stocking (or maybe it was a Bentley parked outside their door).

Being taken to lunch by charming, debonair, handsome Jack was a costly experience. As an experienced heir, he carried credit cards but no money, so I paid for the valet parker, the lunch tip, the coat check, the newspaper, and the paperback books he picked up on the way. Noblesse n'oblige pas. Then he explained how I was actually being offered more money to write for *San Francisco* or *San Diego,* the city magazines he published, than for *Playboy*—*per reader.* To Smiling Jack this seemed logical. (His magazines were read by a few thousand, *Playboy* by a few million.) Also he offered to substitute free hotel space on Mallorca or Hawaii for money, since his advertisers tended to pay in travel chits. "But, Jack, I have children to support," I whined.

"Whose fault is that?" he asked.

If standard-issue Bohemia is layabout and live-off-the-land artistic, Upper Bohemia is the same, but with greater emphasis on style and patronage of the arts and a less revolutionary form of dropping away rather than dropping out. The Upper Bohemian likes to find an agreeable corner within reach of the family lawyer's offices. What the Hamptons and Woodstock are to New York, Mill Valley to San Francisco, Coconut Grove to Miami, the neighborhood of La Jolla has been to San Diego—a dramatic and pleasing terrain with enough eccentricity to raise agreeability to the highest power. There are drugs and music for the questers; molto money, with allegro spending of it. Upper Bohemia offers a comfort which the original scavengers and coughers, memorialized by Murger and Puccini, couldn't imagine singing about.

California, a place of fantasy, attracted Bohemians before the name existed. "Eureka, I Have Found It!" is the state motto. Seekers came for the dream of land, gold, freedom, escape. An early Spanish writer cried: "Know thee that on the right hand of the Indies there is an island called California, very near the Terrestrial Paradise"—just what the doctor ordered. California presented an ecology of expectation from the time Europeans first arrived, when a person could hardly take a step without walking on flowers. And the sundown sea dreamed beyond.

La Jolla (The Jewel) was once a straitlaced, conservative, moneyed neighborhood of a straitlaced San Diego. Contemplating the ocean, the climate, the vegetation, and the sunsets from the terrace of La Valencia Hotel were the prevalent art forms. La Jolla was, someone said, the perfect place for old people and their parents.

During the last generation, abetted by the University of California at San Diego, darker linings to this silver cloud appeared—a youthy surfer-doper underground and, sharing the terrain, an Upper Bohemia of the seekers. A gentleman with a rakish white goatee explained to me that his father forced him out of Swarthmore College and into the family business after World War II, but now he has retired to La Jolla to collect things. "And then I got tired of sunsets at the 'La,' so now I'm"—lowered his voice—"writing a book about a dysfunctional family held together by codependency. You've heard of that?"

In my wanderings I had heard of that.

He grinned. "If he were alive, he'd be a hundred and eleven years old. But Dad'd still be pissed off at how I'm spending the family money."

The man with the white goatee is delighted to be in his second Bohemian childhood.

When I pronounced the old-fashioned word *bohemian* in La Jolla, people looked puzzled. Me? Us? Upper *what?* So then I named a few examples of the species: Melissa Elliott, painter, organizer of sketching sessions; Robin Bright, artist, whose family befriended Frieda and D. H. Lawrence in New Mexico; Barbara Saltman, who runs the adventurous Gallery Eight; Dr. Seuss, high in his observation tower; the painter Wing Howard, who did the murals in the Whaling Bar of La Valencia Hotel more than forty years ago and was having a show of new work at La Valencia during my visit ("It's a civic ordinance that any house above a certain size has to have a Wing Howard painting"); one of his sons, Harrison, also a painter and another, a chef, part owner of Issimo, a local restaurant.

Nancy Sprague Rice, sculptor, spent time in Vence, France, writing and getting over a divorce. In La Jolla she studied with Carl Rogers, father of humanistic psychology. Her brother, Hall Sprague, is a filmmaker, musician, colleague of Richard Farson in the Western Behavioral Sciences Institute. Her nephew, Peter Sprague, is a notable jazz guitarist. She lives in a small apartment and does her sculpture and ceramics in a windowless shed in the garden. (She keeps the door open.) "It's heaven," she says. "I show a little, I sell a little, it's all I need. Never bored. Just go to my studio and be happy."

"Why here?"

"It's beautiful and there's a community of artists."

A former psychologist and special education expert, Pam Widden, has become an artist's model. Odile Crick, wife of Francis Crick (the double-helix man), is a painter. The Sushi Performance Gallery—"we do raw material"—presents performances by artists turned down for NEA grants; as devoted eclectics, they also present the work of grant holders. (Someone asked if I wanted to meet a kindly sexual activist who describes herself as "the easy-listenin' lesbian.") Bonnie Wright, graduate student in music at UC–San Diego, explained that she had raised her children, didn't plan to marry again soon, and retired from "the rag trade"—jobs with Levi Strauss and Esprit—to be a composer. Like so many of the women here, she is athletic, lithe, more than handsome, each one the fairest of them all.

This far corner of California used to be known for sea caves, Indian lore, good fishing, soft mountains. Thirty years ago, when I first visited a bookstore named for a mythological Greek animal, it was filled with browsers all in blond—blond hair, eyebrows, and teeth—practicing depth research in surfing and astrological manuals. They looked like fearsomely sexy monsters from the mythological deep of California. When I asked a clerk in cutoff jeans why Ernest Hemingway's *The Old Man and the Sea* was in the surfing section, he asked in return, as if we were playing riddles: "Some dudes still like to catch a wave?"

The style of making statements in the form of a question, with a rising inflection, seemed to begin among the seekers of California.

Good manners, gracious ladies, fast horses, and retired admirals formed the traditional image of La Jolla; plus golf, tennis, bridge, and right-wing politics. But why should old California have this lovely corner of America to itself? Rumor of sun and ocean got out, and so did the children, bringing back easy manners, adventurous flirtation, irregular dinner hours, and solid trust funds. The contemporary blend of upper class and Upper Bohemia is reinforced by the growth of a scientific and university community—UC–San Diego, the Claremont colleges, the Scripps Oceanographic Institute, the Salk Institute. The Greek-myth combination coffeehouse, bookshop, and art cinema has been replaced, probably by condos or office buildings, and those all-blond surfing gentlefolk are in middle age by now. Sea air and the cliffside irregularity of terrain attracts new tides of aesthetic refugees from Manhattan, Ibiza, and the Côte d'Azur.

My espresso complex of sentimental memory was named for the Unicorn. I remembered it as the Phoenix, another apocryphal creature, which has a habit of being born anew out of ashes. The now equivalent of ashes may be condo development.

The Unicorn-Phoenix has been reborn as D. G. Wills Books. I strolled over, directed by gracious Barbara Cole of John Cole's Bookshop, to find a kind of overgrown, irregular shack with a fiberglass roof. The store was locked—it was early morning—but in front of it there was an unprotected portico with bookshelves and piles of books on tables. Anyone could have walked away with them, or driven up and trucked them out. D. G. Wills seemed to be celebrating an ancient and nearly forgotten tradition of not shoplifting.

I knocked. No answer. I waited for Dennis Wills to appear. I wandered off to examine the psychedelic truck parked nearby, covered with mirrors, dolls, spangles, designs, slogans, keepsakes encrusted on every surface. A tearful JFK doll. A child slipping off its diaper beneath the words SMILE YOU'RE ON CANDID CAMERA. "Adam, it's Adam's truck," a passerby explained. "You can recognize him because he wears a World War Two German helmet. Oh, and he's black. If you say, 'Hey, Adam,' and he looks up and he's black, that's the artist with the truck. I think he lives in it."

I returned to D. G. Wills, knocked again, and like the genie out of the bottle, Dennis Wills appeared. I complained about the temptation to walk off with his books. He shrugged. "Wouldn't do you any good. Books grow like grass. I'd just get more."

And the dampness outside? These books get soggy, Dennis. He shrugged again, offered me a coffee, a cookie, a beer, a bit of heart-to-heart conversation.

The store looks like George Whitman's Shakespeare & Company in Paris, a minefield of used books, stoves, chairs, tables, browsers. Ralph Nader, Laura Huxley, Françoise Gilot speak during informal salon evenings. Gilot's studio space shares the building, which Dennis Wills has expanded by native bookseller-power. A former Russian expert for the air force and the National Security Agency, a student of philosophy at Oxford and Columbia, he decided he would rather be a Zen seeker than a CIA man. He's a bachelor in his forties who keeps the store open every day of the year except Mother's Day, when he closes to take his mother to lunch.

Besides Françoise Gilot, Richard Astle, a writer, and Karen Ulrich, a playwright, live here, along with passing and resident cats. We sat in the patio on a funky collection of chairs and discussed the ghosts of the cats buried here in the garden. Sometimes old surfers wander in, identifying themselves as characters from the Pump House Gang. There's a Café Pannikin—D. G.

Wills Axis. Warming my hands on a nice mug (actually, cooling my hands in the sunlight around a nice brew), I knew I had found Full Classic Bohemia in La Jolla.

Later, I sat in Pannikin over my coffee, reading the epic, cast-of-thousands novel which is the Personals pages of the San Diego *Reader,* from

> BEARDED BOHEMIAN, 35, very nice guy, financially secure, looking for bright, beautiful, bubbly lady to dream with, travel with . . .

to

> GORGEOUS BLONDE, seeks a man so good-looking it's scary. If he's successful and tall, I'm the reward.

until I came to:

> PUBLISHED AUTHOR with joie de vivre sought by petite blonde, 38, sophisticated, multilingual, well-travelled, unencumbered, sensitive, warm, affectionate, playful, communicative . . .

and wondered how she knew I was visiting La Jolla. I *meant* to call her, but got distracted by the après-rendezvous messages of all these lonely people: "LESLIE. I enjoyed last night. Et tu? B."

Pannikin, a coffeehouse like Arabica in my hometown of Cleveland, the Paris of northeastern Ohio, or the Picaro in San Francisco, or Lanciani's in Greenwich Village, uses espresso to bring together classes, generations, and life-styles for a community caffeine high. During my stay, Pannikin housed a show of the work of Harley Gaber, offering graphics labeled Surfing Is Harder Than You Think, and a large-lettered manifesto: I ALWAYS WANTED TO BE A FAMOUS MALE LESBIAN ARTIST.

I asked a fellow lingerer if the nearby Cove Theater shows art movies. "If you call French art," she said. "If you call Depar-doo art."

"Depardieu," I pronounced reflexively: "Cyrano de Bergerac."

"That's what I said. Foreign. Art."

Trying to keep the dialogue going, I asked who is really special in the community besides, oh, Dr. Seuss (now gone) and Jonas Salk. "The Torrey Pines," she answered. "And his wife, the former Mrs. Picasso."

The Torrey Pines are not a family but a rare tree, unique to the area. Françoise Gilot, painter, writer of famous memoirs of Picasso, now married to Dr. Salk, works in that studio above D. G. Wills's year-round bookstore and salon.

As the day passed, Pannikin played host to tattooed teenies, ACT-UP AIDS activists, university profs and students, scribblers in notebooks, readers of books, correctors of music sheets, surfers, backpackers. I met Barbara Zobel here, social patron, model, collector, organizer, and a great beauty. I met Richard Farson, whose Western Behavioral Sciences Institute has been involved in projects ranging from the future of education to the liberation of children. I met his former wife, Dawn Farson—another of the astonishing beauties who are more prevalent than the Torrey Pines in this beneficient climate. She is working on a book about the problems of being a Second Wife. I met a former high-ranking U.S. Navy officer who now carries an Irish passport "because Ireland is a generation behind in the devolution of mass society." I met a young man who was organizing the minority at UC–San Diego which was in favor of the U.S. intervention in the Persian Gulf.

I met Katherine Relf, who gave me a copy of her instant book, *My First Book of Political Animals,* which she desktop-printed in nine copies to oppose the war. She used illustrations from a children's book she bought at Von's supermarket. "Appropriation is my theme," she explained.

She's a writer, softwear designer, and a protester. Her parents are Republicans, she said. Her name is Welsh, but her spirit is Californian.

Hidden in the alley behind Pannikin is Projects, an "art space" which brings Polish, British, Hungarian, Romanian artists to live and work in La Jolla. It's not a gallery, it's not a museum, it's something fanatically else. When I knocked at the door on a

Saturday afternoon, the shades were drawn and the door was locked. But Michael Krichman opened. He was sitting on the floor surrounded by photographs. He let me talk myself in.

Along with his partner, Mark Quint, they choose to do their thing here in La Jolla for a sensible reason—"because we can." Warehouses, spaces, artists, resources are available, "plus good weather. Right now we're bringing artists from Eastern Europe. They experience La Jolla and we experience them."

La Jolla doesn't resemble your red-checked-tablecloth, spaghetti, candle-in-wine-bottle traditional Bohemia, nor is it a standard-issue California grass-and-Jung New Age driftaway resort. There is lots of recreational equipment, Ralph Lauren and Victoria's Secret personal decor. Golf is not a four-letter word, though it has only four letters. In some ways La Jolla is a teenage art dropout's nightmare: a place of *adult* teenage dropouts. These grownups, marking out a portion of blitheness as their due, stake a claim to the freedom of youth with an unanswerable argument: *Why not?*

The Pump House Gang, described by Tom Wolfe more than a quarter of a century ago, still exists. Many of those young wave-riders are now middle-aged weekend surfers with responsible inside jobs. There are second- and third-generation Pump-housers. The Surfing of America didn't quite happen, any more than the Greening did, but a Beach Boy golden oldie tradition carries on. Windansea Beach, once world headquarters for Southern California dropout youth—beer, waves, rock music, and not caring very much—considered the rest of the world to be composed mainly of dorks. Some of the original Pump-housers still drop by after hours as teachers, real estate salespeople, parents, the dork professions. The beach Bohemia hangs in there, firm in its time warp, although communal living and group marriage seem to have been a failed experiment, like LSD.

When I shambled onto the rocks, feeling like Richard Nixon, dorklike among all these tanned beach creatures, I noticed a carved butcher-sculpture totem, an Old Man of the Sea, standing on the deck of a nearby house, staring at the riders wailing down their waves. "What's that?" I asked a young man.

Saint Christopher? Neptune? Some ocean deity?

In his rubber wet suit, toting his board, the young man squinted into the light, trying to be helpful. "I think it's called Tom Wolfe."

I think it's called the generation gap. An ecologically aware woman with a house on the beach—deck, barbecue, telescope facing out toward Tahiti and Bali—thought she had found the solution to her generational pest problems. She projected baroque music out across the sands to drive away a crew of dope-smoking heavy-metal surfers. Rueful results. Like garlic and camel urine against snails or aphids, Bach and Vivaldi brought only partial success. It attracted a ragged crew of dope-smoking middle-aged ancient-instrument surfers, including one who knocked on her redwood door and said, "Hey lady, this gets to be a drag. What about a little Guillaume de Machaut for variety sometimes?"

He was studying composition. His hair was long and sun-bleached, receding rapidly at the temples but advancing onto the shoulders; his thighs were sinewy, his suit was rubber, and his musical preference was either Philip Glass or post-Gregorian intervals and variations. "The waves give me the rhythm, man, but I graduated years ago from the Beach Boys and Windham Hill. New Age gets old pretty fast, ma'am."

Like the rain forest, La Jolla has been attacked by nefarious powers. According to William Murray, novelist and horse hand-icapper—he manages to combine these two metiers by writing about the world of the track—boom times eroded its spirit. Once going its separate way, La Jolla has been attached to San Diego by the glue of development. Funky cafés, art theaters, bookstores and galleries—"but not enough of them"—can still be found in Hillcrest, the gay district of San Diego, or in Del Mar, a community where some artists still find cheaper if not cheap enough loft and garage space.

The movable feast is under pressure to move. "Bohemia is fragmented," says the distinguished novelist/horse handicapper. "You find hangouts here and there, and on the campuses."

The danger is that an Upper Bohemia like La Jolla—a Carmel

of the south, a Hamptons of the west—might become a fun ghetto, a mere taste museum, a pleasure workout studio. Alexandra Whitney, a prize-winning sculptor, doing mainly portraits in bronze, makes a nice distinction about the La Jolla where she grew up—"artsy rather than Bohemian." The La Jolla Museum of Contemporary Art has small but important collections in the pop, minimalist, and conceptual areas—Edward Ruscha, Andy Warhol, Frank Stella, that group. From not too many other art museums can you also observe both whale migration and aboriginal beachperson surfers. (The beach at nearby Encinitas, below the Self-Realization Fellowship Temple, is called Swami's.) The Athenaeum Music & Arts Library, supported by the well-born and well-financed traditional community, plays host to jazz, pop, and classical musicians, shows local artists, lends out music and art books. But for Axie Whitney, whose father owned La Valencia Hotel, "It's a *small* community." She now lives in New York City, a larger community, not defined by blessings of climate, beach, sun, and old California money.

"Artsy" seems to mean amateur or unserious. Researchers at the Salk Institute don't qualify as dilettantes. Françoise Gilot, aka Mrs. Jonas Salk, has plenty to write her memoirs about, having done a tour of duty as wife and distressed spouse-equivalent to Picasso. In the community, she joined Yen Lu Wong, a choreographer, to collaborate on outdoor art performances and installations. A member of their group says that Ms. Wong, who lived for a time in adjacent Del Mar, "was interested in exploring humanistic spiritual concerns and ceremonies. But then she moved to L.A."

Moving to L.A. seemed to interfere with humanistic spiritual ceremonies and concerns.

Of the making of Bohemias there is no end; the Upper Bohemia typified by La Jolla is an extreme outcropping in the Bohemian archipelago. These dropaways, nourishing themselves with art and fantasy, are far from economic rejects. They have made a choice to strew flowers in the way of history and to place a few

petals on their own pillows, too. They are less interested in shock-
ing the middle class than in exercising the prerogatives of privilege. A hundred years ago Gelett Burgess's map of Bohemia
depicted provinces of Peace, Truth, Youth, Vagabondage, and
ports on the Sea of Dreams. Enemy nations, such as Sham and
Vanity, surrounded the happy kingdom. Generally art students,
would-bees, dropouts, gypsies, and, more recently, beatniks, hippies, punkers, occupy the front lines, but there have always been
gracious and wellborn charmers who opted only a little way out.
They retired early with their inheritances, or exasperated families
decided to support the errant branch, since they couldn't be
hustled off into the army, navy, or the Church. In La Jolla and
environs, they choose a sweeter order of life, somewhat this side
of disorder. A person can be just as melancholy with nice things,
can't he or she? Does grief require discomfort? They can pass with
deep feeling through this vale of yearning and still afford the best
miracle hair-care products.

One of my informants, reached by phone at bedtime, giggled,
"I've had a bottle of champagne—very good champagne, by the
way. You *know* what the bubbly does to me. I'll have to call you
back."

But very responsible, she did so, early the next morning, around
noontime.

Bohemianism offers eternal childhood and potentiality, a waiting around for the perfect lover. It promises a kind of antideath
in the form of changeless sitting over wine, coffee, or the tabula
rasa; a paradise, a purgatory—there is no hell in this universe. Or
if there is, it's one for strutting in, a Roseland Ballroom in eternity.

The layabout Bohemian may enter with pouting self-indulgence, believing that his impulses are to be gratified as soon as
possible by whatever means available. And then gradually he/she
lowers his/her standards. This is not the same procedure taken by
the idealistic Bohemian, who aims at nothing less than the pla-
tonic ideal of truth and beauty, contemptuous of those who settle
for what is merely attainable. The despairing idealists agree to
settle for divinity. And then gradually they raise their standards.

The several factions meet for discussion while an audience

listens and (they hope) pays the check. These are folks who like going to bed with a good book, especially if they can read it along with a warmhearted companion. They once wrote a good book, or if they didn't, that's a mere detail. They intend to. They are open to redefining what they mean by the blessed things of life. They like nature, such low-tech sports as fishing, but prefer to come up with poached salmon.

What borrowing, stealing, and light living were to the poor Bohemians of *la vie de bohème* in Paris, trust funds and tax-free bonds are to their cousins in Coconut Grove or La Jolla. Just because they call to Romeo and Juliet from a redwood deck doesn't mean they don't Suffer. They have souls to nurture; they are seekers.

The redwood and mission Bohemia of La Jolla, at the intersections of Remittance and Dropout, provides a congenial ground for drastic eccentrics in a distant corner of the U.S., about as far to the southwest as you can go without sliding into Mexico or the ocean. Psychologically and spiritually, there is an element of isolation; geographically, it is special. The Upper Bohemians of this part of San Diego County are free to be wastrels or geniuses, pleasure-seekers, time-passers, or even, if it happens, original thinkers.

Joseph Diliberti used to be a successful home builder and contractor. He's still a home builder, but the home he has built in eastern San Diego County is a ceramic dome house, made of clay, straw, and water, cooled by a series of what he calls wind chimneys. It resembles a warm-climate igloo. Recycled bottles and broken glass are transformed into light-gatherers and view-seekers, what the ordinary world of the military-industrial-commercial complex might name windows.

He cooks in a stone pit outside, draws water from a well, and fishes or tends his garden for food. He also grows his own dreadlocks. He plays the flute. With a group of friends he hopes to create an experimental village in which bread, electricity, education, art, and philosophy are communally generated. As part of this environment of simplification, he has already dropped his last name. Just call him Joseph.

He is not a childish hippie communard. A wanderer, a veteran of Vietnam, he arrived in middle life at a decision to go to the margin of society, but to go there productively, creatively. He is willing to accept ridicule; he fights back. He is not dragging along the careworn paths of mandala-worship and inner-life questing. Joseph's hands are work-worn.

The Protocols of the Elders of Bohemia include certain regulations: a vastness of expectation, an earnestness of frivolity, a ferocious concentration on style (sometimes expressed as antistyle), eccentricity, pleasure. The Bohemian masses exist in the aura of those few leaders who actually originate music, fine art, literature, fashion, or, as in the case of Joseph Diliberti, architecture and community. The would-bees take their honey from the flowers of creation.

10

California Nation—``Eureka! I Found the Water''

In 1960 I met a young Frenchwoman who had floated from Paris to North Beach in pursuit of the real America—Jack Kerouac, Dean Moriarty, and the father of our country, Kenneth Patchen. She was learning her English on Upper Grant in San Francisco. When I asked what she was doing here, she answered: "Digging ze scene."

Recently the daughter of an old friend, departing the crass and wicked east (Baltimore) for a career in the truth and beauty pastures, intended a crash entry into the tradition. She telephoned to ask where she, her boyfriend, and their surplus U.S. mail truck—they had prepared for the life of risk by learning to use a stick shift—could find a congenial world of fellow artists. I suggested Mendocino—art center, nature walks, resident writers, filmmakers, printmakers, and community activists. "Is it a really artistic place?" she asked.

"Well, it's on the sea."

"What sea is that?"

"The Pacific Ocean."

"Oh yeah, I read about it in geography. Is it spiritual?"

"Pardon?"

"Is it a really spiritual place?"

And so she and her seeker spouse-equivalent sailed out in their truck filled with art supplies. "You're right!" she called (collect) to inform me. "I've been accepted! I have dozens of friends! This is home!"

She had put down roots in Mendocino for six days. But now she's in Bolinas, where the sixties energy is high and it's correct spiritually, besides. "I've got a new boyfriend. We're living in an Indian igloo."

"Do you mean tepee?"

"Right! Far-out! You've heard of it!"

Bolinas was the place, as it is for many who want a corner of Bohemia to the max. As in a beehive, there are those who gather the honey—writers, artists, craftsfolks—and those who make nuptial flights or guard the portals with a low warning group roar. The seeker from Baltimore came with a dream. She has found a cozy hotbed of attitude.

Within the vortex of Dropout, Flower Child, Artist, and Flake can be found that tanned and relaxed, sometimes pale and twitchy phenomenon, the California Bohemian. Eureka, he/she reinvents the Golden State's version of a tribal rite, Discovering the Self. Some do it by practicing a discipline in congenial surroundings, working hard at what the world calls play, childish things like putting paint to canvas or walls, elaborating paradoxes and expressing griefs, telling a version of time through the recombinating of musical notes. Some join the herd of independent minds.

That telephone call from the young woman in Baltimore asked for information not found in the *Mobil Travel Guide*. Most noticed during the sixties, people are still going through what a French psychologist has called "the crisis of juvenile originality."

It's hard to tell during the teen years who is crazy, who is talented, who is questing and who merely lazy, who is creating. Often these rebels are many different things. Like Walt Whitman, they contain multitudes.

Animals don't go through a turbulent adolescence. The animal which has the longest childhood is the human. During that period of doubt, learning, and separation from family, an extended growing up, adolescents break patterns in both the psychopathic and the renewing ways. The Bohemian sometimes decides to extend his juvenile questing all his life long, wearing funny clothes, adopting strange anthems and theories, gathering to debate the end of history and the age of science fiction, drinking too much espresso. And the rest of us, to our surprise, learn from them—take on some of their clothes and manners, listen to their music, read their poems. We follow their bliss.

California is dotted with Bohemian encampments, country and city, mountain and seaside, even in the dense agricultural central valleys, so that recruits to the life of art and metaphysical seeking needn't follow their lonely bliss without company. For those who want Upper Bohemia, there are La Jolla, Mill Valley or Sausalito, the canyons and beach communities of Los Angeles. For those who need urban grit and cheap eats amid the lower depths, it's the Mission District of San Francisco, successor to the North Beach of the beats, the Haight of the hippies; or the Sunset Strip, Silverlake, and Hollywood districts of L.A.; or a bit of Del Mar for San Diego. For the San Jose area, Santa Cruz is not too far, where university, psychedelic, and dropout Bohemias intersect on the earthquake-damaged mall. Every California university has its college-town edges, all-night cafés where bleary exam-crammers can meet bikers, clubs for the most recent musical treats, rap or heavy metal, jazz or folk-rock revival. In Davis a permanent floating writing seminar used to meet after midnight in the twenty-four-hour Denny's, sometimes greeting rosy-fingered dawn with projects for publishing an honest magazine.

For California Bohemia Classic, the world thinks Berkeley, of course. But there are communes in the Sierras, group houses in Eureka, veteran seekers encamped in the gentrifying old towns of Sacramento and the gold-rush settlements. Marijuana country, Humboldt and the Russian River, shelter retired journalists or advertising wordslaves finally writing that novel. Truckee is hospitable to flower ski addicts; I know a young woman who house-sits in winter while she quilts and occasionally works phone reservations for gambling resorts across the border in Nevada. I met her while hiking one summer. She was living in a tepee, picking berries, digging holes for waste purposes (ecologically careful: a circle around her tepee, seven holes, one shitter for each day of the week, so that the ground water wouldn't be polluted.) This was her summer practice because she liked the out-of-doors, Mountain Zen, only heading down to Squaw Valley in her blue VW bug for occasional bouts of shopping (Walgreens Zen). When she finally got hepatitis, she said it was due to cloudy karma, using sunscreen made from lanolin. "Lamolin comes from *lambs.*" Had they but told me.

Lambs with those cute faces which gradually become sheepish. Squeezed and exploited by the military-industrial complex to produce sunscreen for the bourgeoisie.

I suggested that hepatitis might come from drinking from the Tahoe area streams.

Her face, already more yellow than her hair, darkened with reproach. "You don't know me very well, do you?"

"What person ever knows another?" I admitted. Although I had stumbled into her camp when she was cooking her rice and beans (no faces) naked over an oven pit she had dug beneath the pines, naked didn't mean I really knew her. A Dolores who calls herself Solar Luna because it was revealed to her that Dolores means sad—a stone karmic bringdown—is essentially a woman of mystery. Rice and beans have no faces because they are probably not animals.

Whatever the top shaman of Squaw Valley might have told her about her hepatitis, she seemed unclear on the concept of viruses.

"I've been to college, two years at Sac State. Don't patronize me, Herb."

I brought her plenty of bottled water.

A Bohemian census map of California, country and city, town and university—the houseboat communities of Sausalito, the beach nymphs, mountain trolls, and forest druids, the sexual-freedom bands of the Castro, West Hollywood, and the gay neighborhoods of every city—would show California thickly settled by adopted gypsy converts. We are seekers of peace and crusaders (I include myself in this immigration). The forever- springtime climate of much of the state, a persistent habit of hope, an acceptance of change, the checkerboard map of settled communities with hidden corners and new lands with no defined tradition has given Bohemia the chance to conquer. Those who have forgotten history are condemned to repeat it?

Not here. Not in California. And it was a dead white European male who said that stuff about history.

For the Bohemian hordes of the Golden State, history lies ahead; we'll capture it by brute optimism. I can go in for wind-surfing or eccentric punctuation and the universe is open. If my drumming doesn't get me into a decent band, at least I can discover my inner child. (The kid emerges with his hands over his ears, hearing loss due to amplified self-definition.)

Sometimes motorcycles, male earrings, and the smell of grass are part of the decor. There's a proletarian Bohemianism—laid-off aircraft workers with soul, cops and firepersons with notebooks for private jottings—and a senior-citizen division of Gray Panther activists, thrift shoppers, nongolfers who hike and hostel. Each small settlement of the hot, dry, irrigated farming valleys has its hangout bar or café where the local eccentrics come to wile away the century.

Bohemia made noise in the sixties—the flowering of rock music, the youth-culture vibrancy, a whole lot of revolutions shaking. ("I'm not puttin' down the Vietnam war," said a Berkeley free-speech crusader I later met in the Haight. "After all, it brought us together so we could all smoke dope.") It's quieter now. The thirtysome hippies are fortysome, fiftysome; yuppie mania is discouraged by economic facts; grace and meditation turn out to be ecologically sound and energy efficient. A lovely story has crept up on us—*Bohemia everywhere in California*—although like every story not invented by dolphins, we manage to live it out imperfectly. That's part of the human deal.

Often the new workaday Bohemia seems to be backed up, like a movie story, by a musical score. Muzak is for malls, unhip dentists' offices, but your Transformational Bohemians prefer New Age, George Winston, Windham Hill emotion-enhancing. That's cool. For hotter folks, there are the heirs of the Talking Heads, punk and heavy metal, or chirping Japanese electronic sound environments. In these times the rebellious life doesn't just have a sound track; it often seems to *be* a sound track.

. . .

In the early sixties I had a friend who left New York, where his career as Greenwich Village Explainer was going poorly, to resettle in a Bohemian encampment upslope from the Sunset Strip in Los Angeles. Bernard Wolfe was a good writer fallen upon difficult times. He had introduced the word *hipster* to literature in his novel *The Late Risers*, about those who occupied the night of Manhattan; he had ghostwritten Billy Rose's newspaper column, composed pornography at a dollar a page for private collectors, counseled such contemporaries as Saul Bellow and Ralph Ellison in the meaning of things in general, befriended Henry Miller, collaborated on one of the best books about jazz, *Really the Blues*, which was published as the memories of Mezz Mezzrow, written highly praised science fiction, and barely eked out cigar and ethnic-food money by charming millionaires. He had run through his millionaires, broken a love affair, piled up debts, and translated himself to Los Angeles, bearing all his day-sleeping wisdom with him.

I learned from Bernie some of the secrets of the universe, such as that the price of cigars is like currency, exactly calibrated to value, and that fine dining can be provided by going to the cheapest nationality restaurant within walking distance but ordering the most expensive item on the menu. Bernie, who had worked one summer as a bodyguard to Leon Trotsky in Mexico, was mentor to a generation of prebeatnik Sheridan Square artists.

So now there he was transported to Horn Avenue, scratching his gray chest hairs alongside a greenish pool shared with refugees from the Other Coast, charming movie moguls, talking stories, drumming up a few assignments. None of his movies was ever made, but he survived. Among Sunset Strip writers, actors, directors, fresh would-bees crazed with ambition and veteran hope addicts just as crazed, he continued Greenwich Village by other means. Hope never died. Whether or not the Horn Avenue radicals did actually bivouac with Fidel in the Sierra Maestra, as some of them thought they remembered, Bernie actually did spend a vacation from Yale with Trotsky in Mexico. (His novel *The Great*

Prince Died came out of the experience.) Most of the flicker Bohemians around the Horn Avenue pad lived on more ephemeral credentials, such as once lighting a joint for Marlon Brando's sister at a party. ("Very talented actress. Liked a treatment I told her, said she'd tell her brother. It's perfect for Marl.")

In the great tradition, even Bernie's imaginary credentials were real. Once, in Cyrano's—a Greenwich Village coffeehouse transplant on the Sunset Strip—a producer eavesdropped as he talked his way through one of his adventures. The producer bought the story on the spot as Bernie scribbled out a summary on a sheet of paper. At the bottom of the page he inscribed, "I hereby surrender all rights," and signed with a flourish. He created fun. He didn't thrive, yet he lived grandly. I invited him to a party in San Francisco for publication of a novel and he didn't have airfare for the trip, so he persuaded David Jannsen—a television star of the period—to fly him up in his private plane.

That's the Bohemian in action. (What's your favorite wine? "Other people's.")

At Cyrano's, the Greenwich Village exiles—actors, directors, and writers—gathered along with those who liked to watch them gather. "Hollywood" needed its Bohemian coffeehouse—oranges, smog, and money left a few traditional hungers. The rites of public search and brooding over the private truths required this stage. A film producer, driving a wooden sports car, often dropped by because he liked a little snack before bed and liked to pick up the young women ("girls") in black stockings, black turtlenecks, the Juliette Gréco look which still defined Bohemia before the psychedelic rainbow came into fashion. The sort of set designer who never bought the six-pack of Coke, only one bottle at a time, because he was going back to New York any day now. The sort of actor who only wanted to do plays at La Mama or gritty live television in Manhattan but owed it to himself to look things over on "the Coast." A few beaver-eyed teenagers with the haunted look of seventeen-year-olds afflicted with existential philosophy and raging hormones.

Instead of reciting "Angst, anomie, existential despair, the death of God, if not now, when?"—the tunes I used to hear when

I sneaked in for lectures at the New School on West Twelfth Street in the Village—the mantra at Cyrano's seemed to be more on the order of: "Cinema Verité, hand-held camera, good career move. If Cassavetes, why not me?"

What amazed me then, amazes me still, is the indomitable dream. In other Bohemias, would-bees can secrete their air castles out of mere genius, money not required. In the movies, even to conceive of shooting your loop, filling your reel, takes piles of cash.

A young director spent two years completing a feature from a story of mine, using borrowed money, credit cards, actors he knew, film processors whom he sweet-talked into giving credit. He lived in a basement whose window revealed only the feet of passersby outside. He sold 150 percent of the film in return for supplies and services. It would be nice to say he revolutionized the industry, but he turned out not to be Spike Lee or John Cassavetes. His only print was destroyed in a fire. He still lives the dream.

Briefly I fell in love with an actress who seemed to be working as a star of stage, screen, and television until she could find a secure job as a hair stylist. When I asked what she wanted to do after dinner, she said, "Go shopping?" I bought her a copy of *Under Milk Wood* and she moved on to the producer with the wooden sports car. He was clearer than I was on the concept of shopping.

Once, sitting at an outdoor table at Cyrano's with James Baldwin, who had been brought to "the Coast" to work on a script for Marlon Brando, we watched a banker from the Happy Mortgage Savings & Loan across the street do a double take. The famous black writer! Oh my! And he hustled off to a nearby bookstore, returning with a bagful of James Baldwin's books, asking politely, "Mr. Baldwin, would you endorse these books, please?"

Jimmy graciously signed. I asked if he had written "For deposit only," and he said, "He should have bought your books, too, Herb. How rude."

Where Cyrano's used to be now stands a Tower Records. But when archaeologists explore this corner in the future, they may find the shards of forgotten Bohemian ancestors—roach clips, a Capezio shoe, and a copy of *Under Milk Wood,* by Dylan Thomas.

During the flower-child period, the Sunset Strip became a focus for hippie Bohemia's Aquarian victory parade. L.A. rock music, L.A. drugs, and L.A. nervousness needed a place where people could congregate without cars and freeway. You could settle near the Strip, eat, dwell, *share*—it became a neighborhood. The Source, a commune-sponsored restaurant, served vegetarian, zeitgeist-correct food. Lenny Bruce performed in a jazz spot which later became the Playboy Club and is now merely a real estate speculation box. Other L.A. neighborhoods, the Silver Lake district and West Los Angeles, got the idea. Westwood, with its UCLA connection and proximity to the canyon dwellers of Beverly Hills, developed the upscale inland version; Venice and Malibu took care of downscale and upscale by the beach. It became possible to move without wheels in Beverly Hills, feets doing their work, without being arrested for open pedestrian behavior.

The beaver-eyed groupies, who did not yet have that name, staring at the celebrities in the cafés of the Strip, hoping to be discovered, were delicate and unworn, with faces unmarked by yelling at babies and arms that had not put up with the whacking of offspring, the toting of laundry. Their blessed innocence broke the hearts of the middle-aged men who took the trip to Cyrano's as the Bronx bagel babies and the Harlem A-Trainers took the trip into Greenwich Village in the late fifties, early sixties, trolling in the Limelight, the San Remo, the Figaro, the Five Spot, the Cedar Tavern. The times were a-yearning; it was the driving urge of the post-Eisenhower cosmic shift.

The meeting of imported and native California Bohemianism warmed the city which seemed to be America's first experimental space station on earth. While it's easy to name the excesses of Bohemian nesting and swarming, the facts on the ground are these: street life; people saying phrases to other folks who speak phrases in return; galleries, studios, live music, discussions; eccentric works of imagination and compassion; dreams uttered aloud. Bohemian community made Malibu more than a place for surfing, dope smoking, and the depth analysis of bikinis. L.A. became something very like a city in a way it needed to be. Those are still the facts on the ground.

Now when I travel to Los Angeles in search of my Bohemian roots, I find the café called Hugo's in West Hollywood—spiritual heir to Cyrano's—where "industry" hopefuls gather to exchange news of auditions, options, theater stopgaps, and the rainbows they glimpse in the sky. On my first visit, I happened to meet Andrea Marcovicci, shuffling sheet music at the next table, who spoke of a dream of reviving the grand old songs in supper clubs; and then proceeded to do so, employing the gifts God gave her— sweet voice, long neck, and glittering intensity—as God intended them to be employed. In Venice, a few old-time hangout bars and cafés still hang on as the canals gentrify amid sushi and trendiness. A community art center imports poets for readings; neighborhood poets appear at open-mike events. Mental defect is neither a qualification nor a barrier to acceptance among Bohemian communities at their extremity in places like Bolinas, Venice, and the Mission District of San Francisco. People try to remain neutral on the virtues and defects of madness; they take it under consideration on a kind of free-trial examination basis. As a Venice street poet asked me, "Why be a slave to the military-industrial complex when you can get Aid to the Fundamentally Disabled?"

Those organized enough to apply for and cash their welfare checks have found an arts subsidy Senator Helms doesn't directly threaten. But when the street poet asked, "Can you spare a dollar for self-empowerment?" I realized he was not so pure a soul as I had hoped; wracked by ambition, like any other entrepreneurial American.

To the next passerby he said, "I never have sex anymore. This is the nineties. I'm trying to preserve the sanctity of my horniness. Would you care to . . .?" And went into his pitch for empowerment; amazingly, the visitors hung around long enough to reward him for his speech.

Cyrano's is gone, and the apartment complex where Bernard Wolfe and other struggling writer/actor/director/hooker sorts came to settle down temporarily is occupied by a different group:

call girls/script doctors/performance artists/rock musicians. History moves sideways, like a crab. Book Soup on Sunset serves Sunset Strip survivers, cave dwellers dug in like remnants of the Imperial Japanese Army on conquered South Pacific islands, and the film moguls and mogulettes searching for the magic property which is hot, offbeat, and not yet optioned, hoping to jump-start a career or a weekend, whichever has priority.

At Hugo's, a few miles away, I find something which is a cousin of Le Petit Café, the Trieste, or the Picaro in San Francisco. The Source, the commune-run restaurant, now semivegetarian (you have to consider fish a vegetable), still exists, but the spacey New Age communal waitresses have been replaced by noncommunal 1990s versions of the same. Proprietorship is no longer in the hands of God. An East Indian now owns the place.

The last time I asked a waitress, she answered, "Uh, from Punjab? But I think he's got a screenplay he's trying to peddle."

He qualifies.

If there is a Bohemian field command post in California, it is Bolinas, located on the unmarked road which runs between Dream and Megalomania. More specifically, it's on a road just north of Stinson Beach, and the reason the road is unmarked is that the settlers want no tourists or realtors to find their way here. Even Dogtown, Population 6, just before Bolinas, tends to lose its road marking, which was installed by a resident who had found the name on an old map of gold-rush California.

Capital of poets, artists, dropouts, sixties hippies, and feral yuppies, Bolinas is leavened by a few senior fifties beatniks. When I used to visit regularly, the poets-musicians David and Tina Meltzer and their family, the writer Richard Brautigan, who shot himself there, the writer Aram Saroyan and his family, and a doctor who dropped out but was known to be a pretty good doctor if you got sick before noon were pillars of the community. I watched Joanne Kyger, poet, author of *Just Space,* former wife of Gary Snyder, mow the lawn in front of her cottage, brushing wisps of blond hair away from her lovely aquiline face; hair tickles.

My relationship to Bolinas, like that of all noncitizens, is troubled by an exclusionary policy—sort of like Saudi Arabia and carousers. When I've written about the community, I've received death threats; magazines printing the forbidden word *Bolinas* receive denunciations from the local ayatollahs. Once, after a particularly virulent campaign, I was strolling across a meadow when I met Gerard Malanga, Warhol artiste, occasional actor, model, and poet, who cried, "Oh, you're not supposed to be here. Go home!"

"I'm here," I said.

"It's dangerous for you!"

"Well, here I am."

He looked puzzled. "I may have to tell people," he said.

"Do your duty, Gerard."

And I strode down Main Street, feeling like Gary Cooper. It was High Noon in Aquariusland. The seagulls whirled, wheeled, said caw-caw. There were no doves or owls. I felt eyes watching from behind the curtains at Smiley's and Snarly's.

In the tradition, it was considered right, proper, and organic to live off the land. As in Henri Murger's Paris, housing and heating problems were resolved by *déménagement par la cheminée*. The artist stopped paying rent; ducking eviction, burned the furniture for heat; then quietly departed in the dark of the night, casting grateful gazes over his shoulder at the blessed sliver of moonglow. The French phrase back there can be translated as "moving through the chimney."

The ferocious place-pride of Bolinas, originally a Portuguese fishing settlement, takes a more aggressive posture. The baroque doctor, increasingly groovy as the afternoon wore on, speculating about developing hypodermic needles made of redwood, harkens back to a tradition of otherworldly fancy. A Bolinas single mother asked if I ever tried cooking without clothes on; that's how she keeps the vitamins, enzymes, and great spirits intact. I urged her not to fry pork chops in the nude.

In the afternoons there is often a community meditation at a spring in the meadow. Peace, Om, far-out, share my serape, and keep the zoning laws strict. If you're from elsewhere, you can be stalked by haggard sixties thought-police who resemble the Saudi officials who searched through my books, sniffed my glass for a hint of rum, when my flight landed at Riyadh Airport: "Scamper. Move. Get out of town."

This embattled outpost is less Bohemian in the classic sense, more tribal dropout, despite a roster of genuine artists, poets and writers, motorcycle metaphysicians, café and bar pataphysicians, adherents of the Rhinocerus party. It's a classic holy place for the fellowship of revolutionary anarchists. Validated by village intimacy, they are mellow and they are rabid about it. They've got something good going. Naturally they want to keep it for themselves.

Traditional Bohemians seem to thrive on cities and city connections, building their encampments in the low-rent parts of town, developing a congenial neighborhood until the middle class notices and drives up the price of hearty eating and lodging with bicycles in the halls. A little city chaos gives an edge to things. Geniality is not the business of Bolinas, this sweet promontory of California, facing the ocean, playing in the sand and making the revolution.

One of the most un-Bohemian of California places is the Bohemian Club and the Bohemian Grove encampment, that redwood spread on the Russian River where such dainty artistes as Richard Nixon, William Buckley, David Rockefeller, and Gerald Ford come out to play amid fireside conviviality. "The Greatest Men's Party on Earth" is famous for national leaders pissing on trees and throwing off marital traces, plus campfire singing and harangues from Henry Kissinger, who used to be *the* Henry Kissinger. Originally, of course, about a hundred years ago, the club included actual writers and artists who gathered to exchange ideas and drink too much. "Weaving Spiders Come Not Here" remains the motto, although who is to stop, say, the various Bechtels from making a few useful contacts?

When I was invited as a guest at the Bohemian Club in San Francisco, along with Ernest Gaines, author of *The Autobiography of*

Miss Jane Pittman, we drank cognac, inhaled cigar smoke (*good* cigar smoke) and listened to a quartet of insurance company vice presidents sing "Up a Lazy River" in Mills Brothers blackface. A famous industrialist punched Gaines on the shoulder and said, "Hey boy, bet you played football in college, am I right?" I said to our host, "I don't think we're true Bohemians," and Ernest Gaines and I retreated for a pensive nightcap elsewhere. Not Clubable seemed to be our consensus.

Bohemian and *artist* are fuzzy words at all the edges. Take the case of Daniel Ramos, who grew up in the projects of L.A. He liked to write "Chaka" in fat, looping letters, taller than he is, on walls, traffic poles, railway cars, any surface he could find; and when arrested, he was accused of doing half a million dollars of damage as he practiced his art up and down the state from Orange County to San Francisco. Back when, in those distant days of radical chic, Norman Mailer wrote a book entitled *The Faith of Graffiti.* Some of us accept the witty or political scrawls on bathroom walls as a form of literature; spray-can markings on buses and buildings no longer look like folk art, partly because we want to make public decisions about public places without being bullied. Should Mr. Ramos be rewarded by county jail for his creative expression or does he belong in the honored line of superior creatures who mark the world with disturbing revelations?

Recently, a visiting German publisher and I came upon a graffiti artist performing his message on a storefront. The publisher, an outspoken woman, cried: "You stupid! Dirty your own front door!"

The artist and his companion, who functioned as the police and critic lookout, approached us, saying, "So we're going to knock you down. But since you're a woman and we're gentlemen, we're only going to punch out that dude."

"That dude" equaled me.

"You stupid, zat dude not say anyzing," cried the German lady.

In the confusions of chivalry, the two artists stared at each other. They took their spray cans and their skateboards and sailed away in graceful swoops to combat the bourgeois world elsewhere.

Even Vincent Van Gogh, who shaved off an ear in frustration, found the matter of artistic rebellion to be fairly complicated.

Every college community in California provides a nucleus for some kind of mini-Bohemia (or, in the cases of Berkeley and Santa Cruz, maxi-Bohemia). There is usually a coffeehouse called something like the Roma or the Stone. There are the dropouts, the disaffected graduate students, the young profs, the emeritus codgers with their nail clippers, shuffling the morning paper for evidence of Armageddon. Feather River College, a two-year institution up the Feather River, which had a president whose academic training included golf instruction to another president, Dwight David Eisenhower, kept a Trotskyite on the premises, plus a talented wheelchair-bound novelist who called himself Super Flower Crip. Despite the increasingly anxious career pursuits of students, no institution lacks those who dream of making films, novels, poetry, art, music, or *something,* and act accordingly. If you find a person in a tie-dyed tee shirt, he or she is likely to be a tenured professor, but youthy abstention from the conformity ladder—now more like a stalled mall mobility escalator—still attracts California rebels. At UC–Davis I knew a student whose art form was to crusade against the green Historical Bike Lanes on Davis roadways. He wasn't against bicycles, he wasn't against reserved bike lanes. He was against History. "We have no History in Davis! It's a lie!" he wailed.

Truth-trumpeting is one of the characteristics of the Bohemian which the middle class time-server finds disagreeable. As a smug French critic said, "These people think their words matter. They think people should care."

My quixotic friend the student cared. He also listened to Bob Dylan—showed respect for History despite himself.

The Santa Cruz mall, rocked by earthquake, is recovering as a haven for a lively and exasperating community of dropouts, flakes, speedfreaks, radical compromisers between country communard Bohemians and big-city wild-ball trendsetters. The bookstores, cafés, walkway gardens, and easy panhandling among dewy students have created a backup Bohemian community—more of one, in fact, than was absolutely needed. A UC–Santa Cruz student, studying toward a career as feminist activist, told her father about a female street poet whom she regularly befriended with a dollar donation. Her father grunted. "But sometimes, Daddy, when my allowance is late, I just give her a hug. She likes that just as much."

Her father deeply resented this. He imagined the street poet in army-surplus blanket, her manuscripts lining it for warmth, and although he didn't resent his daughter's allowance money going to a nonrelative, he dreaded the results of those end-of-the-month economy hugs. "Hepatitis," he said. "Other diseases."

"Daddy, you're so uptight."

A woman friend of the father counseled him. She explained that hepatitis seems unreal to an eighteen-year-old. But even for a future gender leader, hair care is important, urgent, *real.* "Tell her she'll get head lice. No, don't tell her that. Tell her if she gets head lice, not to worry, there are remedies, kerosene, DDT, or she can just shave off all her hair."

He did so.

"Yucch!" cried his lovely eighteen-year-old. We think the hugs may have stopped.

Santa Cruz houses a vigorous women's Bohemia in communal living arrangements, the anticircumcision front, and a nationally known crusade against the Miss America pageants. With its spectacular site on the California coast, a certain number of theater and art majors move only the few steps from campus to the town after they graduate or drop out. The wooded hills surrounding and towns like Soquel shelter enclaves of sixties-revival explorers of inner space.

Nearby Carmel still claims its reputation, but this Bohemia of Hansel and Gretel cottages and art-ridden refugees from teaching or corporate jobs has been priced onto another plane. Debates about whether tourists in Hawaiian shirts should be allowed to eat ice cream cones on the street replace debates over whether the long line of Robinson Jeffers's verse is really poetry or Nietzschean megalomania. Clint Eastwood seems to be more famous than George Sterling, Ambrose Bierce, or Jack London. The haiku "Carmel is quaint like other places ain't"—seven syllables short, unnecessarily rhymed—doesn't evoke the redwood ruminations of artists and roisterers who once gathered rosebuds while they might. Stuck in traffic behind a red-bearded fireman in a Volvo with his left arm extended straight out, I asked, "Are you making a left turn?"

"No," he said, "drying my fingernails."

A contemporary working Bohemian in the traditional mode, Henry Robbins, was first known as the hard-core hunk vocalist of the California band Black Flag. He likes to keep busy; getting tattooed doesn't fill the idle hours. He has self-published twelve of his own books since 1984. He travels on "talking tours" with the Rollins Band. He records music. In his spare time, he has created a small press, publishing books and tapes for Lydia Lunch and Exene Cervenka. In his *spare* spare time, as a public service, he kind of manages Hubert Selby, Jr., the beatnik star who wrote *Last Exit to Brooklyn*. He lifts and does weights to keep fit. He's into health, has to be, a revolutionary counterculturalist of the nineties. His ambition lies beyond becoming a world-famous artist. His ambition is to dive headfirst into the Millenium.

"Money is a tool!" he says. "Give me more money. I don't want a car, I want a better laser printer."

Lately this admirer of Henry Miller, Hubert Selby, Bob Dylan—the revered ancestors of a thirty-year-old with a sense of history—has discovered a new dimension to his literary gift with its ransacking of the taboos, masturbation, mutilation, suicide, violence, race riots, *politesse*. Speaking to an interviewer before one of his "talking shows," he confided a new secret activity: *rewriting*. A person can change the words. It's not necessarily dishonest. A person can think and rethink. A person can push against the boundaries and push again. Henry Robbins now sees no limits to what he will do.

While the ideology of a Henry Robbins seems genuinely open-ended, others express more doctrinaire intentions. They preach because they want to change the world in a specific direction, as in gender politics. One of the incidental delights of gay and lesbian openness has been the separation of Bohemianism from sexual liberation. It used to be that Bohemians were also thought to be homosexual; sometimes they are, of course. But now unclosed gays can be insurance executive Republicans; the Bohemian style is not defined by sexuality. There are still ideologues like Harry Hay, a pioneer gay activist, founder of the Mattachine Society, who insists—tugging at his tasteful string of pearls—that the true teachers of love and cooperation to the world are the homosexuals. He takes something away from the Bohemians.

Recently he founded a new group, the Radical Faeries, devoted to tearing off "the ugly green frog skin of conformity to find the beautiful fairy prince underneath." From his headquarters in Los Angeles, near the age of eighty, he is still conducting a rebellion against the suburban middle-class family.

"What are the social rebels of Bakersfield up to?" I asked a blithe young woman who had made the quantum leap from Telegraph Avenue in Berkeley to marriage in the Central Valley.

"They run triathalons."

"Okay, you and your group. What do *you* do?"

She considered, this poet and former graduate student, sometime folk-rock singer at the Freight & Salvage in the lower depths of the Bay near Emeryville, trekker in Nepal and acid-dropper in Knightsbridge, who had once interrupted a Fourth of July party at the U.S. embassy in Paris by crying, *Down with hegemony!* Now she has taken on a bit of sun, muscle, and money. "What I do," she mused. "I run pretty good for an over-forty. I drive to Ellay to get my eyes done. I still subscribe to *The Realist.* I met a man who was on the bus with Kesey, he's a contractor now, knows how to build you a neat weekend place if you can afford it. . . . Herb, have I lost my concept?"

Her done eyes grow a little misty and soulful. She knows there are still adolescents in Bakersfield like the one she was, heading first to Berkeley and then to what destiny might bring them as they flowered up and out, opening to the universe.

Gelett Burgess's hundred-year-old map of Bohemia, encompassing the kingdoms of Peace, Truth, Youth, and Vagabondage, also included the enemy regimes of the Philistines, with their cities of Sham, Vanity, and Crudeness. Bohemia maintained ports on the Sea of Dreams, implying the possibility of refuge immigration. Outlying islands included the Delectable Archipelago.

One could update this atlas in California by getting the National Bohemian Geographic cartographers to explore the following centers and outposts: the peninsula of San Francisco, with its beatnik remnants in North Beach; its hippie remnants in the Haight; its islets on Potrero Hill and Clement; its New Yorkish South of Market with heavy-metal yuppies and as many graphic designers as there used to be poets on Upper Grant; its major energy in the Mission, where coffeehouses, bookshops, a lesbian version of the Castro, artists' studios, galleries and performance spaces, theaters and rehearsal warehouses have found a sense of place in the traditionally hospitable Latino world. What spaghetti and red wine were to the beatniks of Italian North Beach, burritos and beer are to the children of the nouveau beatniks and hippies who hang out at the Picaro or the Macondo on Sixteenth near Valencia. A call-to-revolution graffito in the People's Room of the Picaro says: *Thumbsuckers of the World, Unite!* I counted thirty-four bookstores within an easy walking district; some of them very specialized, Arab, lesbian, Maoist, Marxist but *not* Maoist, but most of them dusty and eclectic dream warehouses where every revolution and delight known to personkind can stock their manifestos.

A fanatically square friend in San Francisco defines the Sausalito bargeoisie as the houseboat dwellers at Gate 5 on their leaky fantasy vessels, doing collage, doing dope, doing redundant sexuality. The Greek artist Jean Varda navigated the islands of Bohemia for eighty years, sailing the Mediterranean, docking with Picasso, floating to Black Mountain College, then Big Sur, until he came to his final roost on a houseboat at Gate 5 which he shared with the Zen popularizer, bongo player, and former Anglican priest, Alan Watts. Before the phrase "role model" came to bedevil civilization, Varda was treated as one by Henry Miller, who also intended to climb out of the abyss of time by his skill at always being merry and bright.

Varda built boats, stitched his scrap sails of many colors, dealt with leaks in the vessels by making sure they were tended by eager young bailers. When he heard the siren song, this Ulysses did not strap himself to the mast. He stopped the boat, invited the sirens aboard. "You are merr-maid!" he would cry. "I dash myself into the deep beneath your feen!"

But the sirens of the San Francisco Bay did not wish his destruction. They wished his spaghetti, his wine, his lectures on the meaning of life (laughter, garlic, art, and kindness to old artists).

Varda perceived retired plumbing equipment as outdoor sculpture, making toilets into baroque gods of imaginary religions, laureling them with roots, vines, and flowers. He built tree houses to get closer to the sky. He played like a child in the detritus of the world. He snipped off a piece of one of my shirts to glue into a collage depicting Avicenna the Philosopher with index finger raised as an admonition to mankind.

What did the Persian philosopher, Avicenna, writing in Arabic, have to say to us? From North Africa and a distance of almost a thousand years, as reinterpreted by the Greek-Sausalito artist Jean Varda with the aid of a swatch of green-and-white checked gingham shirt? A person may live only eighty or ninety years, so better make the most of it. It's okay to be indignant, but stop not having fun. The message was one which Varda elaborated tirelessly, indignantly, joyfully. He had heard the rumor that all human beings are mortal. He wasn't sure this applied to him.

Defiance and cunning are necessary to Bohemian survival. Varda also needed money. He must have reasoned that I would be forced to buy his *Avicenna the Philosopher* if I didn't want my shirt to hang on some alien wall; I still own my shirt and Varda's *Avicenna*.

Near the end of his life, this devoted painter, collagist, boat carver, sculptor, jokemaker, and collector of teen angels suddenly set to work on a series called *Celestial Cities*, painted collages which turned out to be his greatest creations. How does such a thing happen? I asked him. He was close to eighty, he had suffered a stroke, the laughter and gaiety were intact. A kind of genius appeared as he lumbered stiffly about his studio.

"All my life I have been charr-latan," he said. (When he spoke

English, he spoke Grik.) "Through charr-latanry I have become arr-tist."

The houseboat on the Sausalito mud flats was filled with wine, talk, bird cages, California Byzantine archaeological relics, hand-maidens. "Your eyes dee-stroy me," he said to the woman I brought to one of his Sunday-afternoon spaghetti feeds. "Because of your eyes I must go to monastery."

And he did. During his monthlong ascetic retreat in a mission in the Carmel Valley, he wrote her a love letter every day—thirty days, thirty erotic poems in a bouillabaisse of languages.

My friend was confused. Bakersfield was not like this. "Ride with it," I said. "You don't have to answer."

"I think . . . is it a compliment?" she asked.

"Ride, Margaret."

Then he came home and proceeded with his life, his art, and his pursuit of other eyes to be destroyed by.

Varda collapsed while running toward a woman in the Mexico City airport. For an eighty-year-old the altitude was too far from sea level. He was used to thicker air for breathing; paradise is on earth, the celestial cities are in the hungry eye. They *say* he died, and in fact we scattered his ashes from his last boat onto the San Francisco Bay, but every once in a while I find a message in fluent Grik on my answering machine: *Her eyes dee-stroy me, I must go to monastery.*

The old Bohemian, maximum admiral of the Sausalito bargeoi-sie, is not forgotten. His *Celestial Cities* burn and glitter on the walls of fortunate collectors. Through charlatanry he stubbornly worked his way with the proper Bohemian indirection toward immortality.

And isn't this one of the primary intentions of the artist? To assert a defiant vision hardwon out of ignorance, to rescue himself and others from the abyss of time passing, of loss? The fact that all of us die anyway (the rumor turns out to be true) is a mere detail in the celestial glow of imagination. The artist's eyes destroy death.

.   .   .

The contagion of Bohemia has spread throughout California, so that even molecular biologists at Genentech and Chiron listen to heavy metal; a successful investment adviser, specializing in Silicon Valley start-ups, throws the I Ching as regularly as he tosses a softball with his kids in the hills of Los Altos. Beatniks, hippies, flower children, grandchildren of the lost and frequently found generation, continuing the Bohemian tradition, have contributed a good part of the style, fun, and options for Strange which continue to make California the promised land. Computer millionaires, each one supporting his own guerrilla filmmaker, recognize the need for Strange. At the wasteful edges of drugging and sexual carelessness, Boheem stragglers and too-muchers charge a tax against society. There is no pain without gain, no new style without somebody's outrage. Cappuccino at two-fifty a cup in a Humboldt County coffeehouse probably means dropout marijuana farmers are bringing their parallel-economy money into town. The fancy saddles and Nepalese evening wear surely indicate that these dropouts do more to earn their keep than play pickup rock'n'roll in the Two A. M. Club.

Old Bohemians sometimes remove their identifying marks and seem to settle into the disguises of normal life. They attend law school, work at advertising agencies, cut their hair and have babies. The teen angels on Jean Varda's houseboat turn up later as teachers, nurses, mothers in El Cerrito. Recently I met a wild creature who had taken the name Meadowland when she was a teen angel; now she is a surgeon, and when we had dinner for old-time's sake, to talk about the years passing, those matters that old friends talk about, about Jean Varda and his *Celestial Cities* and why our friendship would last forever, her beeper interrupted us because she had a heart patient in recovery.

When she came back to the table, she said, "You're the only person who still calls me Meadowland."

"*Doctor* Meadowland."

"Go ahead, say it again."

On Varda's houseboat we had known the happening-maker/ poet Gerd Stern, who later became a prosperous cheese-importer/ poet. We discussed the problems of names, which are usually not self-created, so that Delmore Schwartz imagined himself in the womb listening to his mother thinking, *Delmore, Delmore, such a pretty name,* and D. W. Snodgrass cried out to the Creator: *God! Snodgrass is walking through the universe!* I said that I used to be teased about my name; almost everyone is. Gerd Stern composed an instructional verse about correct pronunciation of his name:

> *Not Gerd*
> *As in turd*
> *But Gerd*
> *As in merde*

Even today, the cheese-importing business cannot engage all his energies. He exhibits sculpture, reads poetry in public. In the ripenings of words he recognizes links between the chaos imperative and the need to reorder matters; and when the microbes are done with milk, it's a superior product—cheese. The Bohemian tradition enriches the dairy-products industry in ways we can only guess at. Perhaps my friend the surgeon cares for her patients in a different and more compassionate way because she is twiceborn, once as a teen angel in the celestial city. Meadowland's eyes can still destroy.

In the state whose motto is "Eureka! I Have Found It," the tribe of Bohemia still rushes out of history into the future, daring fate to do its best and worst. Immortality belongs to those who claim it, digging the scene under the sun and fog and the infinite imaginary possibility of California.

11

Greenwich Village, a Palimpsest

More then a hundred years before the words *underground* and *counterculture* wafted through the air of the sixties, America's first Bohemians—the first to take the name—gathered in a basement beer hall called Pfaff's in Greenwich Village and plotted to produce the *New York Saturday Press*. Its stars were Edgar Allan Poe and Walt Whitman. Whitman liked to drink his beer underground with an audience of manly compañeros at Pfaff's; Artemus Ward and Mark Twain also blew foam, told lies, and contributed to the *Saturday Press*.

One of the Pfaff's circle, FitzHugh Ludlow, who competed with Poe as a consumer of opium and hashish, was more successful as a drug addict than a writer. He lives on through the library of psychedelic lore, established in San Francisco in the 1960s and then moved hither and yon, called the FitzHugh Ludlow Memorial Library. The daughter of one of its curators, not to be named here, is a contemporary movie star. "As a result of my strict psychedelic discipline, she's no flakier than the rest of them," declares her proud father.

Bohemians have grown rich in names for themselves—beatniks, hippies, counterculturalists, punks, New Wavers, and more, reflecting changes in the species. Techno-shamanists use virtual-reality machinery and smart drugs to time-trip into cyberspace . . . or back to our origins among the volcanic gods in the Promised

Land of Maui . . . or at least downtown into a cool club which serves Gatorade fortified with extra vitamins on weekend bliss-outs. Of the making of movements there is no end; nor to the naming of them—*techno-shamanism?* Trance-dancing, Ecstasy (formerly an animal tranquilizer), ultrasaturated inner-childism were briefly revived as vanguard innovations of the early nineties. Memory is not the strong suit here.

Real estate sorceror's apprentices have responded to the inflation of demand by extending New York's Bohemia into a half dozen neighborhoods; Greenwich Village begat the East Village, Soho, the Upper West Side, the gentrifying Noho now seeping inexorably toward the Bowery, and Loizaida (Hispanic for "Lower East Side"). What I happen to be revisiting these days is Village Classic, not yet totally zoned for tourism or condominiumized into a safe haven for professionals. Specifically where I'm staying for some months is the far western portion of the Village which has earned its own nickname, the Fertile Crescent, because of the prevalence of handsome young families. It's not all just beautiful models, actors, poets, and crazies. It's also architects with long-legged wives pushing baby strollers into Lanciani's on West Fourth Street for their breakfast coffee and a session of "sharing."

Since this is real life, not a movie, some of the lovely long-legged mothers have short legs. One of them uses the insights gained from Eli Siegel's Aesthetic Realism to manage mutual funds while the kid is in day care. Those are mere details.

The first time I found the Village, as a teenage runaway from Lakewood, Ohio—bidding formal good-byes to tearful parents and declaring my intention to explore the world, so it was more wanderjahr than runaway extrachromosome fugue—I stayed at the Mills Hotel on Bleecker Street. Fifty cents a night, and cubicles hosed down with disinfectant every morning, so you had to carry your bundle all day and reapply for admission in the evening. I was kept awake by coughers hacking, spitters spitting, and religious fanatics throwing Bibles at each other, and couldn't afford the fifty cents anyway, not to complain of the germs or all-male sexual harassment offered a seventeen-year-old. I moved into a hot-sheets rooming house, one boy among the whores—it was healthier and more congenial. An older woman of nineteen shared her frozen Mars bars with me.

Now the old Mills Hotel has evolved into some kind of arts center, nextdoor to the Village Gate, which I sometimes visit for its jazz or when Garry Goodrow is performing. For a while just before he took his life, Abbie Hoffman used to broadcast his shrewd, brave, goofy calls to revolution from underground at the Gate. It was pirate radio but listed on your FM dial. Due to plastic surgery while a fugitive, plus the plain passing of time, he had lost his heroic incendiary look.

In that dreamy chaos of my seventeenth year, I worked first as a Mercury messenger and then as a busboy, hurrying back and forth over the Minetta stream without knowing it was buried there. I tramped past artists—berets, capes, beards—and knew they were weird and I liked them. Their real lives were as secret and hidden from me as the Minetta stream.

Years and years later, I suavely took beer or meals at the San Remo with Anatole Broyard the writer, or at the Lion's Head with David Amram the Renaissance musician, or with the actor and poet Garry Goodrow at the Rio Mar on Little West Twelfth Street, or Indian vegetarian food with my actress daughter Nina or with the novelist Jerome Charyn, or muffin and coffee breakfasts at Lanciani's with the theater director Arthur Sherman and whoever happened by until the consensus seemed to quarrel with management (maybe someone tried to escape without paying and was rudely yelled at), or escorted various women companions to various up- or down-scale places in the rituals of courtship and trying to seem *interesting*. The traditional Village has seeped east and west, and south to Soho, Noho, and TriBeCa. Bohemia in Manhattan is a spreading stain. Brooklyn Heights, the Upper West Side, and even distant Hoboken catch the urban overflow.

Recently I sat at Art D'Lugoff's Village Gate with Art D'Lugoff, being treated, and remembered the Mills Hotel next door, where they didn't treat. At that time I fretted about the nickel subway fare, half the cost of pea soup with two slices of rye bread and good sweet butter in a nearby Sheridan Square diner. Now I complained about people asking if I used a word processor. A writer shambled up and asked if he could telephone my publisher to ask for a free copy of one of my books. "Sure, that's the best way," I said.

"Who's your publisher?"

"Souvlaki, Burrito, and Knish."

"Are they good? Would they like to see a road novel that blows Kerouac, Burroughs, and Bukowsky right out of the water?"

"That's just what they're looking for, man. Tell 'em I sent you."

He gazed at me fondly. "You're a terrific dude. . . ." The four dots implied: for a guy who has lived too long, taking up room in the world which rightly belonged to him.

In the late fifties, sex and abstract expressionism came together for me when I was sprung out of Detroit and a dire marriage. First a beautiful heroin-addicted Scandinavian dancer, unspeaking and mysterious, seemed willing to undertake a rescue mission. But Lenka also engaged in secret communications with my wife. She asked one of her jealous lovers to spy under the blinds and report to my wife what he saw. You might say I was restarting sex and love on the bottom rung.

After I left Detroit for the Village, first one and then another abstract expressionist painter taught me that actual companionship could be brought to the play of sex; a weather of goodwill could remain steady rather than as merely an intermittent prayer by one or the other huffing partner. There could be friendship.

The spacey dancer decided the opportunities for jazz and metaphysic were greater on Thompson Street in the Village than on Cass Avenue near Wayne State University in Detroit. She floated back into my scene, her wafting at me seemed unfinished business. I still wanted her. She couldn't be mad, I decided, because she looked into my eyes so hospitably, pitilessly, when we made love. Yet I gradually discovered that she was also the girlfriend of a famous heroin-addicted black jazz drummer, that she used too, that her other lover sent her onto the streets to earn money for smack, that she still wrote pain-giving letters and made pain-giving telephone calls to my former wife . . . that she was mad. She was a would-be who sought destruction. She looked at me coolly as I groaned, wondering what it was like to be alive.

To learn so much about harm from someone whose eyes became the eyes of God when we made love was an instruction in my lack of immortality. I could fail myself and others. I could lose. I'm still learning that lesson with the losses time brings.

Pernicious and premature nostalgia was one of the felonies of the Bohemian life; nameless longing merely a misdemeanor, punishable by being forced to linger at café tables, gazing at representatives of whatever dream of fulfillment passed by. The passersby were probably committing the same error, only with different fulfillments in mind.

Otto, an old-time nostalgist, used to murmur in Julius's and the San Remo, "Too many dances have ended," perhaps misquoting Wallace Stevens or even making it up for himself. I urged him not to surrender. But the generalized torporous grief was real (as real as generalized torpor). If Otto and the other poets weren't heard by America or answered by God, it was because they couldn't murmur louder than the shouting jukeboxes stacked with Jerry Lee Lewis, the Temptations, Fabian, and Frankie Avalon. Whatever Renaissance of the Arts was happening in the Village, the music seemed to express the Renaissance of South Philadelphia and the marriage of Italian and black pop soul music. There were still only a few blacks in the Village—mainly the A-Trainers who came on weekends to pick up the Bronx Bagel Babies—but there seemed to be a thin Harlemesque sultriness in the air. The few blacks that actually lived around Washington or Sheridan Squares were treasured as emissaries and pioneers. We were the Indians greeting them on the beaches. The highest levels of colonizing blacks were the few who attended lectures at the New School on West Twelfth Street. As a Jew, one from the Midwest, I had a minimum cachet for the long-tressed young beauties out of Smith and Bryn Mawr. The black guys had the maximum. Even the ones strolling round and round the fountain in Washington Square, the beatnik naval basin, could pretty much get what they wanted while not giving up that ungiving pout, the inward silence, which later became the fashionable face for Black Panthers and Black Muslims.

Of course, the previous is false and misleading as all true generalizations are false. Ted Joans was a jokey, affable, easygoing charmer, a poet, a survivor, offering unabashed fun for himself, for me, apparently for the women he loved, and even for the many children he sired. Ted Joans had the charm of a man in a role that fit him perfectly, hustling poetry and merriment.

The rest of us were busy being not what we had been, although not quite sure what we would be busy with when we became what we dimly imagined we were supposed to be. We were less snug in our new roles. I had the advantage over some of knowing what I *wanted* to be, a writer. It was an edge I shared, of course, with a working percentage of artists. But my evolving condition of would-be-ness didn't seem different to the world from those whose final resting place was in the ultimate stasis of would-be. Even those of us who occasionally finished a story, a painting, a song, had to start from zero again after the brief throb of satisfaction. Virginity grew back anew each time the moon was full.

The smoky dusks of the Village, the smells of wine, coffee, cigarettes, and girls—I cite the now-forbidden word because that used to be the name for these bearers of magic—the hope and desire and dreaming, the anguish of time passing without results despite our convictions of immortality. . . . That's what the Village was to a fellow traveler of the Beatnik party in the late fifties.

JUST A BOY WITHOUT A DOG

I've known three Greenwich Villages, and yet I'm still just a boy without a dog. The first was when I came to New York as a teenage midwestern kid, finding my best level running up and down the avenues for Mercury Messenger Service. On my first delivery I knocked at a door on Washington Square, answering the question, Who was I? with: "I'm Mercury."

"Then where are the wings on your feet?" said the artist who received me. It was still the Village of caped poets, red-checked tablecloths in cheap spaghetti restaurants, and pale huge-eyed seekers from elsewhere. When the Minetta stream, flowing beneath, burst into a basement of MacDougal Street, I realized that this had been farm and pasture land, not so long ago, before e. e. cummings came to mope and sing on Patchin Place.

Then, as a young writer in the fifties, I slipped into "the Village scene" of that period, playing softball with painters from the Cedar Tavern, hanging out at the Eighth Street Bookstore, engaging in nonfights with literary pugilists at the White Horse Tavern, where Dylan Thomas topped himself off with fatal alcohol. When I sneered at the man at the next table, or he thought I had sneered, he put up his fists and said, "Come on, fight." Reluctantly I went along with the program, lifted my hands. But then, before the first blow could be struck, he asked, "What's your name?" and when I answered, said, "Hey, I kind of like your stuff."

He told me his name, Seymour Krim, and I kind of liked his stuff, too, so we knocked down a pitcher of beer instead of each other.

During the explosive sixties period of be-ins, storefront psychedelic religions, street poetry readings, adolescents of all ages on the move, *Evergreen Review* published an advertisement for "The 10,000 Franz Kafka Challenge . . . *From Old Bohemia Comes This Amazing Offer!*" Followed a list of 200 hip names, ranging from Gershon Legman to Antonin Artaud, Pauline Réage to Allan Kaprow, and if you could identify all 200 of these Bohemian heroes, "I, Franz Kafka, will send you my personal check for $10,000." You didn't even have to offer proof; a postcard saying, "I did it!" would suffice. The only catch was that it had to be postmarked by June 4, 1924.

In fact, the 200 names were a pretty good collection of the camp icons of the time: Anaïs Nin, Antoni Gaudí, Alice B. Toklas, Richard Brautigan, Jean Shrimpton, Timothy Leary, with a few ringers thrown in, such as Toussaint l'Ouverture and Vikki Dugan, a pinup model famed for roller-skating in her New York apartment. (Pauline Réage is a pseudonym for the author of *The Story of O.*) If the young read novels, they read *Steppenwolf.* If they went to the theater, they preferred the Living Theater's audience participation revolutionary romps. In a late-sixties happening, a team of demolition artists attacked a VW Beetle while a poet read (inaudibly), a rock band played (loudly), and a Master of Revels threw live chicks and mice at the participants. The door was locked so we couldn't escape: squeals, panic, bloody critters underfoot. Mason Hoffenberg whispered to me: "I dreamed I went to a happening in my Maidenform bra."

He was worried about the neighbors calling the police (noise) or the SPCA (trampled mice and chicks). Since he was on a probation for sale of a consciousness-raising substance, he wanted to go home early.

Now, when I return to the Village in the early nineties, Sam Kramer, the death's-head jewelry maker of Eighth Street, is still dead, and Anatole Broyard, Mason Hoffenberg, and Seymour Krim have gone to the Great Happening on High, too, but the Minetta stream in its secret channel beneath Sixth Avenue, Fourth Street, MacDougal Street, Minetta Lane, still occasionally invades a basement to signal that nature exists, insists on it, in this determinedly urban place. The Lion's Head and the White Horse Tavern carry on a literary tradition. In the far West Village, newer joints, like Florent, or a coffeehouse like Lanciani, appeal to the upper-scale artists, theater people, gentrified Bohemians who haven't relinquished the palimpsest of America's Oldest Living Bohemia.

Truth to tell, the Bohemian hordes have long overflowed the boundaries of the Village. To the south, Soho, Noho, and Tribeca have attached themselves; for many years the Upper West Side and Brooklyn Heights have been suburban annexes for families needing larger apartments. In beatnik and hippie times, the East Village began to play the old role—cheap eats, cheap digs, youth, stringent causes, galleries, and radical street life. When I stay with my actress/waitress daughter on Avenue B, near Tompkins Square Park, I don't know if I'll be awakened by antilandlord rioting or dope dealers whispering, "Smoke, smoke," outside my window. Sometimes I've even awakened by the wan yellow first sun of the morning which says, There's still time, there's a whole new day out there, you can do anything. Get into the Daffodil

Café and start working on a bowl of Ukrainian kasha and an epiphany.

"What time is it?"

"Three-twenty." I was standing in the West Fourth Street subway station.

The questioner fumbled in his pocket, taking out a piece of paper which might have been a prescription for glasses. He needed to prove a point with me. "I don't want you to think I'm high or anything. See, my eyes are funny like this because they just give me eyedrops, see, and they make my eyes funny—I'm not high."

"I appreciate that. You're not high."

"So you better not fuck with me say I'm high, mister."

Now she might be called the painter, my Significant Other; then she was Alice, my girlfriend, long neck, black black hair and ivory skin, close-bitten fingernails. I met her at the Eighth Street Artists Club, which met in a loft on Fourteenth Street, where I had gone to hear a talk by Philip Johnson. Alice said she liked words and I told her that's what I did, I wrote words. And I told her I liked paintings and she said that's what she did, she painted paintings. I asked if she would give up smoking for me. She said we could discuss it. But we mostly discussed words, colors, shapes, and each other, and I forgave her the smoking. She forgave me my smug forbearance.

But without my mentioning it, she stopped biting her fingernails. Her hair was long and glossy, her stride was long and quick, we liked each other. She had come to the Village from Indiana, I from Ohio and Michigan, and we both had metabolisms stirred by the intention to be merry and bright.

During that long-ago sojourn in the fifties, Alice lived in a studio off a courtyard on Commerce Street, with a tree rubbing its filmy leaves on her filmy window, frost edging the glass, a lot of snow falling during that winter. The new year was exceptional for its sudden night blizzards, leaving the Village clean and silent in the morning, bringing kids out with Christmas sleds and red Christmas hats and mittens. We would wake with that unearthly white light reflected into the room from the snow-edged tree, the snow-filled courtyard; and the silence also pouring in. By silent agreement we didn't put on the usual Nonesuch baroque wake-up music, trumpets, flutes, and a rhythm that worked like coffee or rock and roll: no music this morning. The snow made her think of Turner or Brueghel, it made me think of Henry James on Washington Square, but we were both thinking: clean snow, nice snow, it's good to be together.

She had a job as a photographic stylist. I walked with her to Jim Atkins', the diner on Sheridan Square, for pancakes, eggs, and a wake-up blast of breakfast noise. The *Times*, the *Voice*. Other couples, one dressed for work, one dressed for hanging out. I said good-bye to her at the subway entrance, wrought iron, elegant, Manhattan Belle Epoque, but already smelling of aging snow and pee, and then walked east to my own apartment on Waverly Place, kicking at clots of rapidly graying slush, hoping to write a few good words.

The dope dealer in the doorway at the corner of Waverly and Sixth was already at his station for a day's patient waiting for business. He was wearing a long black overcoat, had an umbrella furled at his side, his hands in his pockets, and wished me the top of the morning, as usual. A few good words, I prayed, and once he took my mumbling, trying out the words, for a business inquiry. I wrote a few okay words. I waited for the mail, a letter from an editor or my daughters in Detroit, or the telephone to ring, or that metabolic surge which came along with words I really liked.

At night, alone together after the day apart, Alice and I slowed down, made toasted cheese sandwiches in a pan on her stove (cooking wasn't what she came from Indiana to the Village to do; it was too early in history for the man to do any cooking), and confided some of our deepest thoughts to each other. Some of them we kept in reserve.

If we wanted sociability and a hot meal, we wound long scarves about our necks and trampled through the snow to the okay hot meals available on Bedford Street at Chumley's, a dark cavern down a few steps with hardly any announcement that it was a public place. A few steps away was the narrowest house around, the Edna St. Vincent Millay house, barely room for a witty couplet; the Cherry Lane Theater stood nearby, still does; and another friend—a Catholic philosopher who liked to think about Jews and borrowed my leather jacket to stimulate his meditations—lived in the smallest house in the Village, a tiny pile of two rooms in a courtyard on Barrow Street or maybe it was Jones. Once, in need of inspiration and a shiver, he asked if I would buy a package of condoms while he watched from outside the drugstore.

My friend, the Catholic philosopher, still lives in the Village, has a wife and children, and continues to write about the Jews. Goes to Zionist meetings, Jewish book fairs, synagogues, and hangs at the edges, observing. When I moved to San Francisco, he took the plunge and bought his own leather jacket.

This was a peculiar community, it still is, and people move here because they want some of both its peculiarities and its community. The Village mobilizes to fight for libraries, end police harassment of sexual minorities, prevent prison barges from being moored in the Hudson River nearby; it mobilizes to promote health foods and blood pressure testing; the Seventh Day Adventists can have West Eleventh Street closed to traffic for a weekend street fair of clean living. The Village builds studios fit for sculptors and painters but at prices suited to pre-October 1987 yuppies. Even the B. Dalton bookshop on Eighth Street has gotten "sensitive"; stocks poetry and local writers. When I arrived, the manager hastened to beg the computer to deliver up some of my books.

It would only be a few days. Then I could lurk outside, waiting for the thrill of spying someone picking up a book, reading the jacket, glancing here and there, buying the book. Maybe I could ask my old friend, the Catholic philosopher, to repay me for letting him watch the purchase of three Trojans with the red-helmeted warrior on the package.

Passing a spell in Greenwich Village during the late eighties, I used to walk for breakfast to a truck-driver's joint, the West Coast on West Street near the river. The prices were like the East Village, cheap bran muffins, skimpy on the raisins, bargain eggs, although it seemed to me they put more sugar than absolutely required in the muffins. Probably teamsters burn quick energy faster than combustible novelists. Part of the pleasure of my morning stroll from West Eleventh Street was a regular visit to *The Pathfinder* mural in progress on the wall of a building at West and Charles Streets, bringing Lenin to the People, also Marx, Castro, Malcolm X, Mother Jones, icons and leaders of revolution. The building contains the offices of Pathfinder Press, which has outlets in Chicago, San Francisco, and other warmbeds of overthrow.

The artists painted from high scaffolding along the wall. It was a game to figure out who some of the less-familiar faces were— Nelson Mandela (that was easy), John Reed (not looking much like Warren Beatty), César Sandino, Thomas Sankara of Burkina Faso, Maurice Bishop, a whole variety-pak of national and international heroes blending into each other in a rainbow coalition created (this was part of the theory) by artists from many nations. Some of them had trouble getting visas to visit the U.S.

This was America. Occasionally skinheads or Village right-wingers came in the night to splash rival graffiti on the mural or to harass the gay men from the meat-rack piers nearby. Lights and guards were installed. I saw a trio of transvestite male hookers singing "Amazing Grace" under the spotlight in memory of a colleague brought down by AIDS. They said they were demanding that Charles Ludlum of the Theater of the Ridiculous be painted immediately onto the wall. They said they'd also like Joan Baez and Judy Garland, but they could wait for them, and then they sang "Over the Rainbow."

The Pathfinders Project was alive, it was a happening thing. Gradually Trotsky, Zinoviev, Bukharin, and Karl Radek came out of the mists. The sketches were filled in with honest, courageous, proletarian primary colors. Pipes, guns, flags, and parades. The mural was eclectic and ecumenical. Pathfinder Press is an equal opportunity revolutionary press. Pete Seeger helped to raise funds. The heroes and heroines were marching into a wind-furled banner which proclaims A WORLD WITHOUT BORDERS in French, Spanish, and English.

Both the too-sweet West Street muffins and Revolution via Mural Action express something of the old-fashioned values of Greenwich Village. In the East Village, agitprop art tends to be more about local issues, such as the La Lucha antigentrification murals. They are all inspired by Diego Rivera, the honored ancestor whose portraits of Lenin and Abraham Lincoln were painted out of Rockefeller Center when Nelson Rockefeller decided it was not the People's but the Rockefellers' wall. Downtown, things are different.

Sitting at the outdoor terrace at the Figaro, waiting for my daughter to come dancing across Bleecker Street with three or four or five of her hungry Loizaida friends, I suddenly started. *Lenka!* I saw her, the graceful, lovely, heroin-addicted dancer with her sunny hair cropped furiously short, and here she was again floating down MacDougal toward me. Whatever else she had done, however she had caused unnecessary hurt, she had pulled me away from a disastrous marriage and suggested the idea of pleasure. It had previously occurred to me as a rumor, some kind of distant ideal, but Lenka brought her downy hair and dreamy eyes to bear on the subject.

I jumped up to greet her and called her name. She paused, she smiled her heart-breaking smile—she smiled so rarely, lost in her internal ballet, fixed and floating there, that it always made me think everything could be done anew and better—she opened her arms to the intensity of my joy, my forgetting that she had gone from me to the drug-dealing jazz drummer, and then from him to me, and then from me to him again, and then at his urging to any paying customer in the club. I forgive, I forgive, I still love you, you saved me!

She smiled and smiled. "I'm not Lenka, but I do look like one, don't I?"

Lenka was dead many years now. But the young woman on the Village street with the smart Village mouth lived, still lives, and I saw her. She gave me that sweetness of smile. She shrugged. She continued on her way.

And then my daughter clattered up with a band of her colleagues, actors and dancers, to be taken to an Indian restaurant for yogurt, spices, vegetables, and brown rice.

12

Travels in the East Village/Loizaida

On the sidewalk in front of St. Mark's Place Bookshop, amid muttering thieves market commerce in books, clothes, and automobile radios with connecting wires hastily frayed, an urban balladeer street busker wearing a Nashville Iveco Diesel baseball cap (visor on back of head) pulled at his electric guitar. He sang. He celebrated country-western grief:

> *I got tears*
> *In my ears*
> *Lyin' flat on my back*
> *Cryin' over you.*

This was a Lower East Side, funky streets, country-western busker who was establishing a career in the East Village in the ever-popular suffering troubador trade. He had dropped out of the nerd and geek classes. He pronounced "you" correctly as "yew." He was Korean, making his break from the all-night cold-eyed grocery business.

I knew how he felt. For many years I've regularly gone on safari into the Lower East Side of Manhattan, sometimes merely camping out, sometimes marooned in the jungle by various hurricane weathers, such as love or a shortage of money. The first friend I visited there, a generation ago, was the pioneer poet Allen Ginsberg, my college debating partner when we competed over poetry awards and sexual definition. We've remained friends and sometimes feed together in the no-cost Ukrainian restaurants. I grant him his poetic eminence, he grants me my heterosexual conviction. We have learned tolerance and to be buddies, and it always does my soul good to hear him chant his Buddhist rock songs, such as the great ditty which I recall as:

> *Eat when you eat,*
> *Drink when you drink,*
> *Live when you live,*

and then his warm dark baritone uttering those necessary words:

> *Die when you die.*

In the days before Loizaida was so named by the Hispanics who were moving in among the Jews and Slavs, during the beatnik fifties, I used occasionally to walk there in search of magic mushrooms—there was a shop with a cactus and toadstool sign—before they were discovered to be illegal by the concerned authorities. I might meet Alan on the street. I was also looking for the archaeological remains of the places where my father slept when he came to America at the beginning of the century. He used to rent eight hours of a bed on Hester Street, sharing it with two other immigrant boys who each got to sleep during a slot of time. My greenhorn father earned his living carrying buckets of water to the workers on scaffoldings. It was thirsty work building the early skyscrapers. I imagined this dizzy adolescent balancing buckets on his shoulders, frightened of the immense tumble if he slipped, carrying a dictionary in his back pocket.

For a brief period during my runaway year at age seventeen, I had found a job as a busboy in a basement Romanian-Jewish restaurant, then moved up in the world when I achieved the position of winged-footed Mercury messenger. I saved the subway fare by running with my packages from delivery to delivery. Later my father said: "You're just like me, only dumber. You had to do that shit, but I really had to do it."

And now my daughter had chosen to leave cozy San Francisco and find her career on the Lower East Side. From generation to generation we seemed willing to take the tumble if we slipped.

On Avenue B, near the crack street where my friend the actor Garry Goodrow was mugged and my actress daughter ran to her dance classes and rehearsals, I stood in a Korean grocery as a glittery-eyed young man in the all-black kung fu art uniform entered his new role, Retail Purchaser, with a commanding linguistic confusion: "Hey Papa-san, where the Beeg Pepsi?"

The grocer multiplied emanations of impassivity.

"Beeg-a Pepsi, Papa-san! Pepsi Grande? Hey, Papa-san, you sleepin'?"

Staring silence. No need to hear this.

"Hey, Papa-san, love-ya, love-ya, but got a thirst can't be satisfied without the largest, the biggest, El Pepsi Returnable Bottle Grande, man! Come on, Papa-san! I ain't got the patience to walk to the next fuckin' Korean bodega, Papa-san! Okay?"

And then quietly to me: "What you lookin at, dude?"

I handed him the monster-sized Pepsi cannister. He put money next to the grocer. Kim and I watched him leave. I wondered if Kim was the father of the country-western troubador of St. Mark's Place. Since my daughter was determined to carry through her ambition as an actress, I bought the economy-pak, four rolls of toilet paper, as a house present.

In the summer of 1991 my three college-age children were encamped near each other in the East Village, supping at the thrill of Loizaida Bohemia. Ari was doing film, Ethan was working on music, and Nina was rehearsing a process play which was being developed without a script by the director and actors. In his room on East Ninth at Second Avenue, Ethan explained about the clubs, the reason one stays up all night, in case I had forgotten. Watching his face, I remembered the thrill of loping at dawn through gritty streets, not mean but full of meaning. Suddenly, as he paced near the window, he said in particular low voice: *"Dad."*

I ran to the window. There below on the sidewalk a man reeled with a knife in his chest. Fresh blood stained the cement, a crowd gathered, the medics were prompt. When we went downstairs, the body had been taken away, but the blood was still copious and wet and one shoe remained near the gutter. I asked a cop what had happened. "Homeless beef," he said, making it sound like a utility cut of food. Then I realized he meant an argument between two homeless men, and felt relief, and felt shame for my relief, because therefore the knife had not been intended for my sons and daughter.

This new Bohemia is not one of pure gaiety and charm, streets pungent with woodsmoke and metaphysical quest, moon dreamers waking each other at dawn.

I admired the artifacts collected in the Lower East Side apartment of a man who had written a prizewinning novel with the help of methamphetamine. The medical history of the novel explained something about its rapid transitions, the blooming swarthy fantasies, the sudden close-ups and empyrean speculations, an expressionist rhythm and engaging craziness. It wasn't the speed which really did it, of course; it was the talent.

In his apartment Ferd—call him that—accumulated Lower East Side street sculpture, found objects, symbols of our civilization to which he gave titles and names; for example, a wrinkled Coke-bottle top, matted, framed, and almost audibly rusting behind its glass. He liked the process; said he could hear it crackling at him during the night. He called it: "Oldest living Coke-bottle top." On a curatorial hunt just before sunrise one morning, he had carried off a blinking roadwork lantern and wooden horse. The lantern flashed its eerie red glow over his room with its pressed-tin ceiling, books on teetering boards supported by bricks, hardworking and agitated cockroaches. What do you call this one? I asked. "Haven't decided yet, still thinking. Major project for my fall season."

It was a problem. But before he found its name, he had to complete a sculpture which existed not only in space but also in time. Staring into the blinking one-eyed red lantern, he said, "There's a battery. I need to see how long it lives."

After his successful first novel, he was unable to complete another. "Gave myself a little speed lobotomy," he explained. "Had to relearn my telephone number. Would have had to relearn how to drive, but I lost my license."

"You're recovered now, aren't you? You're still smarter than most people. You're still quick, buddy," I said.

He meditated on this as the lantern blinked and swayed a little in the traffic vibrations from one-way First Avenue outside. "I've come back," he admitted. "Permanently, I guess I've only lost about thirty IQ points. Do you think I can work in television?"

I stood in front of a battered red-brick building on East Fourth Street, studying the graffiti and festive banners which blew and billowed in the breeze overhead. Since I was reading so intently, examining the Keith Haring-styled spray-painting, cave drawings for the hunters and gatherers of our time, a few passersby gathered, as New Yorkers do, to watch me watching. RENT STRIKE. KILL RAGAN.

"What do you think?" asked the proud owner, arms akimbo, of the canvas on which the message had been lettered.

"You're sending mixed signals," I said. "Rent strike is one thing. Kill Reagan is another. And besides, he's not President anymore."

His arms disakimboed in a little dance of happy hostility. He shrugged. He had a mind so fine that several ideas could float belly-up in it at the same time. "Hey man, the military-industrial complex is where all this garbage comes from."

I knew, I knew. Plus the Trilateral Commission, the CIA, and the International House of Pancakes, all getting together in a plot to gentrify lower Manhattan. "Okay, granting your point, but also you misspelled Reagan's name."

That proud pity called disdain crossed his face. He was earning his keep on earth through brilliance; what was my excuse for living? "Don't you understand what a statement is?" he asked. "Making a statement, 'sole. Used to pronounce it *Ree*-gun. Now pronounce it *Ray*-gun. What'd he ever do for AIDS or the homeless problem I got to be polite to him?"

Bohemia has always been about statements both simple and

complex, and about hanging out on the streets to explain to noncomprehending passersby, and about working through confusion to make sense, working through sense to make confusion, affirming the wakefulness of moon dreamers and magik ladies. My friend Ferd, the speed-damaged novelist, started another book shortly after the battery went out on the blinking red lantern dangling from its wooden-horse barrier. The symbols of art don't inexorably apply to fate and biology.

But the building with the graffiti and the rent-strike banner was bought, remodeled, condominiumized, and is now being occupied by young and ambitious folks who like the idea of affordable housing in a place with a perilous history of artistic striving. Some of them are artists. The nearby bodegas now carry the Great Undiscovered White Wines which these new residents require, plus this year's herbs and spices, in addition to the normal Loizaida beer and saltines. There are bed and breakfasts for tourists poking around with guidebooks, looking for Allen Ginsberg. The old lady carrying her dog and muttering, "This is my baby who I love," is answered by a muttering editorial copy editor: "Whom. Whom. Takes the objective case."

TICKERS

We gathered for the memorial service at St. Mark's in the Bouwerie Church, perched like a shipwrecked relic of Auld New York on its grassy and concrete island. The church was the site of famous poetry readings, demonstrations, and happenings, a center for both the beatnik and the Christian faiths. It was an appropriate place to celebrate the memory of John Clellon Holmes, novelist, essayist, poet, friend and contemporary of Jack Kerouac and Allen Ginsberg, best known for first using the word *beat* in its now-traditional sense in an article for the *New York Times Magazine*. It was autumn, the trees were sere, there was a country smell of burning leaves in the air. There was sadness and that mood of banding together for a community affirmation of life despite death.

I walked through the Village and the East Village with David

Amram, composer, innovator in jazz and modern classical forms, performer along with Jack Kerouac in the cult film *Pull My Daisy*. Herbert Huncke was there, street hustler, poet, sometime junkie, now living on welfare. Gregory Corso, John Tytell, various biographers and autobiographers of the beat epoch. Many brought cameras, tape recorders, video equipment, and some brought notebooks. The young tended to be dressed in beat mourning wear, gray sweatshirts with the image of handsome, prebloated Jack Kerouac, the James Dean of this secret society. Since some of them require several icons, James Dean was also their Jack Kerouac. A band of young women in black mourning leathers swept through the crowd, looking for Diane de Prima, who used to conduct poetry readings here, or Ellen Stewart of La Mama, or Judith Malina of the Living Theater; in this society of boys, there had been women leaders, La Pasionarias of the beat generation. Maybe Viva would show up (she still lived at the Chelsea Hotel and had been spotted dreamily roller-skating through the halls with her daughter). Maybe the ghost of Anaïs Nin, who always liked gloomy celebrations. This was a church with terrific karma.

The band of leather women ignored the ex-girlfriends of Jack Kerouac, even the ones who had written books. Book-writing girlfriends weren't their thing.

What seemed festive, besides the Halloween dress-up and crisp autumn air, was the crowd of gawkers, autograph hunters, academics from various Departments of Beatnik Studies, toters of video equipment, interviewers poking recording devices at anybody who looked old enough to be a contemporary of anybody else. But this wasn't a networking uptown party; few of the mourners exchanged cards. The eulogies began, with interruptions by speakers impatient for their turn. Some eulogists, such as Allen Ginsberg, remembered John Holmes as a kindly, even avuncular beatnik chronicler. Others seemed to remember themselves. Piercing vocal interjections came from the air surrounding Gregory Corso, often the emitter of piercing notes at public gatherings. He didn't want to hear this shit about how Johnny Holmes settled in Arkansas to plant the flag of freedom. He wanted to tell about how he and Johnny and Allen and Neal and Jack—but especially

Gregory—had revolutionized, scandalized, and had a great time because God loved him, Gregory.

Allen patted my arm and in his hoarse whispery baritone counseled patience. Of all the beatnik wildmen, he is surely the kindest and gentlest. He even beamed with a kind of masculine maternal indulgence at the buzzsaw interruptions of Gregory Corso, claiming attention, whining through the lyric spaces where teeth used to sit. It was John Holmes's funeral memorial, not Gregory's, but Gregory seemed a little jealous of the notice paid someone else. "Shush," Allen said as I fidgeted. "Gregory's moved. That's how he is."

Seeking to stay my irritation, I remembered Gregory's most touching poem, an epithalamium for the marriage of two beat figures, a painter and a writer, in which he imagined their permanent happiness while he, Gregory, in his old age, would be sitting alone in some furnished room with pee-stained underwear.

Seymour Krim, one of the original virulent ravers, whose image as the near-sighted cannoneer helped to define the public perception of the beat epoch, limped slowly forward, painfully stooped, and declared: "The Beat Revolution in America was the equivalent of the Spanish Civil War."

Some of us muttered. We hadn't suffered starvation, cold, or death from the skies as we kept busy wearing black, smoking grass, courting wan ladies, and complaining about our parents. This didn't seem like the historical equivalent of the sufferings of Guernica.

Sy Krim, peering through his specs, hoarse, very ill, scanned the church and called out the names of the ancients there present. "I see Allen . . . Gregory . . . David . . . Herbert Huncke . . . Herb Gold . . . and we walk a little more slowly now . . . and our tickers don't work so good . . ."

I whispered to David Amram, recently married, happy father of a couple of new babies: "Didn't we walk here pretty briskly?" His ticker worked good. My ticker worked good. Poor Sy Krim's ticker didn't, so it became "our," in that communal sharing of the problems of one by all.

Still, David and I wanted to tell the young folks crowded into

St. Mark's for a share of history that we could stand our ground, and run away from them if necessary.

And still and still, peace to John Clellon Holmes, a departed friend. Forgive us, John, for suffering from the vanity from which you seemed exempt.

GHOSTS OF THE FAN PERSONS

The landmark novel of the dusking of the Age of Aquarius after its beatnik-hippie, speedfreak-pataphysician, revolutionist-artist Lower East Side decade-long summer of love—be-ins, psychedelics, dumpster prospecting, tenement squatting—is William Kotzwinkle's *The Fan Man*. It catches the light off the last spasms. It memorializes the detritus of the early seventies, beatnikery sunk under geological layers of hard living but the fossils still damp, the flower age shriveled to instant nostalgia while the schools graduated or ejected new recruits wearing Peace, Save the Dolphins, and Rain Forest buttons and looking for someone to share a joint with. "If you remember the Summer of Love, you weren't there"—but that didn't mean you couldn't start a new East Village Other, or Eye, or join the Weatherpeople, as West Village folks in the forties and fifties joined the Trotskyites, Schactmanites, or Reichians.

Despite accelerating violence in the streets, despite the obsolescence of once-original fashions, the lure of the island of Loizaida beckoned. Poverty helped; it was America's very own Haiti, Burkino-Faso, Nepal, complete with hepatitis. Runaways, nonconformists, street activists, artists and would-bees found their way in search of a place at the watermargin of American city life. You could live here cheaply and in danger—a bracing tradeoff for colonizers. Bookshops, storefront galleries and studios, coffeehouses, group marriages and communes struggled to survive among the street people, the crazies, the violence, the drugs. A certain amount of intermingling was inevitable. The idealists organized neighborhood gardens where there had been impromptu dump sites, mortuaries, and shooting or smoking galleries; the addicts liked taking their drugs amid the ecologists' tomato plants. Botanicas sold love potions *and* marijuana *and* crystals *and* old copies of *Fuck You, A Magazine of the Arts.*

Personal discovery is always new for the discoverer. The pattern was satisfying. Bohemia was sometimes different, but always like this.

The Lower East Side, a Slavic, Jewish, and Hispanic Manhattan backwater, hospitable to Bohemia, was devolving in the 1970s into a welfare and teenage drug slum. The level of rape, mugging, and random violence was becoming unbearable. The rage of America's self-outcasts seemed to save it, much as it saved San Francisco's Haight-Ashbury. Block by block, they fought for the streets with banners, strikes, street fairs, neighborhood watches, and hammering on the doors of the mayor and the police. Even the Guardian Angels passed through, and gurus chanting Om. A great voodoo mambo from Haiti and Brooklyn spread her skirts and commanded the crack dealers of East Sixth to be gone. If Mother Theresa didn't already have a full dance card, she'd have been invited, too. This was an ecumenical save-the-turf effort. The avid souls of real estate speculators also responded, upgrading tenements now named The Hearth or Artaud Arms. In the real world there is always a price, and the price here was condominiums.

The process continues, a ferment and battle for turf. The St. Mark's Place Bookshop moved across the street into larger and cleaner countercultural space. While the Ukrainian and Polish fill'er-up restaurants still provided thick borschts and fatty plates of cheap comfort food, conducive to narrow arteries and broad behinds, sidewalk seating was available at a café with future Meryl Streeps waiting on the tables. It was on East Sixth; it was called The Sixties. NYU film and theater scholars hooked their bikes to the ironwork with eighteen-pound Kryptonite locks; others arrived for their sprouts, tofu, and yogurt by skateboard or rollerblade. The Doors, Bob Dylan, the Byrds, and Richie Havens blared from the speakers. One could weep for the dear dead immediate past while chatting up the immediate present. Some of these rough and worn young nostalgists eating fresh fruit salads had been conceived by their parents to the tune of "Light My Fire" or "Sad-eyed Lady of the Lowlands." I know this on good authority because I invited three of my artist children to the café for a kind of Disney theme ride into their father's life during the several-year Summer of Love which led to their birth.

Maybe it was "Mr. Tambourine Man" or Corelli's "La Folia." Who paid attention?

At a reading in a basement café on St. Mark's Place, an out-raged poet evoked T. S. Eliot for an audience which nodded and smiled its recognition:

> *Let us go, you and I,*
> *When the evening is spread out like a patient etherized on a table*
> *And offend community standards . . .*

It was the time of trouble in the National Foundation for the Arts. Senator Jesse Helms was Hitler of the Month. Books were not being burned, but grant awards were being overruled. Carnivore indignation thrived alongside vegetarian, gender-indifferent Zen peace in the mean and fertile streets of alphabet city.

After the reading, I strolled down Second Avenue, enjoying the lingering tropical glow of Indian summer, the Third World street action, and stopped with voyeur's antenna quivering at the sight of a couple nibbling at salad at one of the outdoor cafés. The young woman was showing a sharp-featured older man nearly poster-size nude photographs of herself while he stared noncom-mittally. I didn't look closely at the man, but suddenly he said, "Herb!" and it was the painter Larry Rivers. I accepted an invita-tion to join the couple.

The woman, Phoebe Legère, was asking his help to choose the photo for her record album. Briefing me on dynastic history so far, she described herself as "queen of the downtown scene, Herb," not just in the *Voice* but also the *Times* and the movie *Mondo Manhattan.*

"Who doesn't know that?" I lied.

The three of us studied our salads and the photos. She decided I could help arbitrate. "Hey, you like me like this? My hands? Stuck there? Like Madonna, only badder? Whaddya think?"

I thought. She absently brushed a bean sprout from my beard.
A silence of judgment spread over the table. Three persons of our
time were trying to decide if her fingers down there made a strong
statement. The very fingers which had brushed the bean sprout off
my chin.

Phoebe Legère, singer, actress, performer, multipurpose downtown queen, grew impatient. She had only a few years to define
her place on the planet and in the scene. She asked Larry Rivers
in a strong outer-borough accent: "Larr-ry! Do you wanna go
back to my slum and—?" She completed the offer.

He stared. He continued chewing on his salad.

"Larry? So? Do you wanna?"

"I'm thinking," he said. "I'm considering it."

A few years ago there were peyote button and karmic vegetarian
shops; then came the storefront galleries; now there are ghosts of
both periods, psychedelic and aesthetic wake-up storefronts, and
more cafés, stages for public hanging out. The Country Eggs &
Surplus Cheese Never Open Outlet (not its real name) is still alive
behind its dusty, fly-specked pane of glass, still closed most of the
week. The Botanicas are selling love potions and stock market
stimulators in little pink jars. A carved wooden statue of Baron
Samedi, the Guardian of the Cemetery in Haitian voodoo, looks
out across a display of Sure Thing Lottery Bottles being carefully
examined (for what?) by Bush-era mystics trying to get "in touch
with the energy." Baron Samedi shows suave indifference in his
painted eyes.

The fill-up Ukrainian and Polish restaurants, such as the Yo-
landa or the twenty-four-hour Kiev, still stoke with fuel the Slavs,
the junkies, the artists, the students, the cheap-livers. What spaghetti used to be in the West Village, what burritos are in the new
Valencia Bohemia south of Market in San Francisco, blintzes and
borscht and mushroom barley soup are to the Loizaida refuge of
the youngest, poorest, most adventurous, most bedraggled of contemporary Bohemians.

At Tompkins Square Park, Bohemia drifted all the way down
into the homeless encampments. Most of the residents of the

lean-toes, tarp piles, soggy sleeping bags—the winos and druggies, those conversing with invisible angels and devils—have passed beyond the boundaries of Bohemia. It's still hard to draw the actual limits, but in Gelett Burgess's expeditions, the map of Bohemia includes the Delectable Islands, the Kingdoms of Peace and Arcady, Mountains of Veritas, the Hills of Fame. Very little evidence of such in Tompkins Square Park—mostly Vagabondia and Dolor.

Just before Tompkins Square was cleared by the city police, as I walked through with a young actress/waitress, she was panhandled by a healthy young man whose age she abruptly asked. It turned out that they were both twenty-two. "Why should I give you money?" she demanded. "I work as a waitress."

"I'm an anarachnist poet," he said. "Jobs are against my belief. . . . Well, actually my mom and I don't get along, so she won't send me my ID."

With Tisch-trained dramatic incredulity, the young woman asked: "You're an anarchist poet who waits for your *mom* to get your papers?"

"Yeah, listen honey, I hear where you're coming from, but I take care of people, too. You ever need anything, someone hassles you around here, that old guy—"

"—he's my dad."

"—yeah, well, okay, he hassles you, molests like those old fart dads tend to do, you just call for me. Brick. Just call out my name, Brick, hey Brick! and I'll be there for you like my fuckin' mom ain't there for me."

"Terrific, thanks, Brick," said my daughter.

The legend DEAD DEATH was painted on his leather jacket. A former skinhead hairdo was growing out like a marine boot-camp trim. He enjoyed our conversation, but another visitor was crossing the park and needed attention. "Spare change for an anarachnist poet, Sir?"

"Anarachnist" sounded like a science-fiction film combination of spider and freedom-lover. I sought to continue the conversation. "Do you mean arachnid or anarchist?"

"Hey man, I'm a poet. Poetry talks to God and He-or-She's not hung up on lingalistic bullshit like some assholes around here, you dig?"

I dug.

"So now leave me the fuck alone so I can tend to my little spare-change business."

13

Bohemian Diaspora/Bohemian Archipelago/The Territory Ahead and Behind

"Strive to be where you are," said the Zen Bohemian at Tassajara in the Las Padres forest of northern California. Since she had taken a vow of silence in honor of the anniversary of her parents' divorce, she gave me this advice by pointing to her breast. She had ironed the decal letters onto her tee shirt. Later she joined a crew of workers flapping towels and tee shirts to chase the flies out of the dining room at the Tassajara Zen Center, flies that were only striving to be where they were.

In a postindustrial world which clings to the values of useful action, Bohemianism devotes its life force to expressing rather than doing; only essence is real, and effectiveness is reduced to an incidental, irrelevant function of soul. The resemblances to pietistic religion are striking. There is no strict code of observance. The rituals of sharing shift according to local needs and histories. The intention to join is the chief credential asked. There is no main office, no citizenship board; instead, there are charismatic leaders, gurus, gods, and devils. What we have here is a rigorous open-enrollment policy.

But despite this apparent loose acceptance to a tribe and tradition on the grounds of declared faith, Bohemians are left to face the darkness alone. When effective action is an atavism along with the normal supports for esteem, when the justification of history by accumulation of goods, usefulness to the community, the routines of marriage and children is abolished, the Bohemian still meets the changing reality of the mirror. Dialogue with the self may be a reduced dialogue, but it is still dialogue—the concept of monologue is only an abstract metaphor. Free spirits must tell themselves they are making something, doing something, in addition to telling the world they are "creative, revolutionary, real, in touch," whatever the language they come to use—it was *cool, groovy*, at a time in recent history.

The pre-Raphaelite Brotherhood took on the manners of London layabouts, but then lay about actually painting, and soon they were professional artists who had worn capes and velvet at a certain period in their gestation. Now they were artist-Bohemians rather than merely Bohemian (artists?), and continued to don capes and velvet upon occasion. Defiance of the hardworking was part of the deal; embracing the stigmas of rebellion is one of the tenets of Bohemian faith. A person wants to dress so he can't be mistaken for a worker in an office, and he wants to lean against the plate-glass window as a reproach to those who labor and shop. He is not necessarily intending to break the window. He is expressing himself. If the window happens to break, well, that was a probe, and maybe Marshall McLuhan from his grave in Toronto will mutter in his nonstop monotone that it was sending a message through the medium of plate-glass window testing.

There's a San Francisco panhandler, occasionally ejected by the smiling Chilean juice squeezer at the Macondo Café on Sixteenth off Valencia, who wears a tattoo that reads YUPPIE with the afterthought VOID inked over it. He exchanged conversation for my quarters. "Are you a former yuppie?" I asked.

"I'm a Void," he said. "It's the nineties, brother. I'm the living image."

At this minimal level, he was expressing himself, leaving it to his audience to decide if he was also communicating a perspective on social realities. His palimpsest poem reading VOID, one-word long, one-seventeenth of a haiku, with its yuppie shadow behind it, absorbed all his energies. Unlike the mere graffiti artist, he carried it to his audience on daily rounds, using smiles, teeth, repartee. He was not an addict. He was a chemically challenged performing artist in need of fellowship and perhaps a substance unknown to me to push the damp wind of outdoors off his chest. His smile offered fellowship in return. We've all felt that wind on our hearts.

Traditional Bohemians are intended to respond to emergency with greater assertiveness. Kosmik Lady, who has been handing me her poems on the street for many years, believes Void should give up minimalism. She utters many syllables. Her gospel requires floods of explanation, much photocopying.

Russian art rebels at the time just before World War I and the Soviet revolution reflected the passions of St. Petersburg and Russian desperation. The art movement named futurism has a place in history, but the full raucousness of these visionaries can be evoked by the usual splinter group called Everythingism, the café named The Wandering Dog, and perhaps most eloquently by the newspaper called *Murder Without Bloodshed*. When people talk about murder without bloodshed, one can expect a bit of murder with bloodshed. Revolution came hard to Russia, and Bohemia was one of the most stringent victims. At first its self-defense guerillas established outposts of hope.

Tiflis in Soviet Georgia briefly became the Paris of, well, Soviet Georgia, welcoming an ingathering of artists and rebels in such meeting places as the Little Fantastic Cabaret. Some of the Tiflis painters, poets, collagists, and designers made their way in exile to Paris, the Tiflis of France. More died; turned out there was bloodshed after all. Yet during the bad times, the sixty years of the Soviet Union, improvised café life persisted even when there were no cafés. People gathered at tables in apartments to deal in forbidden thoughts. The impulse survived the regime.

In the mid-sixties I smuggled a copy of Henry Miller's *Tropic of Cancer* into the Soviet Union. It had been printed by Barney Rosset of Grove Press in a Russian translation, 2,000 copies, because he thought Russians also deserved to enjoy this chaotic autobiographical sexual romance. He advertised *Tropik Raka* in Russian émigré newspapers all over the world. Thanks to this crash campaign, Grove Press sold six copies. When Rosset suggested I smuggle the remaining 1994 copies into the Soviet Union, I claimed a sore back. Don't have enough underwear to hide one thousand nine hundred and ninety-four copies of a book, Barney. But I agreed to take four of them.

En route, stopping in Paris, I was warned by a frequent visitor to Moscow that it could be dangerous for me. I had studied Russian. I had enough underwear to hide one copy. Anyway, I decided that one copy, allegedly for my own goofy reading pleasure during lonely nights in the workers' paradise, could be justified to the KGB if they found it.

I got through customs safely. I carried the book everywhere, trying to figure out whom to entrust with it. I felt like that Dylan Thomas protagonist on his way to London with his thumb caught in a bottle, but this was Moscow, not London, and I had a duty to shake the bottle off into the proper hands. The sexual liberation of a great people depended entirely on me.

Finally, in Leningrad, I met a lover of jazz and the blues, Billy-Goliday and Dizzy-Gillespie, who had done hard time in labor camps. I approached the subject delicately. Shambling together along a canal in the midnight glow of June, I asked the musician directly: How would he feel if Fate happened to offer him the chance to read the book called *Tropik Raka* by Genry-Miller?

He would be confirmed in his suspicion that God lives. He could die happy.

I passed him the package wrapped in newspaper. He turned pale and scurried off. I was alone without my burden under the midnight sun. I tried to think of Peter the Great opening a window onto Europe in this stony city. At least I had opened a peephole.

When I saw my friend a day later, three people had already read the book, staying up all night, taking turns, drinking coffee, charmed, aghast. "Words!" sobbed the musician. "Such words I have never seen printed in Russian!"

In Moscow in 1991, during the chaotic breakup of the Soviet

glacier, an artists' club—painters, sculptors, musicians, writers, film makers—took to gathering in the apartment of a painter named Nina Maksudova. Like Jim Haynes, she asked a little money for food and drink. While hunger, cold, and despair radiated through Russia, an eclectic group warmed itself with conversation, dreams, the Rolling Stones, William S. Burroughs. They debated about whether it was acceptable to paint over a collage. They danced, they showed their work, they recited, they played guitars. They went home at sunrise.

Years ago a Soviet actor—call him Tabakov—pointed to invisible sounds in the sky outside his apartment, directing me to birdsong and speaking the miracle word "Nightingale! . . . Nightingale! . . ." after a long summit conference of drink and laughter. He made gestures of turning up the volume so that those who tapped his walls would get a good record of the dialogue between bird and universe.

After all this time I still sometimes awaken to that chanted Russian word from a dream of survival celebration: *Solovyay!* . . . *solovyay!* . . .

The reality of Russian streets is still gray and cold, but this enduring traditional reality also exists—companionship in art, satire, fun, shared revulsions. There is an Everythingism for the nineties. One evening, when a masquerade was prescribed as the remedy to gloom, the filmmakers of Nina Maksudova's salon ransacked the Mosfilm warehouses to dress up in homage to their history—as old Bolsheviks, as Che Guevara, as Heroes of Soviet Labor. A womanizing rhythm and blues singer came in Eva Peron drag. Some guests were berated at the door for insufficient mockery, but then admitted anyway. In bleak and wintry Moscow it was life-sustaining to demonstrate playfulness in the graveyard of conformity and deceit, to dance on the bones. Not even Stalin and Brezhnev had been able to extirpate the roots of Russian Bohemia, which has given the world so many poets declaiming in front of the Pushkin monument, audiences standing silently in the frost to hear them. When underground jazz lovers who had already done hard time in labor camps were willing to risk their freedom anew by worshipping the icon of Genry-Miller, Bohemia nation could be recognized, still alive in the Soviet monolith.

Time sometimes wears out Bohemians; some old bohemians think the race died with their own colorful youth. ("In my day there were geniuses.") Recently I renewed acquaintance with a middle-aged woman who was famous in beatnik early-hippie days as the literary Chinese hooker, hoping to cure the North Beach poets of their weltschmerz. Instead, she tended to pass on her own mysterious distress. Bustling in for dinner at the Lonely Table at the Brighton Express on Pacific, wearing colorful clothes from Takahashi, she gave very precise orders for the cooking of her chop and then set about to create a ruckus—reproaching me for my writing, Janis Joplin for her singing and her net halter (no bra), Dr. Francis Rigney for his practice of psychiatry. (Dr. Rigney wrote an early book, *The Beat Mystique,* on the active and passive prophets of an era, using length of beard as a criterion for judging degrees of aggression or nonaggression. There were statistics. There were tables. This was Science.) Ming-Lee violated the rule of kindness set for the Lonely Table. Occasionally management would eighty-six her, but she didn't take it personally.

Now the retired streetwalker—"I've turned in my hook"—has two children on scholarship at University of California campuses, a retired fireman husband, six cats, and only eats out in North Beach at the beginning of the month. "Anyway," she said, still literary, squinting with severely diminished malevolence through her bifocals, "this beach has been so thoroughly combed it's showing bald spots."

"You seem gentler now, Ming-Lee."

"Just older, Herb. Hey, didn't you used to have that thick black hair?"

I hurried home to look in the mirror. Still have hair, but it's fairer in color. Ming-Lee hasn't entirely lost her way of digging at folks. She says her husband, a jovial old guy with a prostate as big as all outdoors, calls her Marge, because Ming-Lee reminds him too much of her professional days. In our time there were geniuses at the Lonely Table in the Brighton Express.

Upper Bohemians, like rich gypsies, used to be exotic beyond the boundaries. The world has evolved; as "revolution" has become

a term of irony, Bohemianism has been tested and found suitable
even for consumption by the rich. In return, by a nice symmetry,
the secret has been revealed that money doesn't need to be a
disgrace among artists. The "downtown scene" in New York,
almost like the Upper Bohemias of the international set and communities like La Jolla, Coconut Grove, and Mill Valley, embraces
wealth as the ticket to the dropout life. "Poor" painters hire
expensive rock bands for their openings. The look of funkiness is
achieved with expensive leathers and fabrics. Nobody minds the
contradictions (a few may be embarrassed).

Some ideals, something otherworldly and religious is at risk in
this welcome to affluence. The trickster careers of traditional
would-bees often become mere game playing or self-display, with
the promise of good financial results when access to media is
added to the normal self-regard of Bohemians. They already
contemplate their own navels. When they can commission others
to do it for them, there is a lessening of fervor. Painters and writers
probably shouldn't employ publicity agents to explain to the world
that they care for nothing but their art. A "holistic manager" who
approached me a few years ago suggested that I could better keep
my eye on the sparrow if I employed him to keep an eye on
everything else, take care of my accounts and credit.

What came to be known as the downtown style in Manhattan
reflected the institutionalizing of Bohemian fashion, a deathly
embrace of the counterculture of the eighties by the surrounding
consumer society. These were rebels without claws. Cheap eats,
clothes, and furniture became alternate items for serious purchase.
Depression-style diners, clatter, noise, and grease, rivaled in popu-
larity hushed vegetarian health and ecology restaurants. Bohemian was brought *into* the Reaganite business hustle. Maybe art
would also trickle down from self-promotion.

In a *Village Voice* Personals ad, a woman, "slim, natural blond,
one child, independent means, seeks man with one earring, ponytail or moral equivalent." Moral equivalent of a pony tail? Would
a Goodwill couch do? Is this "natural blond" a politically correct
Upper Bohemian seeking to express herself by taking care of an
artist or moral equivalent?

Like carp eating the shoreline garbage, living off the detritus of cities, the urban Bohemians flash their bright tails in the sunlight, in the shade, swimming back and forth, happy to be alive at the water margin where they can both feed and display their talents for flashing in the light or hiding in the dark. A young woman fresh out of Cornell into Noho, Manhattan, complained at being labeled a beatnik "just because I wear black, dye my hair green, smoke and listen to progressive rap. . . . They didn't call Richard Farina a beatnik."

Oh yes they did. Beatniks *liked* to be called beatniks in those days. In 1991 the *Cornell Alumni News* published an article about Farina, author of *Been Down So Long It Looks Like Up to Me*, describing him as "the coolest Cornellian ever?"—with a question mark—because he wrote that book, lived in Collegetown, married several folk singers, died in a motorcycle accident upon publication of his first novel. Dick Farina was proud to be a writer, a beatnik, and a composer of songs for Joan Baez and his wife, Mimi. He also claimed to have fought alongside both Fidel Castro and the Irish Republican Army during his summer vacations from Cornell. And later he really did hang out in Village bars with Delmore Schwartz. If his novel had shown more talent, he might indeed have been the coolest Cornellian ever. James Dean and Jack Kerouac didn't attend Cornell.

The recent college revival of beatnik fashion included Captain Quackenbush's Espresso Café in Austin (coffee, smoke, chess, and debate), the Java in L.A. (mud wrestling among poets, a deconstructionist version of the display of verbal talents), the bicycling "bohos" of Duke (ecology a big fave), the Daily Caffee at Dickinson College in Carlisle, Pennsylvania (poetry but also philosophy, crystals, psychic research, ecology, and an audience of high school students learning from their elders, absorbing the vibes, digging the scene).

For a time, during the Aquarian flower years, California seemed on its way to becoming the conquering Bohemian nation, with San Francisco capital of the empire, leaving colonies and outposts everywhere. Digger and troubadour armies hitchhiked up and down California Route 1; ecstatic, undoomed Mimis and

Rudolfos sang (to amplified guitars) in garrets, basements, and old Victorians; Pieter Brueghel's *The Land of Cockaigne* seemed to advance from being a mere painting to becoming the dream film of our lives, wine bubbling from springs, cookable animals leaping into hungry arms, airy spirits looking for love. A generous food-stamp policy helped. The Vietnam war brought folks together so they could smoke and drop acid. The Aquarian Age was our mother, we would not want.

Shrewd businesses accepted the revolution as another commercial opportunity. PSA Airlines established a no-reservation ten-dollar midnight flight between San Francisco and Los Angeles. It was more than a trip; it was trippy. The protocol seemed to prescribe climbing aboard with a guitar, a joint, and a backpack; shoes optional, but shirt or blouse requested. The flight was a way to make new friends, complete or end a romance, transact business while staying high between southern and northern California. Electra propjets flew on Jungian power, plus cheap oil, and the operation may even have made money. There were mandalas everywhere; also mantras, karmas, and animas.

Once, when the flight happened to land at San Francisco at 1:00 A.M. in a heavy storm, the flight attendant compassionately offered to drive me into town. Lucky Herb. It turned out that she had a use for me, although not the one you may be suspecting. There were no working windshield wipers on her blue VW bug. I sat on the hood (drive slowly, please), clearing off the rain so she could bring us both safely to berth. I got a ride, a thrill, a thorough wetting.

When PSA raised the price of the midnight no-reservations Aquarian shuttle to $12.50, most of the dope dealers, actors, musicians, groupies, students, grokkers, and groovers were able to absorb the cost. When the flight was suspended, the flower times of California seemed to come to a symbolic autumn.

The Green Hornet hippie bus continues to this day, plying the roads between San Francisco and everywhere, Nepal excluded due to intervening oceans and mountains. Bohemian Nation endures. The symbolic end of the Aquarian PSA midnight shuttle was not the same as a real conclusion.

Nothing ever dies in the archipelago of Bohemia, but everything changes, volcanoes roar and go silent, islands sink beneath the seas. Ray Manzarek, keyboard player for The Doors, friend and collaborator of Jim Morrison, now performs in coffeehouses and college unions instead of monster rock festivals. Back then he cowrote with Jim Morrison, stood on floodlit platforms as thousands and thousands gaped and screamed; now he improvises, softly noodling, while Michael McClure recites his beast poems for university beatnik revivalists. "This is the spiritual regeneration of America, the breakthrough of the heart chakra over the lower three chakras," says Ray Manzarek, former rock star.

In his mid-seventies now, Lawrence Ferlinghetti remains an icon for the nouveau beatniks, sometimes called beatniks lite, who frequent cafés named in homage to Frida Kahlo (Little Frida's, in West Hollywood, "for one who painted more than her nails") or the Bourgeois Pig or Van Go's Ear. In the early 1990s, beatnikery became a minor fad in L.A. among college students and a few younger movie stars. Blink your eyes and it may be gone, but for a moment heart was in; the lower three chakras were out.

Life is not a cabaret or a festival of love, much as we might prefer it to be, but Bohemia is at least a busy café of watchers and waiters, doers and don'ters, thinkers and the heedless, men and women possessed of the need to seize the day or plan the future or regret the past, all stubbornly devoted to demonstrating that life really is what good sense tells us it is not. A festival of love or lost love. A dance of the living at the irrevocable spectacle of the massed dead. A territory whose citizens defy time while figuring out what to do with it, how to pass it. Islands where the twice-born are plotting how to be born yet again.

The Bohemian clings to the world of sense and feeling—and his or her particular presence in it—because otherwise experience seems to diminish, fade, decay, die. He wants to write in order to name life in the world, paint in order to guard its shape and color, sing in order to measure time and the heartbeat; or he may simply hang out, passing the years, because he is knocked adrift by both the task and the blessings. The Bohemian makes love, as does everyone, in order to celebrate, evoke a glimpse of festival, a hint of paradise. Sometimes the flesh is willing, but the spirit is weak. Bohemian Nation keeps on trying, inscribing need onto both the silence and the noisiness of our short time on earth. *Forever* is on their minds. "I knew all men are mortal," William Saroyan said in his last hours, "but I didn't realize this applied to me."

Bohemians pick and choose from the garden of delights which they have decided to insist must really be there. Even if the garden is a mirage, they are present in a waystation on the universal voyage. The children playing on the stage of these backyards bring their dreams resolutely front and center. The story of Eden is reenacted with kindly snakes and an endless supply of apples.

The world seems to need this moral ventilation system. Over the years bohemia has expanded its role as the rite of passage from childish eccentricity and yearning into creativity. It offers a permanent ward for those who prefer not to struggle in the world of strict demands. Here there is another sort of struggle for pleasure, pain, and moral justification. Enlistees can find reasons for dropping out, bending genders, scrambling brains. They can even say they chose their fate. (I'm a techno-shaman. I was a Sufi in my previous life. I got sick of Portland, Oregon.)

The synergy between those who venture through Bohemia and those who stay, the tradition of neighborhoods, rituals, locales, lingos, habits, dress, codes of behavior, provides structure for the unstructured voyage. It's an autonomous zone. This parallel world not only coexists with mass society; it seems to play a part in its health, a little like the darting fish that accompany whales, cleaning their mouths, grooming their teeth and crevices.

The system works on principles of reversibility. Bohemians sometimes choose to opt in, the non-Bohemian sometimes opts out. It's convenient to be both a crank and a star—and to be able to do so while being poor, lazy, and full of intention, or rich and lazy and full of intention. A bonus of the game of role changes is that one might even become chic with one's soup cans or tangled wire sculpture. The banker Gauguin was first only a Sunday painter who tended to be rude to his wife; later, a seer.

Some dress-up Bohemians seem to be following Oscar Wilde's advice to make a work of art if possible; otherwise, wear a work of art. They keep busy storing up shadows, gathering them in the hope of finding something thick and lasting, as shadows are not, in the real world, supposed to be.

A chunk of grammar falls from the sky, wrapped in mystery and exhalation, like an asteroid or a turd from a cruising alien. It hits the head of the boy sitting over his coffee with pen and a pile of old menus at Ground Zero & Organic Muffins. He begins to write. In his chest he feels unearthly vibrations. The grammar comes in clusters, growing toward a novel if he keeps going; or if he's distracted and takes aim at another fulfillment, the Great American Rock'n'Roll Song.

It's tempting to describe the negligently nonconforming impulses of Bohemian eccentricity as one of the roads to salvation in mass culture, and let us submit to that temptation. I consent, I hereby so stipulate. As long as these self-chosen ones can build their lives on foundations of play, music, and art, stand up when faced by powerful troubles and bravely run away—and survive— life will thrive at the water margins. If we can't pray, let us at least be ridiculous together. Let us be wasteful. Let us make errors, let us make noise, and occasionally let us hear the music of the spheres.

The young man with the pile of old menus near his coffee mug is happy with his morning's discovery, for he has written: *Strive to have been where you were.*